D1572430

DATE DUE

LESSING AND THE ENLIGHTENMENT

LESSING

AND THE

ENLIGHTENMENT

*His Philosophy of Religion
and Its Relation to
Eighteenth-Century Thought*

By HENRY E. ALLISON

Ann Arbor
The University of Michigan Press

To the memory of my Mother

Preface

☐:

Gotthold Ephraim Lessing was one of the seminal minds of the eighteenth century. In addition to being an important innovator in drama, literary criticism, and aesthetic theory, he was one of the most significant religious thinkers of his time. This has long been recognized by German scholars, who have devoted scores of volumes to an analysis of his religious philosophy, but as is unfortunately so often the case, he has been almost completely ignored by the English-speaking world. This work is, as far as I know, the first full-length study of Lessing's philosophy of religion in the English language, and it is my fervent hope that it will help, in some small way, to stimulate interest in a figure whose conceptions of religious truth and the relation between religion and history underlie much of contemporary theological discussion.

My interest in Lessing was first aroused by the study of Kierkegaard, who despite a vastly different temperment and view of the religious life, readily acknowledged the significance of his German predecessor. It was, Kierkegaard tells us, Lessing who first suggested to him the concept of the leap and the famous formula "truth is subjectivity," and it was also, I believe, Lessing who more than anyone else led Kierkegaard to see the paradoxical nature of Christianity's claim to ground an individual's eternal happiness upon a historical event.

Lessing, however, was far more than one of the numerous influences on Kierkegaard. He was the founder of a whole new conception of religious truth and one of the most articulate and profound advocates of the doctrine of man's spiritual development. Thus, although he was in many ways a child of his age, these basic insights led him far beyond the superficial rationalism of the

vii

Enlightenment's approach to religion. As we shall see, Lessing was the first thinker to separate the question of the truth of the Christian religion from the question of its historical foundation. This distinction enabled him to combine a rejection of the "historical proofs" for the truth of the Christian religion with a recognition of the speculative and ethical significance of Christian thought. This led him inevitably to the development of a relativistic, evolutionary conception of religious truth. In light of this new conception the Christian religion is no longer seen as the absolute word of God, but as the highest expression of the religious consciousness of the race at a certain level of its development.

These speculations are in many ways an anticipation of Hegel and German idealism, but their roots are to be found primarily in Leibniz, the great seventeenth-century thinker, of whom Lessing wrote: "If it were up to me he would not have written a line in vain." The relationship between Lessing and Leibniz and Spinoza has often been discussed in the literature, but never, I believe, adequately explained. Thus, the demonstration of the Leibnizean basis of Lessing's fundamental ideas is one of the main themes of this study. Viewed in this regard, Lessing emerges as the first of a long line of German thinkers—a line which includes Kant, Herder, and Schelling—who rejected the narrow dogmatism of the Leibniz-Wolffian tradition, but whose thought was profoundly enriched by contact with the "true Leibniz," whose main works had remained unnoticed in the library at Hanover for more than half a century.

All of the passages cited are given in English translation. Wherever possible I have made use of existing standard translations, otherwise the English rendering is my own. For the benefit of those who desire to consult the original I have included references to the Rilla edition of Lessing and the Gerhardt and Erdmann editions of Leibniz.

The extent of my indebtedness is great. First of all I should like to express my gratitude to my teacher, Professor Aron Gurwitsch, whose inspiring lectures and many private conversations originally aroused my interest in the history of modern philosophy, and to whose profound understanding of Leibniz many of the ideas expressed in this work are ultimately due. I should also like to thank the Graduate Faculty of the New School as a whole for the honor of awarding me the Alfred E. Schütz Fellowship, which enabled me to complete the work in a relatively brief period of time, and Professors Hans Jonas and Albert Salomon for their many helpful criticisms and encouragement. Special thanks are also due Professor Robert Horn of Union Theological Seminary, who read and commented on my manuscript in its initial form and with whom I have conversed often and never without profit concerning the general period of this study. Above all, my thanks go to my wife, who amid sometimes trying circumstances never failed to provide the atmosphere and encouragement without which this work would never have been completed. In addition, my thanks are due Mrs. Naomi Grob for her help in the laborious job of preparing the index.

Finally, I thank the following publishers for permission to quote from material published by them: Stanford University Press: H. Chadwick, ed., *Lessing's Theological Writings*, 1957; The Open Court Publishing Company: A. C. Langley, translator, Leibniz's *New Essays Concerning Human Understanding*, 3rd edition, 1949; Routledge and Kegan Paul, Ltd.: E. M. Huggard, translator, Leibniz's *Theodicy*, 1951; Harper and Row Publishers: T. H. Greene and H. H. Hudson, translators, Kant's *Religion Within the Limits of Reason Alone*, and T. M. Knox, translator, *On Christianity, Early Theological Writings by Friedrich Hegel*; St. Martin's Press: N. K. Smith, translator, Kant's *Critique of Pure Reason*; Dover Publications: Benedict de Spinoza, *The Chief Works*; and Professor L. Loemker for permission to quote from his edition and translation of *Leibniz's Philosophical Papers and Letters* (The University of Chicago Press, 1956), 2 vols.

Contents

CHAPTER 1

The Historical Background

Gotthold Lessing's thought, like that of any significant philosopher, is both a product of, and a reaction to the age in which he lived, and as such, can only be understood within its historical context. Moreover, because of the highly polemical and occasional nature of his writings this truism is doubly applicable to him. His philosophy of religion constitutes an extended polemic with his contemporaries, and it thus becomes necessary to preface this study with an examination of the main religious-philosophical tendencies of Lessing's age, that is, of that period in the history of Western civilization commonly known as the "Enlightenment."

The most apt general characterization of this period was expressed by Kant, whose oft-quoted words should form the starting point of any study of eighteenth-century thought:

> Enlightenment is man's release from his self-incurred tutelage. Tutelage is man's inability to make use of his understanding without direction from another. Self-incurred is this tutelage when its cause lies not in lack of reason but in lack of resolution and courage to use it without direction from another. *Sapere Aude!* "Have courage to use your own reason!"—that is the motto of the enlightenment.[1]

In its application to religion this motto entailed both a theoretical and a practical aspect. From the theoretical standpoint it implied the necessity of subjecting any alleged revelation to rational criteria. Christianity was placed on a level with the other religions, and its veracity had to be established before the bar of reason. Enthusiasm, superstition, and "implicit belief" of all sorts were universally ana-

1

thematized. The direct result of this rationalistic approach to the problem of revelation was that the truth or falsity of the Christian religion, its claim to be the revealed word of God; was conceived of as a question of historical fact, and as such susceptible, at least in principle, of an empirical answer. Thus, if it can be shown that the events related in the Gospel narratives are true, if God did in fact become man at a certain point in history, in a remote corner of the Roman Empire, if he preached, performed miracles, suffered, died, and was resurrected, then the Christian religion is true, and its doctrines must be accepted by any reasonable man. If, however, the evidence does not substantiate these claims, then Christianity must be rejected as a malicious fraud which has tyrannized over the human spirit for eighteen centuries. Such was the manner in which the problem was understood by all parties concerned, and it forms the underlying presupposition in terms of which all of the arguments for and against the Christian religion were formulated.

In its practical aspect the Enlightenment was marked by a strong resurgence of humanistic values, based upon man's heightened awareness of his intellectual and moral powers. This found its expression both in the tendency, widely prevalent in the rationalistic English theology, to treat the Christian religion essentially as a supernatural sanction for morality, and in the utter rejection or radical reinterpretation of those aspects of traditional Christian doctrine, that is, original sin, total depravity, impotence of human reason, and the vicarious satisfaction, which clashed with the prevailing moral sentiments. In this respect the religion of the Enlightenment can be viewed with Cassirer as a renewal of the struggle between Augustine and Pelagius, Renaissance humanism and the Reformation, Luther and Erasmus, and finally between the ideal of human freedom and autonomy and the belief in the bondage and depravity of the will.[2] This time, however, the liberal tendencies, reinforced by two centuries of scientific discovery, by vastly increased anthropological knowledge, and by the beginning of historical criticism of the Bible, emerged victorious in a Europe devastated by over a century of religious wars and bloody persecutions.

The old religious system, the Protestant scholasticism, which was developed and codified in both the Lutheran and Reformed churches during the latter part of the sixteenth and the entire seventeenth century, proved to be completely out of tune with these new insights. The theology of this period, which was contained in carefully constructed dogmatic systems, was thoroughly rooted in

Augustine (as interpreted by Luther and Calvin), and centered around the two main principles of the Reformation: the emphasis upon "sound doctrine," and the reliance upon the Bible as the sole authority. This led to a conception of Christianity as a body of true propositions, based upon an infallible sacred text, which served as the objective standard of truth. Thus understood, the Bible was in no way a human book, but rather the literal word of God, dictated by the Holy Ghost to men who functioned merely as mechanical transcribers of the divine revelation. Carried to its logical extreme, this infallibility covered not only the religious and ethical doctrines, but also the history, geography, and natural science contained therein. Some went so far as to defend the infallibility of the vowel points in the Masoretic text, and elaborate harmonies were constructed to reconcile apparent discrepancies in the various Biblical accounts. These extreme tendencies were more prevalent within the Lutheran Church but were not unknown within the Calvinistic tradition, which maintained as its supreme principle the omnipotent will of God and its corollary of absolute predestination.[3]

Isolated voices such as Hugo Grotius, and the Dutch Arminians, the German Pietists, Hobbes, Spinoza, and the Cambridge Platonists were raised throughout the seventeenth century against various aspects of this grim, intolerant, and coldly intellectualistic conception of religion, but among the first generally influential representatives of the new way of thought were the English Latitudinarians or rational theologians and their chief philosophic spokesman, John Locke. — spoke out against that concept

I
ENGLISH RATIONAL THEOLOGY AND DEISM

As Leslie Stephen has shown,[4] English rational theology of the seventeenth century provided the presuppositions and laid the foundations for the deistic critique of revelation in the eighteenth century. In their polemic with Rome these divines attempted to construct a rational theology capable of gaining the reasoned consent of an impartial examiner. It was their firm conviction that only if religion is established on such a basis can all human claims of infallibility and attempted justifications of persecutions be utterly refuted. Their theology was based upon the twin pillars of Scripture and natural reason. It was believed that from these two sources a list of universally acceptable fundamental doctrines could be derived, and these fundamentals were identified with "true Christianity." Deism was merely the logical development of this principle. Rather than limiting the true faith to those fundamental doctrines shared by all Christians, it simply broadened the perspective, and located the true faith in the "religion of nature," that is, in those basic rational beliefs shared by all men in all ages. This attempt had already been made by Herbert of Cherbury in his *De Veritate,* 1624, in which he sets forth the five fundamental principles of natural religion, and later by Spinoza, but it was not until the eighteenth century that it became a major tendency in European religious thought.

Locke: This rationalistic tradition formed the intellectual background for John Locke, who in his *Essay Concerning Human Understanding* attempted to give it a firm epistemological foundation. This is undertaken in Chapters XVII through XIX of Book Four, wherein he carefully defines and distinguishes the respective provinces of faith and reason. The key to his position lies in the distinction between propositions which are according to, above, and contrary to reason:

> 1. "According to reason" are such propositions whose truth we can discover by examining and tracing those ideas we have from sensation and reflection; and by natural deduction find to be true or probable. 2. "Above reason" are such propositions whose truth or probability we cannot derive from those principles. 3. "Contrary to reason" are such propositions as are inconsistent with or irreconcilable to our clear and distinct ideas.[5]

Upon this basis Locke proposes to consider faith, which "is nothing but a firm assent of the mind: which, if it be regulated, as is our duty, cannot be afforded to anything but upon good reason; and so cannot be opposite to it."[6] In Chapter XVII Locke presents the framework in terms of which the problem of the relationship between reason and revelation must be understood. It is clear from the above quotation that faith must in some sense be reasonable, or at least not contrary to reason, but the content of this faith and its precise manner of reasonableness are discussed in the next chapter.

Here Locke delineates the boundaries between faith and reason, and assigns their proper sphere:

> "Reason," therefore, here, as contradistinguished to "faith,"
> I take to be the discovery of the certainty or probability of such
> propositions or truths, which the mind arrives at by deduction

made from such ideas, which it has got by the use of its natural faculties; viz. by sensation or reflection.

"Faith," on the other hand, is the assent to any proposition, not thus made out by the deduction of reason, but upon the credit of the proposer, as coming from God, in some extraordinary way of communication. This way of discovering truths to men, we call "revelation."[7]

Thus, the proper content of faith is that which is revealed, the word of God insofar as it has been communicated in history to man, and correlatively the function of reason is to determine whether or not any alleged revelation is genuine. Reason fulfills this function by examining both the content and the external evidences for the divine origin of the revelation under consideration. The external evidences are primarily provided by miracles, which Locke shows in his *Discourse on Miracles* (1702) to be the proper credentials of a revelation,[8] and to a lesser extent by fulfilled prophecy. In the *Essay*, however, Locke's main concern is with the content of revelation. His basic principle is that we can never receive anything as true which directly contradicts our clear and distinct knowledge, for there can be no evidence that anything is actually revealed by God stronger than the certainty derived from the perception of the agreement or disagreement of our clear and distinct ideas.[9] If this be denied, he argues, all criteria of knowledge will be destroyed, leading either to universal scepticism or enthusiasm[10] (in refutation of which he added Chapter XIX in the fourth edition).

Thus, no revelation can be accepted which contradicts the plain dictates of reason. It may communicate certain truths which are discoverable by reason, but in such cases the knowledge that it is revealed can never amount to as great a certainty as the knowledge drawn from the comparison of ideas. This is merely the application of the above principle, but it clearly implies the theologically dangerous proposition that revelation, or rather the proof that any particular doctrine is actually revealed, is always of a lower order of certainty than rational insight.

Hence, by a process of elimination, the proper subject matter of revelation is seen to be the second class of propositions: those which are above reason. However, since one of the main purposes of the *Essay* was to prove that the fundamental principles of natural religion—the existence and providence of God—are rationally demonstrable, the only propositions which Locke can supply as examples of this third category are the doctrine of the resurrection of the dead and the assertion that some of the angels rebelled against God.[11] These and kindred, but not specified propositions, although not strictly discoverable by reason, contain nothing contrary thereto, and when ascertained to have been revealed by God "must carry against the probable conjectures of reason."[12]

The logical conclusion to be drawn from a careful consideration of the argument of the *Essay* is that revelation is by and large superfluous, and this, in fact, was one of the basic principles of deism. However, as a professed Christian, Locke was obliged to maintain both the reasonableness and necessity of the Christian revelation, a task which he undertook in the *Reasonableness of Christianity as Delivered in the Scriptures* (1695).

Locke's avowed purpose is to found the understanding of Christianity upon a "fair and unprejudiced examination of Scripture," a procedure reminiscent of "the plain historical method," advocated so strongly, if not always practiced, in the *Essay*. He begins with a consideration of the Fall, the ultimate basis of the doctrine of redemption, which is in turn the central concept of the New Testament. However, already at this point the conciliatory nature of Locke's theology, and of the tradition which he represents, becomes manifest. There are, he argues, two extreme positions:

> Some men would have all Adam's posterity doomed to eternal, infinite punishment, for the transgression of Adam, whom millions had never heard of, and no one had authorized to transact for him, or be his representative; this seemed to others so little consistent with the justice or goodness of the great and infinite God, that they thought there was no redemption necessary, and consequently, that there was none; rather than admit of it upon a supposition so derogatory to the honour and attributes of that infinite Being; and so made Jesus Christ nothing but the restorer and preacher of pure natural religion; thereby doing violence to the whole tenor of the New Testament.[13]

These two positions, that of orthodox Calvinism and deism, are the Scylla and Charybdis between which the entire tradition had to move. To accept the former was to contradict the clearest dictates of moral reason, and consequently to deny the fundamental principles of the Enlightenment; while to accept the latter was to deny the very foundation of Christianity. Locke navigates between these two poles by means of his unbiased reading of Scripture. The Bible says nothing about original sin, eternal torments, or any such scholastic subtlety. It simply asserts that Adam disobeyed the command of God, and for this was punished with the loss of immortality. Thus, for Locke the Fall is simply a fitting punishment for a breach of contract, which any reasonable Englishman would find equitable. There is no transmission of unwarranted corruption, but since all men have, like Adam, disobeyed God, that is, have not fulfilled the "covenant of works" which God made with Moses in respect of the Hebrews, and which is also ingrained on the hearts of all men in the form of the law of nature, all have died. Clearly, this is no more than they deserve, but the New Testament further tells us that God, in his infinite mercy, contracted a new agreement with sinful man, "the covenant of faith," through the fulfillment of which one may be justified short of perfect obedience. This new agreement does not abrogate the old, for the obligation to obey still remains. "But by the law of faith, faith is allowed to supply the defect of full obedience; and so the believers are admitted to life and immortality, as if they were righteous."[14]

The problem now is to determine the nature of that which is required to be believed by the new covenant, and here Locke once again makes use of his straightforward method of interpretation. The New Testament does not teach us an elaborate system of mysterious doctrine, phrased in an unintelligible scholastic terminology, but simply declares that Jesus Christ is the Messiah, a statement, which is confirmed by his miracles, and by his precise fulfillment of the prophecies in the Old Testament. "This," argues Locke in a statement which epitomizes the Enlightenment's matter of fact approach to the problem of the truth of the Christian religion, "was the great proposition that was then controverted, concerning Jesus of Nazareth, 'whether he was the Messiah or no?' And the assent to that was that which distinguished believers from unbelievers."[15]

The acceptance of Jesus as the Messiah is thus the one essential, positive precept of Christianity, and belief in this, with sincere repentance, constitutes the sum total of God's requirements. "These two, faith and repentance, i.e. believing Jesus to be the Messiah, and a good life, are the indispensable conditions of the new covenant, to be performed by all those who would obtain eternal life."[16]

Having delineated his simple, scriptural, and eminently reasonable account of the Christian religion, Locke endeavors to meet the most common deistic objections.[17] These concern the apparent partiality and arbitrariness of a God who could design a scheme of salvation which deprives a large portion of the human race of an infinite advantage simply because of the historical accident that they either lived before or never heard of the miraculous event, and consequently could not believe in the messiahship of Jesus. Locke divides this general problem in two parts. First, he treats the case of the Jews who lived under the old covenant. Through judicious citation of Scripture he is able to show that God accounted their trust in his future promises for righteousness. The real problem, however, as Locke clearly recognizes, concerns those untold millions "who, having never heard of the promise or news of a Saviour; not a word of a Messiah to be sent, or that was come; have had no thought or belief concerning him?"[18]

This is the crucial point which is raised again and again in eighteenth-century religious polemics. A God who could condemn these untold millions to eternal torments, or even deprive them of immortality because of something which was not their fault, could never be the object of a rational worship. Such a God was in the eyes of Locke and the whole Enlightenment a monstrous tyrant. However, if this is not the case, if God does not condemn these millions, what is the significance of the Christian revelation? This then was the dilemma faced by Locke and all those who endeavored to establish the rationality of the Christian religion. Either it is morally offensive in its exclusivistic pretensions or it is unnecessary since man can be saved without it.

Locke and his successors accept the second alternative in a highly qualified form. Since God had "by the light of reason" revealed to all mankind their immutable obligations, and also his justice and mercy, he who made use of the "candle of the Lord" in order to determine his duty, could not miss finding the way to reconciliation and forgiveness.[19] Thus, acceptance of the Christian revelation is not absolutely necessary, for a man can be reconciled to God by following the principles of natural religion and morality. However, if Christianity is not absolutely necessary, it still has been of great advantage and has filled a practical need. For although man has reason enough to recognize God and his duties, he did not make use of it:

> Though the works of nature, in every part of them, sufficiently evidence a Deity; yet the world made so little use of their reason, that they saw him not, where, even by the impressions of himself, he was easy to be found. Sense and lust blinded their minds in

some, and a careless inadvertency in others, and fearful apprehensions in most (who either believed there were, or could not but suspect there might be, superior unknown beings) gave them up into the hands of their priests, to fill their heads with false notions of the Deity, and their worship with foolish rites, as they pleased: and what dread or craft once began, devotion soon made sacred, and religion immutable. In this state of darkness and ignorance of the true God, vice and superstition held the world. Nor could any help be had, or hoped for from reason; which could not be heard, and was judged to have nothing to do in the case; the priests, every where, to secure their empire, having excluded reason from having any thing to do in religion. And in the crowd of wrong notions, and invested rites, the world had almost lost the fight of the one only true God.[20]

Given this wretched state of affairs, Locke shows that the advent of Christ offered several distinct advantages: (1) the clear revelation which he brought with him "dissipated this darkness; made the 'one invisible true God' known to the world: and that with such evidence and energy, that polytheism and idolatry have no where been able to withstand it: . . ."[21] (2) It established for the first time a clear and rational system of morality, supported by Divine authority (this was evidenced by the miracles wrought on its behalf) and hence capable of functioning as a "sure guide of those who had a desire to go right; . . ."[22] (3) He reformed the outward forms of worship substituting "a plain, spiritual and suitable worship" for the superstitious rites which then prevailed.[23] (4) Through his teachings and his life he brought great encouragement to a virtuous and pious life,[24] and finally, (5) he brought to man a promise of divine assistance: "If we do what we can, he will give us his Spirit to help us to do what, and how we should."[25]

Thus, in lieu of its absolute necessity, Locke is able, through his catalogue of advantages, to illustrate the great usefulness of the Christian revelation. However, in making this compromise he has radically altered his original conception. For the content of this revelation is not, as the *Essay* would lead us to believe, a number of factual statements which unaided reason cannot verify, but rather, those very principles of natural religion and morality, which the *Essay* endeavored to establish upon a firm and evident basis. The content of revelation is now completely rational. It yields only those truths ascertainable by natural reason, but it presents them in such a way that they can be grasped by and rendered authoritative to the plain man, who has neither the time, inclination, nor ability for philosophic speculation. In developing this new conception, Locke makes use of an argument which we shall later see reappear in a radically transformed manner in Lessing. Revelation now functions as an anticipation of and substitute for reason. Its role is primarily pedagogical, giving man the first formulation of truths, which when once revealed he is able to grasp rationally. Moreover, he adds: "It is no diminishing to revelation, that reason gives its suffrage too, to the truths revelation has discovered. But it is our mistake to think, that because reason confirms them to us, we had the first certain knowledge of them from thence. . . ."[26]

From this standpoint, Christ is not simply the restorer, but rather the true founder of natural religion. He made it for the first time a practically effective system, and with his clear promise of immortality and appropriate rewards and punishments, he furnished the only sure foundation for morality. His teachings are so simple that they are readily accepted by any thinking person, but without their divine authority the bulk of mankind would have remained in perpetual darkness. For "the greatest part cannot know, and therefore they must believe."[27]

The theological positions just outlined constitute the prototype of the rational theology of the Enlightenment. The thoroughgoing rationalization of the content of revelation, which is still implicit in Locke, becomes explicit in thinkers such as Samuel Clarke and James Foster.[28] The result is that "reason is apparently exalted to such a pitch that revelation becomes superfluous."[29] Christianity is reduced to a reaffirmation of natural religion and morality, together with a few positive precepts, which are "exactly consonant to the Dictates of Sound Reason, and the unprejudiced Light of Nature, and most wisely perfective of it."[30] However, despite the rationalization of the content, the historicity of the Christian revelation is rigorously maintained, and this very rationality, which shows it to be worthy of an omniscient and benevolent deity, as well as the confirmed facts of miracles and fulfilled prophecies, are used to prove its historicity. The general position was first developed in England, but as we shall see, it reappeared in a modified form in Germany, where it formed one of the main negative influences upon Lessing's thought.

Deism: The rationalistic conception of Christianity forms the immediate background of deism, which originally was nothing more than the development of the logical implications of this view.

Acutely conscious of the irreconcilability of a religion based upon abstract demonstration, such as delineated by Clarke, with a faith grounded in the acceptance of certain historical facts, the deists denied the reliability of these "facts" and rejected the few additional positive precepts defended by the rationalistic divines. Thus, what had already become superfluous—revelation—was explicitly recognized as such, and in some cases totally rejected. From the standpoint of the absolute sufficiency of reason, which was the fundamental doctrine of deism, no historical revelation could be of decisive significance. Moreover, a particular revelation was viewed as beneath the dignity of the Supreme Being, who operates only according to universal laws. Correlative with the a priori repudiation of the concept of revelation was a full-scale, a posteriori attack upon the claims of the Christian religion to be such a revelation. The arguments from miracles, fulfilled prophecies, and the miraculous growth of the early Church (which for Locke and his school constituted the decisive external evidence for the truth of the Christian religion) were systematically repudiated and shown to have been based upon fraud, forgery, and enthusiasm.

A typical manifestation of the latter tendency, often called "critical Deism" is Anthony Collins, *A Discourse on the Grounds and Reasons of the Christian Religion* (1724). This work offers further evidence of the prevalence of the factual approach to the problem of the truth of the Christian religion. This truth, Collins argues, is based solely on the claim that Christ literally fulfilled the prophecies in the Old Testament and is thus the promised Messiah. If the evidence from prophecy be invalidated, Christianity falls to the ground. However, as he proceeds to show in great detail, the scriptural account of the life of Christ cannot reasonably be considered a literal fulfillment of these prophecies. Although Collins declines to draw the obvious conclusion, and instead piously suggests the possibility of a symbolic fulfillment, his real intent is clear. This critical aspect of the deistic controversy attracted the most attention and was conducted with the most vehemence, but its details are of little philosophical significance.[31] In each instance the critics shared the same basic premise with the defenders of Christianity—if certain historical claims are factually correct then the Christian religion is true—and only differed in regard to the evaluation of the evidence cited.[32]

The first major representative of this movement is John Toland, who in his *Christianity not Mysterious* (1696) inaugurated the deist controversy in England. Like many of the other deists, Toland's argument is far more radical in its implications than in its outright assertions. Rather than openly denying either the facticity or necessity of the Christian revelation, he claims to have established Christianity upon a firm foundation by demonstrating its complete rationality. The general tenor of his thought is to be gleaned from the subtitle: *A Treatise Showing That There Is Nothing in the Gospel Contrary to Reason; nor Above It; and That no Christian Doctrine Can Be Properly Called a Mystery.* In the preface Toland delineates a three-fold task. He will (1) show that the true religion must necessarily be reasonable and intelligible, (2) show that the requisite conditions are found in Christianity, and (3) demonstrate the divine source of the Christian revelation.[33] This was to be accomplished in three discourses, of which only the first was ever written.

He begins directly with a statement of the main issue: the claim that Christianity contains many exalted and incomprehensible mysteries and, consequently, that one must humbly submit one's reason to infallible authorities. In opposition to this Toland states categorically that "reason is the only foundation of all certitude; and that nothing reveal'd, whether as to its Manner or Existence, is more exempted from its Disquisitions that the ordinary Phenomena of Nature."[34]

However, rather than proceeding directly to the problem at hand, Toland gives a preliminary analysis of the faculty of reason, which is almost a verbatim repetition of the main argument of Locke's *Essay*.[35] Then, armed with the Lockean epistemology, he resumes the discussion. The main issue, as he clearly sees it, is not whether we can accept manifest contradictions as the word of God—this was explicitly denied by the entire rationalistic tradition—but whether any divinely revealed doctrine may according to our conception of it be "seen directly to clash with our Reason?"[36] In raising the question Toland is challenging the basic premise of Locke's discussion of faith in the *Essay*, and by answering it in the negative he is refuting Locke with his own weapons. For, in terms of the Lockean epistemology, whereby knowledge is given a subjective intuitivistic foundation, that is, in the perception of the agreement or disagreement of ideas, there is no basis upon which one can distinguish between that which actually does and that which only seems to conflict with our most evident notions, and consequently the distinction between propositions above and propositions contrary to reason is shown to be without foundation.

Furthermore, Toland argues, if belief is to be meaningful, if it is to influence our actions, then its objects must be intrinsically intelligible. Thus, all mysterious rites, miracles, and incomprehensible dogmas are to be banished from religion. They have no more right in the realm of faith than in that of knowledge, for ultimately, faith itself is based upon knowledge.[37] As he later asks: "Could that Person justly value himself upon being wiser than his Neighbors, who having infallible Assurance that something call'd Blictri had a Being in Nature, in the mean time know not what this Blictri was?"[38]

Upon this basis Toland criticizes Locke's concept of revelation. For Locke, the divine origin of a proposition was an absolute guarantee of its truth, and the role of knowledge was merely to ascertain this origin through an examination of the content and outward evidence. With Toland, however, this notion undergoes a subtle, but decisive change, for if reason be the only judge, and the intelligible its only object, then the perception of this intelligibility can furnish the only grounds for our assent to a proposition. Thus, revelation loses its authoritative character, or as Toland expresses it: "It is not a motive of assent, but merely a source of information."[39] The direct result of this argument is the rejection of all external evidence. A revelation is to be judged solely in terms of its content, and no supernatural signs can give it an authority which it does not intrinsically possess. In short, we do not believe a proposition because it is revealed but because "we see in its subject the indisputable character of Divine Wisdom and Sound Reason; which are the only Marks we have to distinguish the Oracles and Will of God, from the Impostures and Traditions of Men."[40]

Toland, however, is conservative to the extent that he seems with Locke, to take seriously the notion of revelation as a means of information—the communication of previously unknown, yet essentially intelligible matters of fact.[41] Moreover, he argues at great length that the notion of mystery found in the New Testament and earliest Fathers signified precisely such hitherto undisclosed matters of fact,[42] and upon this basis asserts that the pure, uncorrupted version of Christianity found in the Bible is not mysterious in the derogatory sense, but that this tendency only entered Christianity later, under the influence of the pagan rites.[43] Thus, although he rejects its authority, Toland does not explicitly deny the usefulness of revelation. This step, which was necessary for the logical development of the principle of deism, was taken by Matthew Tindal.

In Tindal's *Christianity as Old as the Creation* (1730) we have the most mature expression of English deism. In the development from Toland to Tindal we can detect a marked change in emphasis from a purely intellectual to an essentially moral critique of Christianity.[44] Eschewing any epistemological consideration, which played such a large role in Toland, Tindal argues purely on a priori grounds from the concept of God, and the presupposition of the identity of human nature in all times and places. Since God is an eternal, immutable, omniscient, benevolent and completely self-sufficient being, it follows that he gave men from the beginning, that religion, the practice of which renders them acceptable to him, and coming from an unalterable and perfect being, this religion must likewise be unalterable and perfect. Moreover, since such a being is necessarily completely fair, he must have provided all men, at all times, with the requisite means to recognize this religion, and consequently could not single out any particular people for a special revelation. Finally, since such a being is concerned only with the good of his creatures, and not with the enhancement of his glory, he could not reveal to, or require of men, anything morally indifferent. Thus, by a simple chain of reasoning from the very concept of God maintained by the rationalistic divines,[45] Tindal is able to establish that the true religion must consist solely in the practice of morality, that it is everywhere the same and as "old as creation," and that a just God must have given all men the capacity to recognize its essential ingredients.

This is the classic expression of the deistic principle of the sufficiency of reason, and it is grounded in a genuine awareness of the irreconcilability of the concept of God implied by the new science with the values of traditional Christianity. The deity of Newton and Clarke and of the Enlightenment in general is the Supreme Mathematician, the sovereign architect of an infinite, and perfectly rational universe, and not the arbitrary, despotic ruler of a tiny Near Eastern principality. Thus, commenting upon the search for fundamentals, in the acceptance of which all Christians could unite, Tindal states:

> Would not one think that a little honest reflection should carry them further, and make them see, that it is inconsistent with the universal and unlimited goodness of the common parent of mankind, not to make that which is necessary for the salvation of all men so plain, as that all men may know it? Though one would be apt to

think, that by the number and oddness of those things, which in most Churches divines have made necessary to salvation, they were more zealous to damn others than to save themselves, or at least, that they thought there was no room in heaven for any, but men of these our narrow principles.[46]

From this standpoint any historical revelation is true only insofar as it conforms to the immutable dictates of natural religion, or, as Tindal expresses it, natural and revealed religion differ only in the manner in which they are communicated: "The one being the internal, and the other the external revelation of the same unchangeable will of a being who is alike at all times infinitely wise and good."[47] Moreover, since natural religion is perfect, any deviation from, or addition to it is inevitably a corruption, owing its origin to the artful deception of priests. Thus, the Christian revelation is true to the extent to which it is a "republication of the religion of nature"[48] and false to the extent to which it deviates therefrom. Furthermore, such deviations or additions are not only not pleasing to God, but they are injurious to men. Following Bayle, Tindal sees that the roots of superstition and persecution lie precisely in the recognition of the belief in, and practice of things morally indifferent as necessary for salvation:

> They who believe that God will damn men for things not moral, must believe, that in order to prevent damnable opinions from spreading, and to show themselves holy as their heavenly father is holy, they cannot show too much emnity to those against whom God declares an eternal emnity; or plague them enough in this life, upon whom in the life to come God will pour down the plagues of eternal vengeance. Hence it is that animosity, emnity and hatred, have over-run the Christian world; and men, for the sake of these notions, have exercised the utmost cruelties on one another; the most cursing and damning Churches have always proved the most persecuting.[49]

Thus, the ethical and the a priori critiques of positive religion are conjoined in Tindal, with the latter laying the foundation for the former. The practice of one's immutable and readily apparent duties is all that is pleasing to God or useful to men, and no alleged revelation which proclaims the contrary can be accepted as divine. This principle leads Tindal (again following Bayle) to a moral critique of various Old Testament narratives, of which the Hebrews'

wanton murder of the Canaanites furnishes his favorite example.
Since this and innumerable similar deeds obviously contradict the
evident dictates of natural law, they cannot have been commanded
by God. Hence, the groundwork is laid for a complete rejection of
the authority of the Old Testament, a task which was systematically carried through by Tindal's disciple, Thomas Morgan, in his
Moral Philosopher (1737).

Tindal concludes with a lengthy critique of Clarke. In essence
he accepts Clarke's analysis of the clearness and sufficiency of the
law of nature, but rejects as inconsistent his argument for the necessity of certain supplemental revelations:

> If Christianity, as well as deism, consists in being governed
> by the original obligations of the moral fitness of things, in con-
> formity to the nature, and in imitation of the perfect will of God,
> then they both must be the same. But if Christianity consists in
> being governed by any other rules, or requires any other thing,
> has not the Doctor himself given the advantage to deism.[50]

With this deism reaches its logical culmination. Christianity is
true precisely to the extent to which it is superfluous. Nothing positive—nothing besides the practice of morality—deserves a place in
the true worship of God, and thus the sum total of traditional Christian doctrine, as well as its historical claims, are not only religiously
irrelevant, but morally pernicious.

II
PIERRE BAYLE AND THE ENLIGHTENMENT

Bayle's relation to the Enlightenment is an ambivalent one. In
many respects he is one of its most important progenitors. His
attack upon superstition and intolerance and his moral critique of
the Bible not only provided the inspiration but also much of the
material for subsequent discussions.[51] However, his radical scepticism and fideism stood in sharp contrast to the prevailing tendencies
of the age and offered a significant challenge to its rationalistic
approach to revelation. Nevertheless, because of his tremendous
historical importance and especially because of his influence on
the young Lessing, we shall here consider both aspects of his
thought.

Superstition: Attacks on superstition are scattered throughout
Bayle's writings,[52] but the most systematic treatment is found in

his first major work: *Miscellaneous Thoughts on the Comet of 1680* (1682). Here Bayle uses the popular belief that comets are divinely ordained presages of misfortunes as a pretext for a general repudiation of superstition. He offers all the standard scientific arguments against this and similar superstitions, but his main attack is formulated from a theological standpoint. If, he argues, comets are presages of evil then they are miraculous, and since they occurred with equal frequency before the advent of Christ it follows that God performed miracles for the sole purpose of strengthening idolators in their ways.[53] This conclusion is acceptable to orthodoxy, which argued that God performed miracles among the pagans to prevent them from falling into atheism. This, however, presupposes that atheism is a worse crime than idolatry or superstition, and it is precisely this claim, together with its corollary that God would act to promote the latter at the expense of the former, which Bayle endeavors to refute.

In support of this paradoxical position, based upon Plutarch's *Essay on Superstition*, Bayle offers a detailed examination of paganism, which reveals a long and sordid history of debauchery and cruelty, combined with a firm belief in the existence of the gods. Such has been the historically verified result of superstition. The consequences of atheism, however, have not been nearly so pernicious.[54] Many atheists have led exemplary lives,[55] and a peaceful and law abiding society of atheists is quite conceivable.[56] Thus, Bayle concludes "that if one considers pagans and atheists by their disposition, either of mind or heart; one would find as much disorder among the former as among the latter."[57]

After showing at great length the moral superiority of atheists to the devotees of superstition, Bayle endeavors to explain this phenomenon in terms of a psychology of religious behavior. Believers can be inhuman tyrants (his favorite examples are Nero and Louis XI), and nonbelievers morally upright men, because belief is not the determining ground of action and prudence in regard to a divine providence is not, as had been assumed by traditional religious psychology, a check upon the passions. All men, whether Christians, pagans, or atheists, generally act according to their present inclinations,[58] for as he later reflects: "If conscience were the cause determining men's actions, would Christians live such wretched lives?"[59]

The most significant consequence of this rather pessimistic conception of human nature is the justification of ignorance or honest doubt, which for Bayle includes atheism. Since the acceptance of a certain set of beliefs is not in itself conducive to the moral life, an atheist may be as good a man as a believer and thus must not be condemned for his error. Superstition, however, since it works upon the passions and fosters the belief that rites rather than morality are demanded by God, has a negative moral effect and inevitably leads to excess and complete corruption.[60] With this Bayle establishes what Cassirer considers to be one of the fundamental axioms of the Enlightenment: the recognition that not doubt or ignorance but dogma, which if believed implicitly leads ultimately to superstition, is the real enemy of both morality and religion.[61]

Toleration: Although Bayle offers various arguments for the principle of unlimited religious toleration, they fall roughly into two classes.[62] The first, grounded in his sceptical denial of the possibility of rationally determining which is the true religion, dominates his earlier treatments of the subject. From this standpoint Bayle attacks the attempted justifications of religious compulsion based upon "the rights of the truth."[63] The Catholic Church had argued that, since it was in possession of the true faith and that without it an individual is doomed to eternal damnation, the veritable charity is to compel him to recognize this truth. Against this view Bayle contends that such a claim involves the confusion of one's persuasion, or subjective conviction of the truth, with the truth itself. An individual's belief is largely determined by the time and place of his birth and the nature of his education, and since the followers of each religion are equally convinced of the truth of their beliefs any claim made in the name of truth, must be reciprocally granted to all contending parties. Thus, for Bayle "the rights of the truth" are equally "the rights of the erring conscience,"[64] and consequently:

> . . . the true church, whichever it may be, is as little justified in using coercion or persecution against the others as the others are in using them against it; for the only thing that could justify the true church in the persecutions which it exercizes against the others consists in the fact that she is persuaded of their falsity. However, the others are no less persuaded of her falsity than she is of theirs; therefore they have the same right.[65]

In the *Philosophical Commentary upon the Words of Jesus Christ: "Compel Them to Come in"* (1686), his major discussion of toleration, Bayle reiterates the sceptical argument, but subordi-

nates it to a positive principle: the absolute primacy of moral reason.[66] This work, which was occasioned by the revocation of the
Edict of Nantes, is prefaced by a vitriolic attack upon the Roman
Catholic Church, but the text itself is devoted to a dispassionate
and logical argumentation. Catholic theologians from Augustine to
Bossuet had used a literal reading of Luke 14:23: "And the Lord
said unto the servant, Go out into the highways and hedges, and
compel them to come in that my house may be filled," as justification for their policy of compulsion. Against this Bayle asserts the
primacy of the universal moral reason which he defines as "a clear
and distinct light which enlightens all men."[67] Although this natural
light has severe limitations in regard to speculative matters, Bayle
states:

> I do not think that it should have any with regard to the practical
> and general principles which concern morals. I mean that we must,
> without exception, submit all moral laws to this natural idea of
> justice, which just as the metaphysical light, "enlightens every man
> who comes into this world."[68]

After some general remarks to the effect that constraint is incapable of inspiring religion and can only lead to hypocrisy,[69] and
that a literal reading of this passage contradicts the entire spirit of
the Gospel,[70] Bayle offers his doctrine of the primacy of moral reason as a key to the interpretation of the Bible. According to this
principle, he argues, any reading which contradicts the plain dictates of morality must be erroneous. Now the literal interpretation
of the passage "compel them to enter" obviously does just that, and
it therefore must necessarily be false.[71]

This is Bayle's most decisive statement concerning the primacy
of moral reason. Its universal authority extends even to the content
of revelation.[72] Religious compulsion is shown to contradict the
dictates of this natural light; thus, it categorically must be rejected,
and any scriptural passages which appear to justify it must be reinterpreted. Moreover, this principle provides a new foundation
for the theory of "the rights of the erring conscience." False beliefs
are now seen to possess an intrinsic worth, based upon the sincerity
with which they are accepted. Each man who follows the dictates
of his conscience in the profession of his religion is acceptable to
God.[73] This position, involves the extension of the Protestant
emphasis upon the individual conscience as the ultimate au-

thority in spiritual matters, to the un-Protestant justification of
the "erring conscience." This extension gave birth to the concept of
the innocence of error, one of the cardinal beliefs of the Enlightenment, and thus it is thoroughly in the spirit of his successors that
Bayle declared: ". . . there is no error in religion, of whatever sort
one may suppose, that is a sin if it is involuntary."[74]

Scepticism: If, however, Bayle may be regarded as a genuine
forerunner of the Enlightenment in regard to his treatment of
superstition and intolerance, his radical scepticism and fideism,
rooted in the thought of Montaigne, Charron, La Mathe La Vayer,
and Gassendi, constitute a complete rejection of its basic conception
of religion. This aspect of his thought was first developed in his
monumental *Historical and Critical Dictionary* (1697, second edition, augmented 1702) and further amplified in the many controversies which occupied the last years of his life.

Bayle's theoretical scepticism, which admittedly stands in sharp
contrast, if not direct contradiction, to his emphasis on the clarity
and universal validity of moral reason,[75] finds its most precise
formulation in the article *Pyrrhon,* and especially in remarks B and
C.[76] He begins with the reflection that Pyrrhonism is a danger only
to theology, but not to natural philosophy or the state. Most
scientists are sceptics concerning the ultimate nature of things and
are content to find possible hypotheses and experimental data.
Moreover, since a consistent Pyrrhonist has no dogmatic political
views, he will readily conform to the customs of the country in
which he resides.[77] In religion, however, where firm conviction
requires absolute certainty, it is a different story. Here scepticism
may constitute a positive danger, but Bayle concludes ironically,
that it is seldom of any great practical effect, because:

> The grace which God bestows upon the faithful, the force of educa-
> tion in other men, and if you will, ignorance, and the natural
> inclination men have to be peremptory, are an impenetrable shield
> against the darts of the Pyrrhonists, though the sect fancies it is
> now more formidable than it was anciently.[78]

This sets the stage for the main presentation of the sceptical
position, which takes the form of a dialogue between two abbés
concerning the contemporary significance of Pyrrhonism. The first,
and orthodox abbé asserts that he cannot understand how "there
could be any Pyrrhonists under the light of the Gospel."[79] In reply,
the second abbé proclaims that a contemporary sceptic would be

even more powerful than his ancient counterpart because: "The Christian Theology would afford him unanswerable arguments,"[80] not to mention the advantages derived from the new philosophy.

After a brief treatment of the sceptical implications of modern philosophy,[81] Bayle proceeds to the crucial issue between rationalism or dogmatism, and scepticism: the "criterium veritatis." If scepticism is to be refuted, there must be an infallible standard of truth. The rationalists, following Descartes, contend that "evidence is a certain character of truth."[82] If this be denied, there is no certainty. Against this, the sceptical abbé makes the radical claim that there are propositions possessing clear evidence, which are rejected as false, and thus, evidence is not the mark of truth, and consequently there is no certainty.[83]

In support of this contention the abbé cites several theological examples, of which two will suffice to illustrate Bayle's method. It is evident, he argues, that two things which do not differ from a third, do not differ from each other. This principle is one of the bases of all our reasoning, but nevertheless, we are convinced by the revelation of the doctrine of the Trinity, that this principle is false.[84] Second, from the moral realm, the abbé argues: It is evident that evil ought to be prevented, and that it is a sin to permit it, when avoidable. However, Christian theology clearly shows us that this is false, for it teaches us that when God permits all the evil and disorders of the world, he does nothing inconsistent with his perfections.[85] Furthermore, the attempt to avoid these difficulties by arguing that the examples depend upon judging the Divinity by human standards is of no avail. Such a qualitative distinction between human and divine reason implies that the true nature of things is unknowable and thus leads us to an even more radical scepticism.[86]

Finally, after systematically demolishing the claims of reason, Bayle offers (Remark C) the pious alternative of faith, as the only sure road to God:

> When a man is able to apprehend all the ways of suspending his judgment, which have been laid open by Sextus Empiricus, he may then perceive that that logic is the greatest effort of subtilty that the mind of man is capable of; but he will see at the very same time that such a subtilty will afford him no satisfaction: it confounds itself; for if it were solid, it would prove that it is certain that we must doubt. Therefore there would be some certainty, there would be a certain rule of truth. That system would be destroyed by it;

but you need not fear that things would come to that: the reasons for doubting are doubtful themselves: one must therefore doubt whether he ought to doubt. What chaos! What torment for the mind! it seems therefore, that this unhappy state is the fittest of all to convince us, that our reason is the way to wander, since when it displays itself with the greatest subtilty, it throws us into such an abyss. What naturally follows from thence, is to renounce that guide, and beseech the cause of all things to give us a better. It is a great step towards the Christian religion, which requires of us, that we should expect from God the knowledge of what we are to believe, and do, and that we should captivate our understanding to the obedience of faith.[87]

Thus, Bayle's scepticism leads to a radical fideism, wherein the claims of reason are rejected before the sure standard of divine revelation. His major application of this position was to the problem of evil, in regard to which he endeavored to establish the theoretical superiority of the Manichaean to the Christian hypothesis, and consequently to emphasize the need to reject the findings of reason and accept the Christian doctrine on faith. This view is developed in the articles: *Manichees, Marcionites,* and *Paulicians,* but it receives its most comprehensive expression in the first of these, which served as the starting point for all subsequent discussions of the subject.

After a preliminary description of the Manichaean dualism and the narration of some of the more sordid details of the sect's history, Bayle states his thesis:

It must be confessed, that this false tenet, which is much more ancient than Manes, and cannot be maintained by anyone, who admits the Holy Scripture, either in whole or in part, would not easily be refuted, if it were maintained by pagan philosophers, well skilled in disputing.[88]

The balance of the article is devoted to a defense of this statement, and this involves a concrete application of the fideism already discussed. By a priori reasons, Bayle argues, the defenders of the Manichaean hypothesis would quickly be routed. All our clear ideas of order teach us that a necessary, infinite, and eternal Being must be one and endowed with all perfections. From this point of view there is nothing more absurd than the doctrine of two ultimate principles, one of which is inherently evil and can frustrate the designs of the other.[89] However, in order to establish itself, a system not only requires a logical chain of clear and distinct ideas, but it must also account for experience. One principle is sufficient to explain adequately the phenomena of nature, but the greatest objections against the unity of God are provided by man:

> Man is wicked and unhappy: every one knows it by what he feels in himself, and by the intercourse he is obliged to have with his neighbors. He, who lives only five or six years may be perfectly convinced of these two things; and they, who live long, and are much engaged in worldly affairs, know this still more clearly. Travels afford perpetual lessons upon this subject: they show every where the monuments of men's misfortunes and wickedness: this appears every where by the many prisons, hospitals, gibbets and beggars. Here you see the ruins of a flourishing city; elsewhere you cannot even find the ruins of it.[90]

However, neither the physical nor the moral world is completely evil, despite the preponderance of misery: "There are every where some things that are physically good and morally good; some examples of virtue, and some examples of happiness . . ."[91] and it is precisely this which causes the difficulty. If there were none but evil and unhappy men, there would be no need to have recourse to two principles. It is this mixture of happiness and virtue with misery and vice which seems to require the dualistic hypothesis and which constitutes the strongest argument for the Manichaean position.

In order to emphasize further the difficulty of refuting this position, and to demonstrate the need for recourse to revelation, Bayle once again resorts to dialogue, this time between Melissus and Zoroaster. Melissus, the Eleatic monist, would undoubtedly contend that his system best agreed with our clear ideas of order. Zoroaster would be forced to admit the a priori superiority of his opponent's position, but would argue that it is unable to account adequately for the existence of evil, and that since the principal requirement of a good system is the ability to explain experience, the dualistic hypothesis, which can do this, must be preferred.[92] In support of his case Zoroaster argues:

> If man is the creature of one principle perfectly good, most holy and omnipotent, can he be exposed to diseases, to heat and cold, hunger and thirst, pain and grief? Can he have so many bad inclinations? Can he commit so many crimes? Can perfect holiness produce such a criminal creature? Can perfect goodness produce an unhappy creature? Would not omnipotence, joined with infinite

goodness, furnish his own work plentifully with good things, and secure it from every thing that might be offensive or vexatious?[93]

The traditional Christian answer to this problem, which Bayle puts into the mouth of Melissus, is based upon the freedom of the will. Since God endowed man with a free will, he is not the cause of moral evil, but only of physical evil, which he justly decrees as a consequence of sin. However, in response to this Zoroaster might well reply that if man were the work of an infinitely good principle, he ought to have been created not only without any actual evil but without any inclination thereto. Moreover, in addition to pointing out the difficulties inherent in the doctrine of free will, he would formulate the decisive question: Did God foresee that man would make ill use of his freedom? If he did, he should have prevented him from sinning, and even if he did not positively foresee it, our notions of a perfect being teach us that he would determine men to moral, as well as to physical good, so as to prevent the very possibility of such a state of affairs. If, reasons Zoroaster, the prevention of possible error by his children is deemed a duty incumbent upon every father, how much more so is it to be expected of the Deity? Melissus would be able to formulate some replies to these objections, but they would not be decisive, and thus, asserts Bayle, the argument would continue without Zoroaster ever being brought back into the way of truth.[94]

Such then is the outcome of the great conflict between faith and reason. Christianity fails on both its theoretical and practical sides to justify itself before the bar of reason, and the believer is advised to reject totally the dictates of his feeble reason and subject himself to faith. This, of course, implied the denial of the possibility of a rational theology such as prevailed in England and constituted a major challenge to the fundamental values of the Enlightenment. The most eminent of the many advocates of reason who accepted this challenge was Gottfried Wilhelm Leibniz.

III

LEIBNIZ AND THE GERMAN AUFKLÄRUNG*

Leibniz: Leibniz's relationship to the Aufklärung is analogous to that of Locke to the English and Bayle to the French Enlightenment. Each laid the foundation and delineated the main direction

* Throughout this study I use the term "Aufklärung" to refer to the specifically German branch of the Enlightenment.

which the movement would take in his country.[95] However, while Locke's *Essay* and Bayle's *Dictionary* were universally proclaimed, the positive influence of the Leibnizean philosophy was confined largely to Germany.[96] This fact helps account for the singular character of the Aufklärung, which while manifesting the practical and eudaemonistic tendencies of the age, never completely lost its metaphysical and religious orientation.

The historical significance of Leibniz's philosophy of religion is based largely upon his *Theodicy* (1710). Here Leibniz endeavored to reaffirm, against Bayle, the agreement between philosophy and theology, or reason and revelation, and thus to provide a new foundation for the fundamental tenet of the religious thought of the Enlightenment. The *Theodicy*, however, was not an isolated production, but rather the culmination of a life-long concern with the problem of the relation between traditional religion and the new science and humanistic values. Moreover, this very concern was itself grounded on the basic concept of his philosophy: the principle of universal harmony. It was in virtue of this principle, which underlies all his thought, that Leibniz continually endeavored to find a measure of truth in every position and to reconcile apparently diverse philosophical and theological standpoints.

In the practical sphere this profound concern with reconciliation and harmony led to a concerted effort to reunite Christendom. Acting as the representative of the Court of Hanover, Leibniz engaged in a voluminous, if intermittent, correspondence with Bossuet (lasting from 1683 to 1702), in a fruitless attempt to arrive at doctrinal agreement, and eventual unity, between the Lutheran and Roman Catholic churches. Although much of Leibniz's effort in this direction was dictated by diplomatic considerations, his treatment of specific doctrines often reveals a genuine philosophic and religious concern with the issues.[97]

It is, however, only in the speculative realm that the full significance of the universal harmony is manifest. It is largely by virtue of this principle that he endeavored to reconcile the main concepts of natural religion: God, providence, freedom, and immortality, with the findings of modern science. He had argued that "in effect metaphysics is natural theology,"[98] and on this basis he repeatedly defended his own philosophy and criticized that of others.[99]

This critical tendency is especially evident in his treatment of Descartes and Spinoza. It has been said with some justification that, from 1671 on, Leibniz's real quarrel with Descartes centered around the religious and moral consequences of his doctrines, which as Leibniz was anxious to show, lead straight to the dreaded Spinozism.[100] Leibniz based his critique upon two specific points: the proposition that matter takes on successively all the forms of which it is capable, and the denial of the relevance of final causes in physics.[101] In regard to the former Leibniz contends that this position ultimately implies a denial of the wisdom and justice of God, and thus was not far from the views of Spinoza and Hobbes. If God produces everything, he argues, and does not choose from among possibles, then there is no ground for trust in providence, and consequently such a conception is the "first falsehood" and the very foundation for atheism.[102]

The critique of the second point, the rejection of the use of final causes in physics, is even more basic. It is here that Leibniz formulates his fundamental opposition to the Cartesian doctrine of God. The true philosophy, he maintains, must provide an entirely different conception of the divine perfections than Descartes', one that will be of use both in physics and ethics. Rather than excluding final causes from physics, "it is by means of them that everything ought to be determined, for the efficient cause of things is intelligent, has a will, and consequently strives for the good." This, however, is far from the sentiments of Descartes, who contends that "goodness, truth and justice are only such because God has established them by a free act of his will."[103]

It was this aspect of the Cartesian position, the grounding of the goodness, justice and wisdom of God in an arbitrary act of will, implicit in the rejection of final causes in physics, which constituted the real object of Leibniz's attack.[104] It was his firm conviction that only if the divine will is viewed as conforming to an objective standard of truth and goodness can God's wisdom and goodness, and consequently the ultimate rationality of the universe, be affirmed:

> For if truth depended only upon the will of God, and not upon the nature of things, since the understanding necessarily 'precedes' the will (I speak of natural and not temporal priority), the divine understanding would precede the truth of things, and thus, would not have the truth for its object. Such an understanding is without doubt only a chimera, and thus, it would be necessary to conceive of God, in the manner of Spinoza, as a being with neither understanding nor will, who produces good or evil indifferently, being indifferent in regard to the things, and having nothing inclining him to the one rather than to the other.[105]

This argument constitutes the theological aspect of Leibniz's critique of Descartes' phoronomic conception of matter. Here he supplements the scientific demonstrations of his own dynamic conception with the suggestion of the superiority of its moral and religious implications. Such a two-sided critique, typical of Leibniz, is another significant expression of the principle of universal harmony. From this standpoint there can be no ultimate conflict, such as the Cartesian scheme implied, between the findings of physics and the principles of natural religion and morality, between God as architect of the physical world, and God as ruler of the moral world of rational beings. Thus, in his *The Principles of Nature and of Grace, Based on Reason* (1714), Leibniz can speak of a preestablished harmony between the realms of nature (efficient causes) and grace (final causes). In relation to the problem raised by the new science, this meant simply that although all events in the universe are mechanically determined, they may neverthless also be viewed as expressions of an underlying purpose. The teleological order is revealed in and through the natural order. The wisdom of God is manifest in the laws of nature.

The Leibnizean concepts of providence and grace, which became generally adopted by the Aufklärung, were merely the results of the application of the general principle of harmony to the special case of rational beings. Because these rational beings or souls are finite images of the wisdom and goodness of God, they constitute, together with God, an ideal society or "City of God," wherein perfect justice and the greatest possible amount of happiness is to be found. Moreover, this marvelous arrangement does not take place through a disruption of the natural course of events, as if God's moral government could conflict with the laws of physics, but rather:

> . . . by the very order of natural things itself, by virtue of the harmony pre-established from all time between the realms of nature and of grace, between God as architect and God as monarch, in such a way that nature leads to grace, and grace perfects nature by using it.[106]

Despite the similarity of terminology, this passage entails a complete break with the traditional, Augustine-inspired, theology. Divine providence is no longer seen as a miraculous intervention in the course of history but as an intrinsic element in the total plan of the universe, and grace is not regarded as the repudiation

of a sinful and corrupt nature but as the eminently rational perfection of a finite, yet basically good one. Moreover, the City of
God, which Augustine limited to the relatively small number of
the elect, is expanded to make room, at least potentially, for all
rational beings. This, in effect, constitutes a total repudiation of
the Augustinian position, and Leibniz further expressed his antagon-
ism to this view in a fragment, which although unknown to the
Aufklärung, epitomizes its religious attitude:

> I am persuaded that it offends the justice of God to believe,
> for example, that infants dying without baptism, or morally good
> men who have never heard of Jesus Christ, are eternally damned
> because of it. Moreover, such irrational dogmas have no basis in
> Holy Writ, and nothing is better suited to undermine Christianity
> than to maintain them.[107]

This fragment is thoroughly in the spirit of the *Reasonableness
of Christianity* and the *Philosophical Commentary*. Leibniz shared
with Locke and Bayle the same basic humanistic values, but he
went beyond them in his endeavor to give these values a firm
metaphysical foundation, by grounding them in the doctrine of
God. Just as in his critique of Descartes, he saw that "it is necessary
to prove that the God who governs all is wise and just and that he
leaves nothing without reward and punishment; these are the
great foundations of morality,"[108] so too, he saw here that the
Augustinian-Calvinistic doctrine of double predestination and un-
merited grace implied a similar conception of the divine decree
as the manifestation of an omnipotent and arbitrary will. In each
case such a conception implied a concrete danger to the basic
principles of morality and religion, and, thus, in each case it had
to be refuted.

It was, moreover, a similar danger, which Leibniz saw in
Bayle's scepticism, and which led him to write the *Theodicy*, his
only full-length philosophical work published in his lifetime. Not
only would such views impede the progress of science and lead
to intellectual sterility, but, more important, the admission of
irrationality into the universe calls into question the wisdom and
goodness of God and thereby threatens the only satisfactory basis
upon which moral and religious values can be upheld.

The recognition of this clear and present danger determines
the standpoint assumed in the Preface to the *Theodicy*, where
Leibniz's purpose is the avowedly practical one of the inculcation

of true piety. This piety, which is identical with felicity, consists for Leibniz, as it does for the tradition, in the love of God. This love, however, is not a blind enthusiasm, but "a love so enlightened that its fervour is attended by insight."[109] Moreover, this kind of love provides the foundation of moral behavior. In and through love the individual comes to the realization that in the fulfillment of his duty he is obeying the will of God, and it is this realization which leads to that concern for the common good which constitutes man's highest satisfaction.[110]

In thus grounding true virtue in knowledge, Leibniz posed for the entire Aufklärung, the "clearing up of the understanding" as the primary ethical task. As Windelband has shown, this follows directly from the conception of the monad, whose perfection consists entirely in the clearness and distinctness of its perception.[111] Furthermore, since the objects of this rational love are the divine perfections, the result of the clarification process is the proper concept of God, and it becomes the task of religion to preserve this concept from infection. As we have already seen, such infection is caused by the emphasis upon God's omnipotent will rather than his supreme wisdom, and it is precisely this which Leibniz sees in Bayle's views, just as he formerly had in Descartes. Thus, in defining the purpose of the work, Leibniz states: "Our end is to banish from men the false ideas that represent God to them as an absolute prince employing a despotic power, unfitted to be loved and unworthy of being loved."[112]

The accomplishment of this task involves the removal of the difficulties raised by Bayle in his defense of the Manichaean hypothesis, and it is to this end that Leibniz devotes the bulk of the *Theodicy*. These difficulties are essentially of two sorts: the first springs from man's freedom, which appears incompatible with the divine nature, but which is nevertheless necessary for morality; the second concerns the conduct of God, who as the supreme and omnipotent creator seems to bear the ultimate responsibility for evil.[113] The first of these problems is given a preliminary treatment in the Preface and is there resolved in terms of the distinction between the different types of necessity. Although divine foreknowledge of future contingencies is granted, these events do not thereby lose their contingent status. Since they are grounded in the fitness of things, they are dependent upon the will of God and as such possess only a hypothetical necessity. The question of evil is posed in terms of the cosmic optimism, which is the logical consequence of the principle of universal harmony. Since the world is the creation of an infinitely wise, good, and powerful Being, it is necessarily the best of all possible worlds, for "this supreme wisdom, united to a goodness that is no less infinite, cannot but have chosen the best."[114]

However, far from resolving Bayle's difficulties, this purely formal response serves merely to sharpen the issue so that the basic question now becomes: why such a world, granted that it is necessarily the best possible, nevertheless contains sin and suffering. To this Leibniz proposes two types of answers, which we can do no more than indicate in outline. The first is based upon the general reflection that partial evil often leads to universal perfection, and that consequently, if the world did not contain the sin and suffering, which it in fact does, it would not be the best possible.[115] The second, and more basic, is grounded in the consideration of the nature of evil, which Leibniz, with Augustine, considers as essentially privative. As such, he argues that its origin lies in

> the ideal nature of the creature, in so far as this nature is contained in the eternal verities, which are in the understanding of God, independently of his will. For we must consider that there is an *original imperfection in the creature* before sin, because the creature is limited in its essence; whence ensues that it cannot know all, and that it can deceive itself and commit other errors.[116]

Leibniz calls this original imperfection metaphysical evil and posits it as the source of both physical and moral evil, or sin.[117] Thus understood, the existence of evil in the best of all possible worlds is not denied, but since it is not dependent upon the divine will, is shown to be reconcilable with the goodness of God, without the necessity of having recourse, with Bayle, to the Manichaean hypothesis.

The second part of the *Theodicy* is devoted to a systematic application of these principles to Bayle's formulation of his position in the *Response to the Questions of a Provincial*, wherein he presents seven theological propositions concerning the Christian concept of God and opposes them with nineteen philosophical objections.[118] Leibniz answers each of Bayle's arguments, but the discussion constantly returns to the same point. In each instance Bayle considers the given positive experience of evil and then asserts that this fact can not be made to accord with the Christian concept of God, while Leibniz responds each time with his a priori conception of finality, so that regardless of the facts the perfection of God is maintained. In the light of this Leibniz is able to formulate a general answer to all of Bayle's difficulties, which suggests the entirely different levels on which the two men argued:

> If things connected together may be separated, the parts from their whole, the human kind from the universe, God's attributes the one from the other, power from wisdom, it may be said that God can cause virtue to be in the world without any mixture of vice, and even that he can do so *easily*. But, since he has permitted vice, it must be that that order of the universe which was found preferable to every other plan required it. One must believe that it is not permitted to do otherwise, since it is not possible to do better.[119]

However, before proceeding to the justification of the goodness of God and the freedom of man, Leibniz must first attack the very heart of Bayle's scepticism, which is manifested in his insistence upon the irreconcilable opposition between faith and reason. This doctrine, which is a renewal of the two-truth theory of the medieval nominalists and Averroists, contains an explicit denial of the universal harmony, and consequently of the goodness and wisdom of God; thus, its refutation is a necessary preliminary to any theodicy from a Christian standpoint.

This task is undertaken in the *Preliminary Dissertation on the Conformity of Faith with Reason,* which serves as an introduction to the actual discussion of the problem of theodicy; in it Leibniz offers the fullest "official" expression of his conception of the relationship between reason and revelation, a conception which, just as did Locke's in England, formed the starting point for all further discussion of the subject in eighteenth-century German theology.

Leibniz's position, both here, and in his other writings, is fairly close to that of Locke and the English rational theologians.[120] He shares with them the fundamental rationalistic tenet that the true religion must have marks to distinguish it from the false, for "else would Zoroaster, Brahma, Somonacodom and Mahomet be as worthy of belief as Moses and Jesus Christ,"[121] and he also seems to accept the fact that Christianity contains such marks. Thus, Werner Conze, in his monograph on Leibniz's historical work, shows that his attitude toward the Bible and sacred history is basically orthodox.[122] The Judaeo-Christian revelation itself, and its essential content, are viewed as well-attested matters of fact, recorded in an infallible Bible, and in this regard Leibniz seems to share with his contemporaries the factual approach to the problem of the truth of the Christian religion.[123]

Leibniz begins the *Preliminary Dissertation* with a statement of his fundamental assumptions: two truths cannot contradict one another, the object of faith is the truth which God has revealed, and reason consists in linking truths together, and, in comparison with faith, especially those truths to which the human mind can attain naturally. This broad conception of reason is shown to include empirical reasoning based upon experience, and in this sense faith itself can be included within the reasoning process, for its credibility depends, as with Locke, upon the experience of those who witnessed the miracles which attested to the revelation.

This broad conception, however, is contrasted with "reason pure and simple," which is concerned only with nonempirical truths, and it is in light of the consideration of the two meanings of reason that Leibniz presents his fundamental distinction between truths of reason, which are absolutely or logically necessary, and truths of fact (positive truths), which are the specific laws it has pleased God to give to nature, and which being grounded in the divine will are not absolutely, but only morally necessary.[124]

Having made this distinction, Leibniz finds it easy to justify the traditional conceptions of both miracles and mysteries. It is clear that neither of these can contradict eternal truths:

> For if it is a question of proof which is founded upon principles or uncontestable facts and formed by a linking together of eternal verities, the conclusion is certain and essential, and that which is contrary to it must be false; otherwise two contradictories would be true at the same time.[125]

However, since the positive laws of nature have only a moral or physical necessity, they are subject to dispensation for a higher purpose (one apparent only to the supreme wisdom), and this is precisely what happens in the case of miracles, which thus become part of the rational order. Moreover, a similar argument can be presented for the Christian mysteries. Since by definition they are contrary to appearances, any merely probable arguments lose their force, for inconclusive reasoning must yield to faith. If, however, such mysteries contain obvious contradictions or manifest absurdities, then they must be rejected as false and not revealed.[126]

Finally, in order to solidify his argument Leibniz adopts the scholastic distinction (which we have already seen in Locke) between that which is above and that which is contrary to reason and shows that this is perfectly in accord with his earlier distinction between the two types of necessity. What is contrary to reason is contrary to the absolutely necessary and evident eternal truths and consequently must be unqualifiably rejected, while what is above reason is not intrinsically irrational, but merely beyond the comprehension of a finite mind.[127] From this point of view the mysteries of the Christian religion are, as with Locke, above but not contrary to reason.

Thus, Leibniz believes that he has shown that there is no real conflict between faith and reason. The traditional mysteries of the Christian religion cannot be demonstrated, for this would imply their comprehensibility, but since they are not contrary to reason their possibility may be explained, and they may be defended against rational objections. This philosophical defense and explanation of various doctrines constitutes one of the most interesting aspects of Leibniz's theological thought[128] and will be subject to further examination in connection with Lessing. It will suffice here to depict two examples which are relevant to the later discussion. The first concerns the doctrine of the Trinity, which Leibniz recognized as a mystery, but which he nevertheless endeavored to defend against rational objections. This defense, briefly suggested in the *Theodicy*, was more fully developed in a youthful essay, *Defense of the Trinity by Means of New Logical Inventions* (1671), written in response to the attacks of the Socinian, Andreas Wissowatius, and first published by Lessing. Here Leibniz does not endeavor to prove or explain the doctrine, but simply to defend it by disclosing the logical fallacies in the arguments brought against it. This was deemed sufficient because in the case of a divine mystery, it is enough to show that it is not subject to any insuperable objections.

The second example concerning the doctrine of the eternality of punishments is of a much more controversial nature. This doctrine, which as we shall see was completely repudiated by the German rational theologians, is defended by Leibniz both in the *Theodicy* and in the preface to the writings of another Socinian, Ernst Soner, likewise published by Lessing. In the *Theodicy* Leibniz's main defense is based upon the notion that the damned continue to sin eternally, so that the eternality of their suffering is "founded on the principle of the fitness of things, which has seen to it that affairs were so ordered that the evil action must bring upon itself a chastisement."[129] Thus understood, Leibniz believes the eternality of punishments is perfectly reconcilable with the goodness and justice of God.

By such means did Leibniz undertake his great task of reconciliation. The result, however, was a somewhat uneasy compromise which proved unable to sustain itself against the more consistently rationalistic critiques that eventually ensued. In Germany the first, and still hesitant, step in this direction was taken by Leibniz's most influential follower, Christian Wolff.

Wolff: It has been often and correctly observed that Christian Wolff's true significance should not be measured by his place within the history of philosophy, but rather by his contribution to the general history of culture. This contribution was primarily pedagogical, for it was he who first introduced the German public to philosophical thinking, and thus made philosophy a general cultural concern.[130] It is because of this that Wolff ranks as one of the dominant forces behind the reawakening of a German intellectual life, which had lain dormant since the Thirty Years' War.

This was achieved through the popular presentation of a comprehensive philosophical system. Its main principles were borrowed from Leibniz, and its primary intent was to provide a philosophical foundation for all the sciences. However, although Wolff's philosophy is based largely on Leibniz and provided the main medium through which Leibnizean ideas influenced the early Aufklärung, he can by no means be considered a mere systematizer or popularizer of Leibniz.[131] The basic Leibnizean principle of universal harmony was completely alien to Wolff, who instead presented an essentially mechanical conception of the universe, emphasizing external physical forces, rather than an immanent teleology.[132] Upon this basis Wolff also rejected the concept of the monad and substituted that of "simple things," which function merely as necessary correlates of composite things, and whose force is a necessary postulate for the explanation of movement, but not a fundamental ontological characteristic.[133] Finally, with the rejection of the monad, the concept of a preestablished harmony is given a much more limited role, being used only to explain the relation between mind and body.

However, despite these fundamental differences, Wolff is essentially at one with Leibniz in regard to his interpretation of the concept of God, and the main principles of natural religion. Thus, Wolff begins the section "of God" in his *Rational Ideas of God,*

the World and the Soul of Man with a restatement of the Leibnizean version of the cosmological argument; based upon the principle
of sufficient reason and proceeding from the contingency of the
world to the necessity of an "independent being" who contains
within himself the sufficient reason for the world.[134] Moreover, the
analysis of the nature of the "independent being" is formulated in
terms of Leibnizean concepts:

> Because God conceives of all worlds through his understanding and
> therefore everything which is possible, the divine understanding
> is the source of the essence of all things, and his understanding is
> that which makes something possible as he generates these con-
> ceptions.[135]

And, just as the divine understanding is the ground of possibility,
"so is the will of God the source of the reality of things."[136]

This, in essence, is a repetition of the Liebnizean formula as
expressed in the *Theodicy*, and it is primarily through Wolff's
influence that these conceptions came to serve as the foundation
and ultimate justification of the ideals of the Aufklärung. However,
since these ideals, at least in their popular form, were basically of a
utilitarian and hedonistic nature, the meaning of the original
Leibnizean conception was radically transformed. This shift is
evident in Wolff's treatment of the problem of evil. Formally, his
solution is identical with Leibniz's. This is necessarily the best of
all possible worlds, and evil is merely original limitation or priva-
tion. However, while for Leibniz this optimism was a cosmic principle, referring to the universal context, Wolff interprets this principle largely in terms of man. Thus, the best of all possible worlds
becomes that in which there is the most possible happiness for
man.[137]

The same combination of substantial verbal agreement with
Leibniz and a radically different emphasis can be seen in Wolff's
treatment of the problem of the relation between reason and revelation. Like Leibniz, Wolff recognized Scripture as a source of
revealed truth, but, unlike him, he sought to show that the basic
principles of his natural theology were found therein. This was
accomplished in his *Theologia Naturalis* (1736–37), by means of
a judicious selection of texts.[138] The logical issue of this procedure
was the theory of the parallelism between reason and revelation,
which became the fundamental doctrine of the theological branch

of the Wolffian school.[139] This doctrine, which had its roots in Wolff's contention that "the Scriptures speak chiefly of actuality, philosophy of possibility,"[140] found its logical culmination in Johann Lorenz Schmidt's "Wertheimer Bible" (1735). Taking this parallelism in full seriousness, Schmidt applied it to his translation of the Bible, with the result that Genesis read like a textbook in Wolffian philosophy:

> In the beginning God created all the heavenly bodies and our earth itself. In regard to what specifically concerns the earth, it was in the beginning completely desolate. It was surrounded by a dark cloud and completely covered with water, over which violent winds began to blow. However, in accordance with the divine purpose there was soon some light. And because this was very necessary, it so happened, according to the plan which God had instituted, that from then on light and darkness continually alternated, and this is the origin of day and night.[141]

Now although such a work was ostensibly based upon Wolffian principles, it is totally at variance with Wolff's fundamentally conservative attitude toward traditional Christianity. It was this conservatism which led him to reject all speculative treatment of dogma. Content to demonstrate their lack of formal contradiction, Wolff recognized the mysterious nature of these dogmas and left their explanation and defense to the theologians.[142]

However, although he did not concern himself with individual dogmas, Wolff was thoroughly convinced of the need of a rational explanation of the general questions of miracle and revelation. Like Leibniz, he attempted to establish the possibility of both within the framework of natural theology, and also like Leibniz, he accomplished this through the distinction between the intellect and will of God. Thus, miracles (including immediate revelations) are possible because they are grounded in the will of God. Although they abrogate the laws of nature, they do not contradict the eternal verities, which are grounded in the divine intellect. Nevertheless, because of his rigidly mechanistic world view, totally alien to the spirit of Leibniz, Wolff endeavors to delimit sharply their actuality. Miracles are indeed possible, but in a well-ordered world they must be a rare occurrence, because God would only disrupt the course of nature for the most compelling reasons.[143]

Nevertheless, Wolff recognized such a miraculous event in the case of the Christian revelation, and this leads him to formulate the criteria in terms of which any alleged revelation must be judged.[144] This generally rationalistic and factual approach to the problem of revelation was, as we have seen, one of the universal characteristics of the theology of this period. It is certainly present in Leibniz, but it finds its ultimate expression in Wolff, who methodically delineated the conditions which any true revelation must fulfill.[145]

The first of these criteria is its necessity. This is based on the consideration of its miraculous nature. Since a revelation constitutes a rupture in the order of nature, it must contain knowledge, which is of the utmost importance to man and not attainable by natural means, "and therefore it is clear that God reveals nothing, which we can learn through reason."[146]

Second, since God cannot will anything not in accordance with his perfections, he could not reveal anything which contradicts these perfections. Consequently, since his infinite understanding is one of his perfections, "that which God has revealed cannot contradict the truths of reason."[147]

Third, since no truth can contradict others, it is not possible that a divine revelation could obligate man to deeds which run counter to the laws of nature or conflict with the unalterable essence of the soul.[148]

In addition, Wolff also posits a series of secondary criteria, according to which it must be shown that the knowledge communicated could not have been arrived at by natural means[149] and that the miracles wrought in support of it were not superfluous.[150] Finally, Wolff goes so far as to determine the appropriate linguistic form of a divine revelation! It must not use more words than necessary, they must be perfectly intelligible, and "the entire arrangement of words must agree with the general rules of grammar and rhetoric."[151]

These criteria are clearly grounded in the Leibnizean concept of God as the infinitely wise and good sovereign, whose perfections are mirrored in the human soul. It was assumed by the entire rationalist tradition that on the basis of this concept the finite mind could determine, at least to a limited extent, the conduct appropriate to divinity. In Wolff, however, we find what seems to amount to the reductio ad absurdum of this view. On the one hand the possibility and the actuality of revelation are maintained, but on the other hand any alleged revelation is subjected to criteria which never have and never could be fulfilled. This resulted in an irreconcilable tension between the respective claims of reason and revelation, which eventually led to the dissolution of the whole "rational supernatural" position. In Germany this dissolution took two forms, both of which were profoundly influenced by the previously discussed developments in English theology: the first form was that of a more thoroughgoing rationalization of the content of revelation (modeled after Locke, Clarke, and Foster), and the second form was a consistent naturalism, which, arguing from the Leibniz-Wolffian concept of God, denied the very possibility of any historical revelation.

Neology: The first development, the complete rationalization of the content of the Christian revelation, was the work of the movement generally referred to as "neology,"[152] which became the dominant theological tendency in Germany during the latter half of the eighteenth century. The development from Wolffianism to neology is analogous to the transition from Locke's *Essay* to his *Reasonableness of Christianity.* In both instances there is a change from the concern with a formal, epistemological analysis of the possibility and acceptable content of a revelation, to a consideration of the rationality of the actual doctrinal content of historical Christianity. Within the neological camp, whose leaders included Sack, Spalding, Jerusalem, and Semler, these considerations took the form of a philosophical, historical, and philological examination of traditional Christian doctrine. Starting with the presupposition of the identity of "true and original Christianity" with the religion of nature, these men rejected the doctrines found to be irreconcilable with this postulate and showed, by means of historical and philological criticism (here Semler is the main figure), either that these doctrines were not in fact based upon a true interpretation of Scripture, or that they were later, and completely unjustified, accretions.

The key to this new standpoint is the reinterpretation of the concept of reason. For the abstract, theoretical reason of the Wolffian school, neology substituted the empirical, practical, and essentially ethical understanding of reason emphasized by the English theologians.[153] Such a substitution was thoroughly in accord with the psychological, practical spirit of the times and was simply the theological manifestation of the same principle which found its popular expression in the "Moral Weekly's," and its ultimate philosophical articulation in Kant's primacy of practical reason.[154]

In its application to Christian dogma this principle meant the final dissolution of the old orthodox dogma, so tenuously maintained by the Wolffian conservatism. For neology the whole body of traditional doctrine was no longer considered a self-contained system of divinely revealed truths, but individual dogmas were judged in terms of their ability to help promulgate piety and virtue. This resulted in a renewal of the quest for fundamentals, which as we have seen, characterized the endeavors of the seventeenth-century English divines. Now, however, the sole criterion became the practical effect of a specific doctrine. The fundamental, genuine teachings of the Christian religion were construed as those which promoted that moral and spiritual perfection which was looked upon as the true destiny of man.[155] Whereas formerly, man's self-understanding and self-evaluation were largely determined by traditional Christian teachings—the doctrine of the Fall, original sin, and redemption—now human nature and its allegedly infinite potentialities became the standard in terms of which the Christian religion was to be judged.

This neological reinterpretation of Christianity contains two aspects. First, its complete rationalization of the content of revelation implied a rejection of the traditional conception. Such a rejection was already formulated by the English deists, but neology differed from deism, for although it emptied the Christian revelation of all of its historic content, it nevertheless accepted, and took seriously, revelation as a fact. Although revelation contains nothing more than the main principles of natural religion, it was still defended as practically necessary. Without its aid, it was generally claimed, these principles would be neither clearly apprehended by nor practically efficacious for, the bulk of mankind. Thus, just as Locke and Clarke admitted the theoretical sufficiency of reason and denied its practical effectiveness, so Jerusalem proved through historical reflections that unaided reason has not, in fact, led mankind to the true knowledge of God. Upon this basis Jerusalem and the whole neological movement was able to overcome the Wolffian dualism. No longer is there a "theologia revelata" added to a "theologia naturalis," but the entire complex of religious truth is seen as both revealed and rational. It is revealed insofar as these principles were first clearly manifested through Moses and Christ, and it is rational insofar as they can all be appropriated, albeit not discovered, by reason.[156]

Second, in virtue of the historical and philological weapons forged by Semler and others, neology provided the means for the

complete rejection of the entire Augustinian dogma complex. This
was achieved through systematic attacks upon the individual doctrines. Not only original sin, but also predestination, the damnation
of heathens, the vicarious satisfaction, and the eternality of punishments were seen to be thoroughly at variance with the new humanistic spirit and were thus rejected. The underlying spirit of the
movement was succinctly captured by Jerusalem, who speaking of
the "nonsense of the melancholy Augustine" asks:

> Where is it found that men should be damned because of their
> inborn depravity? Where, that men who live outside of the Chris-
> tian religion, where that the heathen, where that unbaptized infants
> should be damned? Where, finally, that most terrible of all ideas:
> that God has determined to damn some men for all eternity?[157]

One of the most significant expressions of the general neological viewpoint, and one with which Lessing engaged in a direct
polemic, is found in Johann August Eberhard's *New Apology for
Socrates, or Investigation of the Doctrine of the Salvation of
Heathens* (1772). During the course of this work Eberhard attacked
the entire range of questionable dogmas, from the concept of super-
naturally efficacious grace, which he saw as the denial of the
significance of human effort, to the doctrine of the vicarious satisfaction, which he found to be morally repugnant. Moreover, he saw
more clearly than most, the systematic interconnection of the entire
dogmatic complex.[158] However, despite his comprehensive view of
the problem, his particular concern was with the doctrines of the
damnation of heathens and the eternality of punishment.[159]

These specific problems are treated in Sections VIII and IX,
in light of the previously made general philosophic and critical-
historical objections to the entire Augustinian system. He begins
by analyzing the basic problem into two parts: (1) Must the
heathens necessarily be doomed because of their religion? (2) Is a
heathen necessarily incapable of moral goodness? Both questions
are unequivocally answered in the negative. In regard to the first
he reiterates Bayle's principle of the innocence of error.[160] The
heathens lacked the true concept of God and hence were ignorant,
but, since this ignorance was unavoidable, they are not thereby
deserving of damnation. The proper concept of God requires the
true notion of infinity, and this can only be achieved through long
practice in abstract thought. Moreover, despite their absurd theolo-

gies, the heathens at least recognized the fact that the world depends upon a transcendent cause.[161]

The question of the morality of the heathens is treated in a similar vein. The virtues of the Greeks and Romans are an established fact for anyone with the rudiments of a classical education.[162] It is admitted that their virtues were not the fruits of a proper concept of God, but this does not destroy their moral character. Even idolatry may contain the basic idea of moral worship in an obscure form,[163] and if morality cannot find its support in the public religion, there are yet many other inducements to virtuous action, such as the social order and personal honor.[164] The result of this lengthy analysis is the complete repudiation of the famous Augustinian doctrine that the virtues of the heathen are but splendid vices, which is not only refuted but shown to lead to the absurd consequence that what is called virtue in a moral sense is vice in a theological sense.[165]

Not only, however, did the orthodox condemn all heathens to Hell, but they endeavored to keep them there eternally. Thus, in Section IX the argument shifts to a discussion of the doctrine of the eternality of punishments. This gruesome doctrine of the everlasting torment of rational and sensitive creatures contradicts all conceptions of a wise and just world order, and consequently, from the neological standpoint, could not be considered part of the Christian revelation.

In typical neological fashion, Eberhard attacks the doctrine from two directions. He shows by means of a philological analysis that it is unscriptural. The chief text advanced in its support is Matthew 25.46, "And they will go away into eternal punishment, but the righteous into eternal life," but following Semler, Eberhard contends that the Hebrew and Greek words for eternal mean simply an indefinite period, and not an infinite duration.[166] Eberhard's chief concern, however, is not with the critical-historical, but with the philosophical aspect of the doctrine, and it is to this that he devotes the bulk of his attention.

He begins with a survey of the chief philosophical arguments in favor of the doctrine. The first to be considered is Mosheim's defense, based upon the conception of sin as an infinite offense against God, which thus renders the offender infinitely culpable. In rejection of this, Eberhard draws upon Wolff's concept of offense as an action through which another individual becomes less perfect, either in himself or in regard to his external condition.

When the concept of offense, thus understood, is applied to God, its absurdity becomes manifest.[167] The second philosophical defense of the doctrine of the eternality of punishment is based upon the notion of the infinite continuity of sin, and this, as we have seen, was the view of Leibniz. Against this position Eberhard simply asserts that no finite creature can sin infinitely, but, more important, he accuses Leibniz of insincerity in defending this doctrine. Leibniz, he argued, attempted to accommodate his views to the teaching of the various religious parties in order to win popularity for his system. Thus, he was forced to find a sense in which the doctrine of the eternality of punishments is reconcilable with the best of all possible worlds.[168]

Having disposed of the two main defenses of the infinity of punishment, Eberhard proceeds to formulate his own positive proof of their finite duration. He argues that we cannot conceive of God punishing without love or without an ultimate purpose (sufficient reason), and in the best of all possible worlds this purpose could only be the improvement of the sinner.[169] Now since the eternal continuation of punishment could never lead to such improvement, but rather implies the denial of its very possibility, it must be rejected as a pernicious doctrine which leads to a false concept of God. Finite punishments, on the other hand, serve to improve the moral character of the sinner and are consequently perfectly compatible with the best of all possible worlds.[170]

With this repudiation of Leibniz's treatment of Christian dogma, in terms of the general principles of the Leibnizean philosophy, the neological movement reached its logical culmination. The Christian revelation, completely emptied of its traditional content, was now identified with the basic principles of natural religion. This process was one way in which the Aufklärung overcame the untenable compromise reached by the Wolffian school, but this compromise was also attacked in a far more radical manner from another direction, from the standpoint of a consistent naturalism, wherein the principles of natural religion are shown to be apparent and sufficient in themselves, thus rendering any revelation entirely superfluous. This was the view implicit in the deism of Tindal, and it found its supreme German advocate in Hermann Samuel Reimarus.

Reimarus: Like the entire Aufklärung, Reimarus' thought is firmly rooted in the Leibniz-Wolffian philosophy, and can be seen as the logical development of its rationalistic implications. While

Leibniz admits miracles (including a historical revelation) in the divine plan, and Wolff does not deny their possibility, but insists that a universe with few miracles is more in accordance with the divine wisdom than one with many, Reimarus draws the last consequence and rejects them completely.[171] Creation for Reimarus is the single miracle, and nature the only revelation. Next to this "natural revelation" any positive revelation is at best superfluous.

This sincere commitment to the principles of natural religion distinguishes Reimarus' critique of Christianity from the cynical productions of the French materialists. Christianity, for Reimarus, must be rejected because it represents a barrier to the acceptance of the true and completely rational religion whose practice alone can lead to the happiness and perfection of the human race. Reimarus presented the basic tenets of this natural religion, conceived of as a clear and sufficient body of knowledge concerning the nature and purpose of God and the duties and eternal destiny of man, in his *Treatises on the Foremost Truths of Natural Religion* (1754). Since this work was confined to a seemingly orthodox treatment of natural religion, including refutations of atheism and pantheism, it achieved wide popularity. The real implications, however, which Reimarus drew from this conception of religion, but never dared to make known in his lifetime, are contained in his monumental *Apology for Rational Worshippers of God*. It was from this work, with which he became acquainted during his stay in Hamburg, that Lessing took the material, which he later (1774–78) published anonymously as the *Fragments of an Unnamed*.

Although its complete text has never been published, David Friedrich Strauss has provided a comprehensive analysis of the history and content of the work,[172] and it is in the light of his analysis that I propose to consider the fragments published by Lessing. Reimarus, according to Strauss, prefaced his *Apology* with an account of the reasons which generally led him to the complete rejection of Christianity. These were: (1) The recognition that the Bible is not, as had been commonly assumed, a textbook of doctrines. Reimarus reasoned that if God desired to reveal to man a supernatural doctrine whose acceptance is necessary for salvation, he would have presented it in a clear and orderly manner. The actual Scripture, however, is an ambiguous and varied collection of documents wherein no such clear teachings can be found.[173] (2) The inability either to comprehend or accept the doctrine of the Trinity.[174] (3) The rejection, in terms of a rational understanding of God, of the orthodox conception of divine justice and grace, whereby the vast majority of the human race are doomed to eternal torment.[175] (4) The awareness of the repulsiveness and crudity of the allegedly "chosen people" and the immorality of their actions as depicted in the Old Testament.[176]

All of these objections can be found in the deistic writers, but Reimarus gave them a more systematic, detailed, and scholarly presentation than they had received previously. His polemic with Christianity may be divided essentially into three parts: (1) a general philosophical critique of the concept of a historical revelation, (2) a critique of the Old Testament, both from the standpoint of the content of its teachings, and the morality of its heroes, and (3) a critique of the New Testament, emphasizing the fallibility of its authors and the distinction between the teachings of Jesus and the apostles.

Each of these general lines of criticism is found in the fragments published by Lessing. After a relatively innocuous selection, *On the Toleration of Deists* which Lessing published separately (1774) in order to test the public reaction, there followed (1777) a group of five fragments which constituted the most skillful and passionate attack on Christianity to confront the German theological world in the eighteenth century, and, finally, in the midst of the controversy with Goeze (1778), a last selection from the *Apology* containing Reimarus' historical reconstruction of the life of Jesus and the origin of the Christian religion.

The first of the five fragments, *On the Decrying of Reason in the Pulpit,* is a defense of the role of reason in religion. One of Reimarus' major arguments against the acceptance of any historical religion was that an individual's beliefs are largely the product of ingrained childhood prejudices. This is not only true of the uneducated masses, but also of those intellectuals who are engaged in the serious investigation of religion, but who nevertheless invariably find the truth in the sect in which they were raised. For, reasons Reimarus, what else can account for the fact "that a Mufti, a chief Rabbi, a Bellarmine, a Grotius, a Gerhard, a Vitringa, with so much knowledge and honest effort, could all be equally convinced of the truth of such opposing systems?"[177]

This dominance of prejudice in even the best minds was, for Reimarus, the direct result of the suppression of reason. Rather than the blind subjection to faith, demanded by the orthodox clergy, a completely objective examination of religious questions is necessary.

Moreover, since we are all able to achieve an adequate knowledge of the truth, goodness, and power of God, such an examination cannot help but prove fruitful.[178] Thus, in the first fragment of Lessing's main selection, Reimarus asserts the value and sufficiency of a purely rational religion, and it is this principle which serves as the ultimate foundation of his critique of revelation.

This critique is developed in the second fragment: *Impossibility of a Revelation Which All Men Can Believe on Rational Grounds.* Here Reimarus systematically considers and rejects the possibility of a universally acceptable revealed religion. The argument is presented along basically deistic lines, but the irreconcilability, felt by all the deists, between the supreme mathematician disclosed by the new science and the jealous, tribal deity of the Jews finds an unusually vivid manifestation. Reimarus begins with an analysis of the problem into its component parts. A divine revelation may be given immediately to each man, or it may be directly granted to only some men and communicated to the rest through written and oral tradition. In the latter case there are again two possibilities: either God reveals himself to some individuals among diverse peoples or to one select people.[179]

The first two alternatives are dismissed in summary fashion. A direct revelation requires a perpetual miracle, and this plainly contradicts the wisdom of God. The second possibility is even more absurd, for not only does it still require a great number of miracles, but they do not even directly achieve their purpose, which is the proclamation of the divine message. For this human testimony concerning the revelation is necessary, and therefore "it is no longer a divine revelation, but a human testimony of a divine revelation,"[180] and as such, would never gain universal acceptance. Moreover, since a process of repeated revelations would only serve to increase the possibility of doubt, error and deception, it is clearly contrary to the wisdom of God.[181]

There still remains the possibility that God revealed himself to one people, at certain times through certain individuals, partly orally and partly by the written word. Since the latter alternative is asserted to be the case and to provide the only way to salvation for all mankind, Reimarus proposes to consider it more carefully. This conception of revelation has the advantage over the previous ones of not requiring as many miracles, and it does not suffer from the inconsistencies of the second alternative. However, even here, Reimarus argues, miracles are required for the accomplishment of that which could have been achieved through the normal course of nature. Second, since such a revelation is inevitably obscure and too sublime for reason to grasp, it could never be generally accepted. Third, due to the abundance of false prophets, any such claim must remain doubtful, especially since changes, errors, and a proliferation of sects inevitably arise in the course of time, and finally, it is simply contrary to human nature that all men should believe in a single revelation.[182]

The rest of the fragment is devoted to the elaboration of this thesis and its specific application to Christianity. The key to the argument is the distinction between a "reasoned belief" and a blind acceptance. Only the former can be considered meaningful or pleasing to God, and Reimarus' intent was to show that only a minute portion of the human race could possibly achieve such a belief.

The first class to be eliminated contains all children under ten years of age. They are incapable of forming a proper conception of God, and hence, their religious beliefs are determined solely by the accident of birth and environment. Moreover, drawing upon contemporary mortality statistics, Reimarus shows that only one-third of all infants born live to reach the age of ten, so that on the orthodox theory two-thirds of the human race are automatically excluded from eternal blessedness. Reimarus is willing to interpret these statistics more liberally and lower the number to one-half, but he still concludes that this constitutes a powerful argument against the notion that the acceptance of a revelation is the only means to salvation.[183]

Reimarus next considers the untold millions who lived before the advent of Christ, of which only an inconsiderable fraction (the Hebrews and their neighbors) could have had the slightest inkling of a divine revelation.[184] Finally, he examines the case of those born after Christ and finds that, even here, fully one-half have never heard of Jesus Christ or Christianity and that, among those who have, there are many reasons why most of them could never receive an authentic report thereof, and still more reasons why they could not accept it as a divine revelation. The chief reasons offered for the latter point are the immorality of the Christians and the disunity and mutual damnation of the various Christian sects.[185]

After these numerical considerations Reimarus turns to the basic question of what is necessary for a "reasoned belief" in order to emphasize further the absurdity of making such a belief requisite for salvation. A "reasoned belief" in a historical narrative, he argues, requires a detailed knowledge of philology and history. If one is incapable of grasping the true meaning of Scripture, but is dependent upon the interpretation of another, then one's belief is blind and ungrounded.[186] With this Reimarus achieved the reductio ad absurdum of Protestant scholasticism's concept of faith as the acceptance of an objectively true body of doctrine contained in Holy Scripture. Reimarus' skilled criticism shows that this doctrine implies the very different proposition: in order to be a sincere Christian one must first be a good philologist! Now it is obvious that since the vast majority of mankind are not capable of becoming philologists, God did not intend this as the sole means of salvation.[187]

The next two fragments are devoted to an analysis of the Old Testament. The first, *The Passage of the Israelites Through the Red Sea,* exhibits the absurdities involved in the Exodus narrative. The second, *That the Books of the Old Testament Were Not Written to Reveal a Religion,* contends that the Old Testament not only does not contain, but specifically denies the doctrine of immortality, and concludes that since this doctrine is an essential ingredient in any "supernatural, soul-saving religion" the Old Testament does not contain a divine revelation. In support of this contention Reimarus analyzes the various passages cited by orthodox theologians as implying the presence of a doctrine of immortality and shows that, if read correctly, they fail to do so. Here both the general exegetical principle that the Old Testament must be understood in the sense intended by its authors, and not in light of preconceptions derived from the New Testament or various symbolic books, and the analysis of specific passages strongly suggest the influence of Spinoza's *Theologico-Political Treatise.*[188]

Reimarus' critique of the New Testament is contained in the final two fragments. In *On the Resurrection Narrative,* the last of the main series of five, he points to the many discrepancies and contradictions in the various accounts of the resurrection and concludes with a classic statement of the deistic position:

> Witnesses whose testimonies disagree so much on the most important details would not be accepted by a judge in any worldly affair, even if it were only a question of deciding who has the right to a small amount of money. How then can one demand that the testimonies of four such conflicting witnesses should serve as the basis upon which the whole world, the entire human race in all

times and places, grounds its religious faith and hope of salvation?[189]

The last fragment, *On the Purpose of Jesus and His Disciples*, published separately by Lessing (1778) in order to fan the flames of the already raging controversy, constitutes Reimarus' most severe indictment of Christianity. After having previously demonstrated the falseness of the traditional accounts, he here offers his own conception of the life of Jesus and the origin of the Christian religion. His prime contention is that Jesus had no intention of founding a new religion, but that he was a completely orthodox Jew who observed the law and merely wanted to spiritualize its observance.[190] In support of this thesis Reimarus divides the message of Jesus into two parts: (1) call to repentance, directed against the Pharisees, and (2) the announcement of the immanent kingdom of God.[191] This latter concept, Reimarus claims, was intended by Jesus and understood by his disciples in a purely worldly sense, corresponding to the Jewish messianic expectations. Thus, throughout his lifetime Jesus taught and his disciples believed "that he was a great worldly king, and would establish a powerful kingdom in Jerusalem."[192]

It was, Reimarus argues, only after Jesus' inglorious death on the cross, which completely shattered all their expectations of earthly power, that the disciples stole the body, invented the story of the resurrection, and became the founders of a new and mysterious religion. Upon the basis of this rather imaginative historical reconstruction Reimarus surmises

> that it was only after the death of Jesus that the apostles hit upon the idea of a spiritual, suffering savior of the whole human race. Hence, after Jesus' death the apostles discarded their previous conception of his teaching and deeds, and therefore first ceased to conceive of him as a powerful, earthly savior of the people of Israel.[193]

The result is that Jesus becomes regarded as a well meaning, but deluded fanatic, the apostles clever and self-seeking deceivers, and the Christian religion a colossal fraud. Such a conception is obviously as one-sided as the orthodox view which it combats, but it nevertheless formed the logical outcome of the deistic polemic. As we have seen, both the deists and the orthodox believed that in the last analysis the truth of the Christian religion depended upon the veracity of the Biblical accounts. The orthodox affirmed and the deists denied this veracity, but both sides operated within this general framework: either the word of God or fraud. Reimarus' fragments brought the opposition into sharp focus, but as we shall see, it was Lessing who first provided the standpoint from which this antithesis could be overcome.

CHAPTER 2

Lessing's Philosophical and Theological Development

□:

Lessing's major philosophical and theological works are the products of the last decade of his life (1771–81), when he was ducal librarian at Wolfenbüttel. During this period he directed almost all his efforts to his monumental polemic with the theologians and to the attempt to articulate his own religious-philosophical insights. It was this struggle, induced by the publication of the fragments of Reimarus, which resulted in the *Anti-Goeze, The Education of the Human Race,* and *Nathan the Wise.*

Since these writings, together with other significant works of this period, constitute Lessing's distinctive contribution to the history of religious thought, it is only natural that an interpretation of his philosophy of religion should focus upon them. However, in view of Lessing's lifelong concern with the problems under discussion, it is important that his early writings be not entirely lost sight of. Every thinker undergoes a development, and Lessing is no exception. Hence, before proceeding to a detailed analysis of Lessing's mature views, it will be necessary to suggest briefly the path by which he arrived at them.

I

THE FIRST PERIOD—1748–55

The time from his first residence in Berlin (1748) until his departure for Leipzig (1755) is generally regarded as the first period of Lessing's maturity. Coming from the home of an orthodox Lutheran pastor, he had been thoroughly imbued as a youth with the traditional faith and had even enrolled (1746) at the University of Leipzig to study theology. However, he soon tired of the theological lectures, and under the influence of the freethinker, Christlob

50

Mylius, developed an interest in the stage. The literary fruits of these early years were a few immature comedies, but the first taste of the world of literature induced the nineteen-year-old Lessing to leave the university and attempt to earn his living as an author.

The natural place for such a venture was Berlin, which, under the influence of Frederick the Great, was the center of free thought in Germany. Here Lessing came in contact with Voltaire and La Mettrie, and most importantly, with the writings of Pierre Bayle, who was undoubtedly the major influence on him at that time.[1]

The earliest important indication of Lessing's religious views is to be found in a letter to his father. His pious parents had quite naturally been concerned about the ungodly influence upon their son in Berlin and had repeatedly requested him to relinquish his literary career and return to the university and to the orthodox faith. In response to their admonitions, Lessing replies:

> Time shall teach whether he is the better Christian who has the basic doctrines of Christianity in his memory and, often without understanding them, in his mouth, goes to church and takes part in all the ceremonies out of force of habit; or he who has once intelligently doubted and has, through investigation, finally attained conviction, or at least still strives to attain it. The Christian religion is not a thing which one should accept on trust from one's parents. Most people, to be sure, inherit it from them as they do their property, but they show by their actions what kind of Christians they really are. So long as I fail to see one of the chief precepts of Christianity, love thine enemy, better observed, so long shall I doubt whether these are really Christians who give themselves out for such.[2]

The two thoughts expressed in this passage—that an individual's religious beliefs should be the result of rational conviction and not blind acceptance, and that these beliefs should be morally efficacious—were basic tenets of the Enlightenment and recurrent themes in Lessing's thought. Moreover, since many of his early writings, consisting largely of poems, unpublished fragments, book reviews, and "Vindications" (a species of literature modeled after Bayle), were directed specifically to one or the other of these points, a brief analysis of a typical example from each sphere will suffice to indicate the general nature of Lessing's religious views at this time.

The Ethical Orientation: The clearest expression of Lessing's early emphasis upon the practical aspect of religion is to be found in his *Thoughts on the Moravians,*[3] wherein he endeavored to defend the pietistic community against orthodox attacks.[4] This defense, however, served merely as the pretext for the presentation of his own, Bayle-inspired analysis of the relation between religious belief and moral action. After a preliminary condemnation of the polemical tactics of the orthodox theologians, Lessing states his main thesis:

> Man was created for action and not for speculation. However, just because he was not created for it, he inclines more toward the latter than the former. His maliciousness always leads him to what he should not, and his presumptuousness to what he cannot do. Should he, man, let limits be set for himself?[5]

The balance of the work is devoted to the elaboration and confirmation of this claim. He endeavors to show both that the true end of human life is ethical action rather than empty speculation and that despite this more attention has always been paid to the latter. He begins by illustrating this in light of the history of philosophy. After the idyllic splendor of its earliest period, those "happy times, when the most learned were the most virtuous! when all wisdom consisted of brief rules for living,"[6] a decline set in. The great hero of this primitive stage, Socrates, who taught men to abjure heavenly things and instead look within themselves, was followed by men who completely perverted his teachings, for after Socrates "Plato began to dream, and Aristotle to syllogize."[7] Furthermore, this first stage is shown to be paradigmatic for the rest. Each major intellectual advance was inevitably perverted by the next generation of disciples. In the wake of decadent scholasticism came Descartes, Newton, and Leibniz, who gave the truth a new form, and disclosed many of the secrets of nature, but they were soon followed by the Wolffians:

> . . . who now glorify the mortal race, and believe themselves especially worthy of the name philosopher. They are inexhaustible in the discovery of new truths. In the smallest space, by means of a few numbers united by signs, they can interpret mysteries for which Aristotle would have needed intolerable volumes. So they fill the head while the heart remains empty. They lead the mind to the highest heaven, while the soul is, through its passions, set beneath the beast.[8]

From this myopic glance at the history of philosophy, Lessing turns to the history of religion and finds a similar pattern. Just as in philosophy, the original, simple rules according to which one should direct one's life became lost amid the clutter of irrelevant speculation, so too in religion, after the "simple, easy, and living" religion of Adam, "the essentials were submerged beneath a deluge of arbitrary propositions."[9]

The application of this primitivistic conception to religion suggests the essentially deistic nature of Lessing's views at this time.[10] This "simple, easy, and living religion of Adam" is nothing more than the natural religion of Tindal, and the depiction of subsequent religious development as the perversion of this original ideal is simply a restatement of the deistic conception of positive religion as a corruption of the original religion of nature. Similarly, Lessing's treatment of Christ "as a divinely inspired teacher" whose true purpose was none other "than to reestablish religion in all its purity,"[11] is also consistent with the deistic viewpoint. Here, as in Tindal, the essence of religion is seen to consist wholly in the practice of morality, and any mysterious doctrine or ritual is an unnecessary and even harmful appendage.

After this description of the nature and work of Christ, the history of the Christian religion is analyzed in terms of the previously delineated pattern. The original simplicity and practical orientation established by Jesus, which guided the spirit of primitive Christianity, were eventually corrupted by the political conquest of the Roman Church and the ensuing dogmatic controversies. Once again the concern with religious doctrine led to the total neglect of morality, and the result was even greater superstition and barbarity than had existed previously. The history of the medieval Church provides Lessing with a perfect illustration of this contention:

> As long as the Church was at war, it was concerned to give its religion that rigor, through an irreproachable and extraordinary life, which few enemies were capable of withstanding. However, as soon as it was at peace it lost its rigor, and began to adorn its religion, to bring its doctrines into a certain order, and to reinforce the divine truth with human proofs.[12]

Finally, after briefly describing the Reformation in a similar vein, as an intellectual advance which did not lead to a corresponding moral improvement, Lessing turns to the contemporary scene and finds the situation at its lowest ebb:

> And now for the present—should I deem it fortunate or unfortunate that such an excellent combination of theology and philosophy has been made, one in which it is only with labor and

distress that the one is separable from the other, in which one weakens the other; the former attempting to compel belief through proofs, and the latter to support proofs with belief? Now, I say, because of this perverse manner of teaching Christianity, a true Christian has become rarer than in the Dark Ages. Our knowledge is like the angels, but our manner of living like the Devil.[13]

These rather sweeping historical reflections set the stage for the actual defense of the Moravians, which also serves as an apology for Lessing's own conception of the nature of religion. In light of the proceeding analysis the Moravian community is seen as a greatly needed corrective to the exclusively intellectualistic and dogmatic concerns of contemporary theology. Their theoretical weaknesses are admitted, but dismissed as irrelevant, for their intent was not to change doctrine, but to reform men's lives.[14] Thus, although as an enlightened thinker, Lessing did not feel any sympathy for the enthusiastic excesses, characteristic of this community,[15] he was nevertheless able to apprehend the great superiority of its deliberate cultivation of the inward and ethical life to the barren scholasticism of orthodox dogmatics.

The Rationalistic Orientation: The rationalistic aspect of Lessing's early thought found its chief expression in the *Vindication of Hieronymus Cardanus,*[16] in which he approached the same basically deistic position from a different direction. Both the general plan of this work and the manner in which it is undertaken are modeled after Bayle.[17] An obstensibly purely objective examination of a historical figure is used as the vehicle for the communication of religious-philosophical views. Lessing begins by limiting his task, both in regard to the aspect of Cardanus' thought to be defended and to the particular attacks which he shall defend him against. Traditionally, Cardanus had been accused of being an enemy on three counts: (1) because of a work he allegedly wrote against the immortality of the soul, (2) on the grounds of some of his assertions about astrology, (3) on the basis of a supposedly offensive place in his *De Subtilitate.* In the course of his "Vindication" Lessing proposes to address himself solely to the third point.[18]

This project was immediately occasioned by the Lutheran pastor Johann Vogt, who in his *Catalogues of Rare Books,* called attention to two editions of *De Subtilitate,* noted the discrepancies between them, and pointed to an apparently irreligious passage in the first, which was omitted in the later edition. The basic theme of the work is the comparison of the various religions (a theme to which, as we shall see, Lessing later returned in *Nathan the Wise*). Cardanus presents a hypothetical argument between a Heathen, a Jew, a Moslem, and a Christian. Each propounds the traditional proofs for the truth of his, and the falsity of the other religions, but rather than proclaiming the obvious superiority of the Christian position, Cardanus allegedly concludes in the earlier edition that the question of ultimate victory in the argument must be left purely to chance.[19]

Lessing's refutation of this interpretation, which occupies the bulk of the work, is a minor masterpiece of erudition and polemic, as well as a fruitful source for knowledge of his religious views at this time. After a preliminary display of learning, directed to showing that Vogt was merely parroting a long list of commentators,[20] Lessing presents his German translation of the relevant portion of Cardanus' text.

Within the translated portion the respective claims of the Heathen and the Jew are treated briefly, and the bulk of the attention is paid to the Mohammedan and the Christian. The actual arguments advanced on both sides are quite commonplace, although Cardanus does not fail to include a bit of irony in the speech of the Christian. Thus, in positing the traditional historical arguments for the proof of his religion, Cardanus' Christian maintains that the Old Testament prophecies were fulfilled so exactly by the events in the life of Jesus, that an impartial observer might well believe that they were written after the fact.[21] The arguments from the Biblical miracles, which are greater and better attested than those claimed by the Mohammedans, and from the miraculous growth of the Church are then presented, and the Christian closes his case with the additional claim that his religion contains nothing contrary to either morality or natural philosophy.[22] In rebuttal the Mohammedan emphasizes the polytheistic implications of the doctrine of the Trinity and the practice of image worship and also argues positively from the greater worldly success of his own faith, the moral equality of its adherents with Christians, and the continued presence of miracles among its followers.[23]

After presenting the essence of Cardanus' argument, Lessing questions the reason for its alleged offensiveness. This, he suggests, could be the result either of the very attempt to compare Christianity with the other religions or of the manner in which this comparison was carried out.[24] In rejecting the former, Lessing passionately reaffirms the rationalistic attitude expressed in the letter to his father. "What," he asks, "can be more necessary than to be convinced of one's faith, and what is more impossible than conviction without previous examination?" "Moreover," he continues:

> It cannot be maintained that the examination of one's own religion suffices, that when one has discovered the mark of divinity in his own, it is not necessary to look for them in others. Such comparisons are unnecessary, for when one knows the right path, he has no need to concern himself with false paths.—One does not learn the false from the true, but only gets to know the true by means of the false.[25]

Lessing continues by arguing that since Christians possess the true faith, they cannot possibly be hurt by such an impartial examination and that since the proponents of the false religions will inevitably be made to see the light, they can only be helped by it.[26] However, despite these pious pretensions it is clear that Lessing's real purpose was to cast doubt upon the unique status of Christianity and to show that it is merely one among a number of religions to which rational men have confessed their allegiances. Each of the major faiths can present equally valid or invalid arguments in its support, and none is able to demonstrate its superiority over the others.

This interpretation is amply supported by the balance of the work. Having rejected the first, Lessing turns to the second possibility: that Cardanus' manner of presenting the comparison was somehow offensive. Here again he distinguishes two possible views: either his defense of Christianity was not adequate, or the positions of its opponents were stated too strongly. In regard to the first alternative, Lessing states dogmatically:

> I demand impartial readers; and they should tell me if any of all the innumerable theologians and philosophers, who since Cardan have demonstrated the truth of the Christian religion, have had one proof more, or presented the same proofs in a stronger manner than he. More elaborately no doubt, but not more strongly.[27]

This claim, however, was based not upon the strength of Cardanus' arguments, which were quite commonplace, but rather upon the futility of all such attempts. Lessing's defense of these proofs only adds to the irony contained in their original formulation. Although he treats all three historical proofs, the discussion of the argument from the miracles of Jesus best indicates Lessing's true position. Cardanus' Christian had argued not only that the miracles of Jesus were greater than those of the Mohammedans, but also that they were better attested. Since this thesis was simply asserted as a fact, and in no way proven, it provided the perfect opening for Lessing's irony. Commenting on Cardanus' argument, he writes:

> He declared that they really are miracles and, further, that they were confirmed as such by trustworthy witnesses. Therefore, he distinguished them from the forgeries of a learned deceiver, who presents the unusual as the divine and the ingenious as the miraculous to an ignorant populace. He further distinguished them from the exaggerations of an enthusiast who knows what must have happened; the pity being that no one saw it. Can their credibility be better, or only differently established?[28]

Lessing's conclusion is that they cannot be better established, but the reason lies not in the intrinsic merits of Cardanus' argument, but in the futility of all such proofs. Because all are ultimately worthless, Cardanus' can be said to be as good as any. Thus, we can find in this work the first treatment of a theme which later came to dominate Lessing's polemic with the theologians—the complete rejection of all historical proofs for the truth of the Christian religion. In the present instance the proofs are not explicitly attacked, but the negative implications of Lessing's discussion are nevertheless quite clear.

It is, however, only in the rejection of the last alternative: that perhaps Cardanus' presentation may be objected to because it depicted the other religions in too favorable a light, that the full irony of Lessing's position becomes apparent. Rather than making the opposing cases too strong, he argues, Cardanus did not make them strong enough.[29] Lessing supports this paradoxical contention with the familiar claim for the need to base one's religious convictions upon a thorough examination of the evidence, and in terms of this he justifies the desirability of presenting the various alternatives in their best possible light.[30] With this in mind Lessing embarks upon a vigorous defense of the Mohammedan religion and shows that it is in all respects far more reasonable than Christianity and that all of the common objections, such as the sensuous manner in which it depicts paradise, are equally applicable to Christianity.[31] The result of this "defense" is that Islam is identified with the natural religions of deism, and, as in the *Thoughts on the Moravians,* this simple and rational, natural religion, is shown to be infinitely superior to historical Christianity. It is from this standpoint that Lessing's deistic Mohammedan is able to demand of the Christian, just as Tindal had demanded of Clarke: "You must prove that man is obliged to do more than to know God and be virtuous; or at least, that reason, which was given to him precisely for this purpose, cannot teach him these things."[32]

It is, I believe, significant that Lessing sees no necessity for any further response on the part of the Christian. The defense delineated by Cardanus must suffice, not because it is adequate, but because none can be. Christianity's claim that man is obligated to do more than know God and practice virtue is, for the twenty-three-year-old deist, completely ungrounded.

Philosophical Speculations: Despite the ethically oriented deism, so evident in the *Thoughts on the Moravians* and the *Vindication of Hieronymus Cardanus,* the young Lessing was not totally devoid of interest in speculative philosophical issues. This interest is manifested in the short fragment, *The Christianity of Reason,*[33] a curious document which is one of the most variously interpreted of all Lessing's writings. The scholarly disputes regarding this work are not only concerned with the question of its general significance within the total scheme of Lessing's thought, but also the determination of the sources upon which it is based.[34]

The work itself, although left unfinished, contains a tight argument, and may be conveniently divided into four sections. Sections 1–4 form the general introduction, and deal with the concept of God. God is described (Sections 1–2) as the most perfect Being, who as such can only be concerned with the most perfect thing and, consequently, from all eternity has been engaged in self-contemplation. This account is clearly rooted in Aristotle's analysis of the divine activity as "thought thinking itself,"[35] but it does not necessarily suggest a profound knowledge of Aristotelean metaphysics.[36]

The next section (Section 3) is decisive: "To conceive, to will, and to create are one with God. One can therefore say that anything which God conceives he also creates."[37] This passage contains an explicit critique and modification of the Leibniz-Wolffian concept of God and suggests Lessing's early dissatisfaction with the anthropomorphic implications of this concept, which are evident in its popular formulations.[38] Moreover, this suggestion as to the nature of his dissatisfaction is confirmed later in the work (Section 15), where he states:

God could think of his perfections divided in an indefinite variety of ways. There could therefore be an indefinite number of possible worlds were it not that God thinks always of the most perfect, and thus amongst all these thought the most perfect of worlds, and so made it real.[39]

These two propositions clearly indicate that Lessing's modification of Leibniz was in the direction of a deterministic monism. For if God is only concerned with the contemplation of his own perfections and if the divine thought is identified with the creative act, then the created world is nothing more than the result of the divine self-contemplation and, as such, is not separable from God. The determinism is grounded in the identification of the divine intellect and will. For as Bayle and Arnauld had already argued, an infinitely good, wise, and powerful being must necessarily will and produce the best of all possible worlds.[40]

However, despite the emphasis upon determinism and monism, it is important to see how far this scheme is from Spinoza. Lessing's God is a self-conscious, personal Being, engaged from all eternity in self-contemplation. Although he is determined, this determinism is grounded in his reason and goodness. Consequently, whether or not these views are in any way reconcilable with Leibniz's,[41] they are certainly quite far from the Spinozistic pantheism.

Section 4 states the program to be followed in the balance of the work. God can consider his perfection in two ways: either he thinks of them all together and of himself as the totality thereof, or he can consider them individually, according to their proper grade.

Sections 5–12 constitute the second main division and treat the first alternative mentioned above. Here Lessing presents a speculative interpretation of the doctrine of the Trinity which, with one significant omission, was later reproduced in *The Education of the Human Race.* Lessing's argument is based upon his prior identification of conception and creation in God. Because of this identification, God's self-contemplation from eternity implies the existence from eternity of a being lacking none of the divine perfections. This being, called in Scripture "the Son of God," is the simple consequence of the divine, creative self-consciousness. It is an identical image of God, lacking none of his attributes, and only termed "Son" because of the logical priority of the conceiver to that which is conceived. Moreover, Lessing continues, since the more two things have in common with one another, the greater is the harmony between them, the greatest possible harmony must exist between two things which have everything in common. Thus, by a meta-physical tour de force, Lessing arrives (Section 9) at the concept of the Holy Spirit, which he equates with the harmony between Father and Son.

Such a discussion of the Trinity certainly does not reveal any deep concern with Christian doctrine. There is absolutely no connection between Lessing's Son of God, and the Jesus Christ of the Christian faith. This identical image of God is a purely speculative construction, and not the savior of the human race. Thus, as in the previously discussed works, we see that Lessing had broken completely away from orthodox Christianity, although this fragment provides the first indication that he desired to replace it with something far different from the simple religion of Adam, which was advocated in the *Thoughts on the Moravians*.

Sections 13–21 constitute the third basic division of the work. Here Lessing turns to the second alternative mentioned in Section 4: that God contemplated his perfections individually. Since every thought is a creation with God, the result of this contemplation is the creation of a series of beings, each of which has something of the divine perfections. The sum total of these created beings constitutes the world, which as we have already seen, is necessarily the best possible.

Upon this basis Lessing proceeds (Section 16) to describe the best of all possible worlds in essentially Leibnizean terms. The most perfect manner in which the divine mind can contemplate its perfections is in the form of an infinite series of greater and less, which so follow one another that there is never a gap between them. Furthermore, since for God to think is to create, the world must actually consist of such an ordered chain of being or hierarchy of perfections, and since this chain must be infinite, the infinity of the world is incontestable. In short, Lessing's universe is ordered according to Leibniz's principle of continuity.

Moreover, both the basic elements of this world and their mutual relations are conceived of in a thoroughly Leibnizean manner. For, it is argued, God creates nothing but "simple things," the composite being merely a secondary consequence of this creation, and: "Since each of these simple beings has something which the others have, and none can have anything which the others have not, there must be a harmony among these simple things; and from this harmony everything may be explained that happens among them, that is, in the world."[42]

The third section closes with the pious hope that at some future time "a happy Christian" will extend the sphere of natural philosophy to this point, but that this will only take place in the distant future, when explanations have already been found for all the phenomena in nature, and there remains nothing to do but to trace them each to its source. Such a program of research is likewise Leibnizean in spirit, but the designation of such a researcher as a Christian, must, I believe, be taken ironically, as still another indication of Lessing's alienation from traditional Christianity.

Thus, the first twenty-one paragraphs of *The Christianity of Reason* contain what can only be described as a brief sketch of an entire philosophical system. Much of the content of this system, and its very mode of presentation (in brief paragraphs), are reminiscent of Leibniz, but the young dramatist, journalist, and antiquarian was not afraid to criticize and modify the Leibnizean philosophy on certain important respects.

The final sections (22–27) contain an outline of Lessing's ethics. He begins by characterizing the simple beings, who are the ultimate constituents of the universe as "limited gods." As such, their perfections are similar in kind, although not in degree, to the Deity's. The most important of the divine perfections are God's consciousness of and ability to act in accordance with his perfections. Since finite beings possess similar perfections, albeit to a lesser degree, they can be ranked according to their consciousness of these perfections and their ability to act in accordance with them. Those who are sufficiently conscious of their perfections to act in accordance with them are called moral beings, and this leads Lessing to a formulation of the moral law: "Act according to your individual perfections."[43] The fragment ends abruptly (Section 27) with the reflection that there are beings who are not sufficiently conscious of their perfections.[44]

The key point in these final paragraphs is that moral action is viewed as requiring a certain level of consciousness. One must be sufficiently conscious of one's perfections before one is able to act in accordance with them. This suggests that Lessing's ethic is ultimately intellectualistic. Like Leibniz, he grounded virtue in knowledge, and as a result he also conceived of the "clearing up of the understanding" as the primary ethical task. From this standpoint the statement "Man was created for action and not for speculation" can be seen in its proper perspective. Clearly, Lessing was not here advocating the anti-intellectualistic emotionalism of the pietistic sect. In order to truly be considered moral, those deeds which con-

stitute the true end of man must be guided by rational principles—
by the consciousness of one's perfections. Thus, Lessing's quarrel,
and he is here following Bayle, was not with the use of reason, but
with its abuse. He did not reject speculation per se, but only that
irrelevant brand of speculation which is totally divorced from life,
and hence it is entirely fitting that Lessing's own youthful attempt
at speculative thought should culminate in an ethic.

II
THE SECOND PERIOD—1755–60

Lessing's major concern during the years 1755–60 was with
literary criticism and the drama. Consequently, although there was
an increasing emphasis on purely theoretical questions, the few
scattered reflections on religious and philosophic themes do not
suggest any significant advance beyond the views expressed in his
earlier writings. This period is marked by the full flowering of
his friendship with Moses Mendelssohn.[45]

Lessing and Mendelssohn: In 1755 Lessing collaborated with
Mendelssohn on an essay, *Pope, a Metaphysician.* The work was
occasioned by the Berlin Academy's announcement of a prize essay
on the subject of Alexander Pope's system, as contained in the
proposition: "All is good." The Academy's aim in offering such a
subject was obviously to disparage the Leibnizean optimism,[46]
with which Pope's *Essay on Man* was popularly identified. The
essay of Lessing and Mendelssohn is essentially an attempt to
demonstrate the absurdity of the designated subject. It begins with
a delineation of the difference between poetry and metaphysics,
and it shows by means of a close textual analysis that Pope's
optimism has little in common with the Leibnizean philosophy.
However, although the essay gives evidence of Lessing's continued
interest in Leibniz, it moves entirely on the level of the popular
Theodicy-oriented understanding of his philosophy.

A similar attitude is expressed in Lessing's relation to Mendelssohn's first work, the *Philosophical Conversations* (1755).
Mendelssohn had shown the manuscript to Lessing, who not only
proceeded to have the work published, but also gave it a glowing
review,[47] praising both the succinctness of its style and the cogency
of its reasoning. The main theme of the relevant portion of the
work is the relationship between Leibniz and Spinoza. Its two theses
are that Spinoza is the true discoverer of the preestablished harmony[48] and that, although it is untenable, if Spinoza's system be

understood as a description of the Leibnizean universe, as it exists in the mind of God before the creative decree, it can be reconciled with the basic principles of morality and religion.[49] Both of these arguments are rather superficially, albeit lucidly, formulated, and the first is not even original with Mendelssohn.[50] Nevertheless, they are worthy of mention in this context because Mendelssohn's fantastic interpretation of the Spinozistic universe as immanent within the mind of the Leibnizean God strongly suggests the influence of Lessing's *The Christianity of Reason*.[51] Lessing's apparent approval of these speculations indicates the relatively superficial level of his own philosophical reflections at this time and helps to place his subsequent discussions of Leibniz and Spinoza in their proper perspective.

Still another product of Lessing's acquaintance with Mendelssohn was his interest in the English "philosophy of feeling." This interest was aroused by Mendelssohn's *Letters on Sensations* (1755), in which the attempt was made to find a positive, philosophical basis for a doctrine of feeling. This was formulated in explicit opposition to the Wolffian school, for whom feeling, as grounded merely in the obscurity of perception, was something essentially negative. Mendelssohn was influenced in this direction by his reading of the British empiricists, especially Locke. Lessing accepted Mendelssohn's theory in a modified form and was induced (1756) to translate Hutcheson's *System of Moral Philosophy*. The correspondence of these two men during this period also reveals a lively interest in the problem of feeling, especially in regard to aesthetics,[52] with which both were primarily occupied. The full significance, however, of Lessing's concern with this subject does not emerge until his conflict with Goeze and must there be viewed in the light of the doctrine of the *New Essays*.

Literary Criticism: Lessing's critical interests during this period found their chief expression in the *Letters Concerning the Newest Literature*, in which he collaborated with Mendelssohn and Nicolai. From the beginning of 1759 until September 1760 Lessing was the editor and chief contributor to this enterprise. His main concern was with the creation of a living and independent German literature, which he hoped to promote through impartial and constructive criticism. In the course of this endeavor he felt called upon to defend the basic principles of the Aufklärung against the enthusiasm of the Swiss school, led by Bodmer, Klopstock, and Wieland, and the shallow moralizing of Cramer and Basedow, and it is in these letters that Lessing addressed himself to religious and philosophical questions. Thus, they provide the best source for the knowledge of his religious and philosophical views at this time.

The first relevant reflections occur in Letters Seven to Fourteen, which are devoted to a critique of Christoph Martin Wieland's *Feelings of a Christian* (1755). The general object of Lessing's attack is Wieland's attempt to characterize Christianity in terms of aesthetic feeling. As we have just seen, Lessing was very much interested in the problem of feeling, and he was far from denying its religious significance. He was, however, anxious to distinguish between true religious feeling and the products of the poetic imagination, which Wieland presented as the essence of Christianity. Thus he writes:

> Christian feelings are those which each and every Christian can and should have. And Wieland's are not of that kind. At the most they could be the feelings of a Christian, that is to say, of a Christian who is at the same time a wit, and too, a wit who believes that he is greatly glorifying his religion if he makes its mysteries into objects of aesthetic sensibility. If he succeeds in this project he will become enraptured with his beautiful mysteries. He will be overcome by a sweet enthusiasm, and his feverish brain will begin to believe in all seriousness that this enthusiasm is true religious feeling.[53]

However, this skirmish with Wieland was merely preliminary to the attack upon Johann Andreas Cramer, editor of *The Northern Guardian*, the foremost organ of the Klopstockean school. The essence of Lessing's critique is contained in the Forty-Eighth and Forty-Ninth Letters. These remarks were later supplemented (Letters One Hundred Two to One Hundred Twelve) in rebuttal to a defense of Cramer by Johann Bernhard Basedow, but it is only the original criticism that need concern us here.

In the Forty-Eighth Letter Lessing reflects upon Cramer's proposed reform of religious education. It was Cramer's contention that, since the best method of learning is to proceed from the relatively simple to the more difficult, children should first be taught to consider Jesus merely as "a pious and completely holy man," and only later when their understandings have matured should they be introduced to the doctrine that he is the divine savior of the human race.[54]

Lessing's reaction to this scheme is rather complex, but highly significant, for it clearly shows the grounds of his displeasure with the "modern theology," of which Cramer was an adherent. The remarks in *Thoughts on the Moravians* make it abundantly clear that Lessing had no quarrel with the purely human conception of Christ. However, he realized that the tacit presupposition of the ultimate rationality and conceivability of the doctrine of the Incarnation lay at the heart of Cramer's pedagogical plan. Only upon this basis is it meaningful to talk about a preparation of the understanding, and it is precisely this basis which Lessing vehemently denied. Although at this time he stood completely outside the Christian framework, he saw that Christian dogmas are by their very nature inscrutable mysteries and, consequently, that any attempt to "prove" their rationality is absolutely futile. Hence, in depicting the implications of Cramer's scheme, he is quite consistently able to assume an apparently orthodox guise and assert:

> Does he call that facilitating the comprehension of the mysterious concept of an eternal savior? Rather it is abandoning it. It is putting an entirely different concept in its place. In a word, it is making the child into a Socinian until he is able to comprehend the orthodox doctrine. And when can he comprehend it? At what age do we become more capable of comprehending this mystery than we are in childhood? And since it is a mystery, is it not more reasonable to instill it into the receptive child than to await the time of the resisting reason?[55]

Lessing continues his attack in the next letter, here focusing on Cramer's claim "that without religion there can be no honest men."[56] Such a statement provided the perfect opening for a student of Bayle, and Lessing takes full advantage of it. He begins by demonstrating the inconsistency in Cramer's argument. In the statement of his thesis, Lessing contends, Cramer defines a man without religion as someone who does not accept the Christian revelation, but in the proof of this claim, where he argues that such an individual could not be completely righteous, because he cannot fulfill his obligations to the God he does not recognize, Cramer understands a man without religion to be an outright atheist.[57] As a staunch defender of the natural religion of the Aufklärung, the young Lessing vehemently rejects this equation of the denial of revelation with the denial of God.[58]

However, Lessing's strongest objections are directed to the

second stage of Cramer's argument, in which it is alleged that merely on the human or social level a man without religion could not be fully honest, because he would lack the decisive motive to moral action, that is, the expectation of future rewards and punishments.[59] In reply to this rather banal apology for religion, Lessing writes:

> Since I admit that revealed religion adds to our motivating grounds for acting honestly, you can see that I take nothing away from religion. But neither shall I take anything away from reason! Religion has far higher purposes than to mold the honest man. It presupposes him; and its chief aim is to raise the honest man to higher insights. It is true that these higher insights can and do become new motivating grounds for acting honestly; but does it therefore follow that the other motivating grounds must always remain ineffectual, that there is no righteousness besides that which is connected with higher insights?[60]

In this explicit rejection of the neological reduction of religion to morality, Lessing has combined Bayle's emphasis upon the autonomy of morality with the intellectualistic, essentially Leibnizean conception of human behavior, outlined in *The Christianity of Reason*. Thus, the above passage shows us that despite the apparent anti-intellectualism of the *Thoughts on the Moravians*, the young Lessing regarded the religious life as essentially a quest for truth.[61] Moreover, a similar statement, written twenty years later, graphically suggests that the intellectualistic conception of religion formed a permanent part of Lessing's Weltanschauung. Discussing the ultimate purpose of Christianity, he there asserts:

> The ultimate purpose of Christianity is not our salvation, which may come how it will, but our salvation by means of our enlightenment. This enlightenment is necessary, not merely as a condition of our salvation, but as an ingredient, in which, in the last analysis, our entire salvation consists.[62]

III
THE BRESLAU YEARS—1760–65

In November 1760 Lessing left the "Literary Letters," his whole circle of friends, including Mendelssohn, and the city of Berlin to accept a position as secretary to General Tauentzien in Breslau, where he remained until May 1765. Not overly burdened with official duties, Lessing was able to devote a good deal of time to study, and it was during this period that he acquired an extensive knowledge of the Church Fathers and early Church history and, of even greater importance, began the serious study of Spinoza.

Although the combination of official duties and intensive study precluded the possibility of any major literary production, the Breslau years are generally considered to have been the decisive formative period in Lessing's career. This was recognized by Lessing himself, who in the midst of an illness, wrote to his friend, Karl Wilhelm Ramler: "The serious epoch of my life draws near; I begin to become a man, and flatter myself that in this burning fever, I have raved away the last remains of my youthful folly."[63]

And in the judgment of no less a person than Johann Gottlieb Fichte:

> The real epoch of the determination and fortifying of his mind appears to fall within the time of his residence in Breslau, during which this gifted spirit, without any outward literary direction, and surrounded by heterogeneous business affairs, which to his view only passed on the surface of life, meditated on himself, and struck root in himself.[64]

Despite the lack of any extended philosophical or theological works stemming from this period, Lessing's literary remains contain several fragments which suggest the direction of his interest and level of development at this time. These deal with his philosophical as well as religious-historical studies, and we shall concern ourselves with both classes in an effort to determine both the nature of his understanding of and relationship to the philosophy of Spinoza and his general attitude toward the Christian religion.

Lessing and Spinoza, Metaphysics: Prior to this period Lessing's few scattered references to Spinoza had been generally unsympathetic and thoroughly in the spirit of Bayle's critique and the popular Enlightenment understanding of "the great atheist." Thus, in writing to Johann David Michaelis, the theologian, about Mendelssohn, he praised his friend as a "second Spinoza," who "for complete equality with the first lacks nothing but his errors,"[65] and in *Pope a Metaphysician* he speaks of Spinoza as an "acknowledged heretic" and of his philosophy as an "erroneous system."[66]

The writings of the Breslau period exhibit a marked change

from this standpoint. This change is manifest in the two brief philosophical fragments which Lessing directed to Mendelssohn. The first fragment, *Through Spinoza Leibniz Only Came upon the Track of the Preestablished Harmony*, together with a letter to Mendelssohn (April 17, 1763) which reiterates the argument of the fragment, refers to Mendelssohn's *Philosophical Conversations*. We have already seen how Lessing originally praised this work. Now, however, he expresses himself somewhat differently: "I must confess to you that for some time I have not been completely satisfied with your first "Conversation." I believe that you were even somewhat of a sophist at the time that you wrote it, and I am amazed that no one has yet taken the side of Leibniz against you."[67]

This difference in attitude is only explicable in terms of Lessing's close study of Spinoza, and in both the fragment and the letter he sharply distinguishes between the Spinozistic and the Leibnizean positions. Mendelssohn's theory that the doctrine of the preestablished harmony was anticipated by Spinoza was based upon Spinoza's contention that "the order and connection of ideas is the same as the order and connection of things." Against this Lessing argues that the notion is only meaningful in light of the proposition that "mind and body are one and the same thing conceived now under the attribute of thought, now under the attribute of extension," and upon this basis he chides Mendelssohn: "What kind of a harmony could have occurred to him in making such a statement? The greatest, it may be answered, namely the harmony of a thing with itself. But is that not just playing with words?"[68]

In this connection Lessing emphasized the basic difference between the two positions. The Leibnizean hypothesis of the preestablished harmony is designed to solve the problem of the relationship between two distinct entities—body and soul[69]—and, despite a superficial verbal similarity, it is not to be confused with the radically monistic position of Spinoza. It is true that both men can subscribe to the thesis that the order and connection of ideas in the mind corresponds precisely to the order and connection of bodies in the external world: "But because both use the same words, will they also connect them with the same concepts?"[70]

Lessing answers this question in the negative and illustrates his point, in characteristic fashion, by means of a metaphor. Suppose, he suggests, there were two savages, each of whom sees for the first time his image in the mirror. They both realize that their images make precisely the same movements in precisely the same order as they do, and when they begin to philosophize about this phenomenon both must attempt to interpret this remarkable correspondence in terms of a single principle.[71]

The fragment breaks off at this point, and the metaphor is not carried through. Nevertheless, Lessing's implication is quite clear. The two savages are obviously intended to represent Leibniz and Spinoza, who advocate the two possible interpretations of the phenomenon of correspondence. Either the relationship between the body and its image is to be explained in terms of a preestablished harmony between two disparate substances or understood simply as the correlation of two aspects of one identical thing. Although this part of the argument is not contained in the extant portion of the text, it is quite easy to see where Lessing's preference lies. In terms of the comparison delineated in the above paragraph the Leibnizean position becomes a manifest absurdity, and the monistic conception, wherein the man and his image are the same thing considered under two aspects, presents itself as the only meaningful interpretation of the situation. Thus, we can find in the fragment not only clear evidence of Lessing's thorough grasp of Spinoza, but, even more important, a definite albeit implicit suggestion of his adherence to this mode of thought.

The second fragment, *On the Reality of Things Outside God,* which was also presumably addressed to Mendelssohn,[72] contains a Spinoza-induced development of the basic theme of *The Christianity of Reason,* the identity in God of thought and creation. From this standpoint Lessing proceeds to criticize the Wolffian formulation of the relation between possibility and actuality, a relation which can be seen as the central problem of the Wolffian ontology.[73]

Lessing's own position, the equation of the real world with the world which exists within the divine mind, which Eric Schmidt has labeled "Panentheismus" as distinguished from "Pantheismus,"[74] is here formulated in explicit opposition to the Wolffian ontology defended by Mendelssohn. He demonstrates that on the basis of this ontology it is impossible to conceive of the reality of things "outside God" or in nontheological terms, of their actuality as distinct from their possibility. Hence, Lessing is here making explicit that denial of the distinction between possibility and actuality, which was already implicit in his prior identification of thought and creation in God.

Lessing begins with an analysis of Wolff's conception of actuality as "the complement of possibility"[75] and asks if the divine mind contains a concept of this complement. Since it would be absurd to deny that God possesses such an idea, it follows that the thing itself exists within the divine mind. For what, he asks, can the reality of a thing outside God have which distinguishes it from the reality contained in his idea? Any such distinguishing mark would be something of which God has no idea, and this involves a manifest absurdity. But, if the idea which God has of the reality of a thing contains everything which is to be found in the thing, then this idea is *eo ipso* the thing itself. The situation is basically similar with Baumgarten, for whom the actuality of a thing is defined as "the sum of all possible definitions that may be applied to it."[76] Must not God have an idea of these additional determinations? And if so, this idea is identical with the thing itself. In both instances the positing of a reality additional to the completely determined concept in God is seen as a groundless and unnecessary duplication. Lessing has here quite systematically applied "Occam's Razor" to the Wolffian ontology.

With this, Lessing has grasped the fatal weakness in this ontology: its utter inability to solve adequately its central problem, the relation of possibility to actuality. The distinctive mark of all the formulations stemming from the Wolffian school is that the transition of a thing from possibility to actuality is equated with the acquisition of additional determinations. However, this equation, which is implicit in Wolff's and explicit in Baumgarten's formulation, is based on the fundamental confusion of a thing with the degree of determination of its structure. The thing qua possible has a different determinate structure than the same thing qua actual, and thus the modal change from possibility to actuality is understood in terms of a structural change from less to more determinants.[77] Moreover, this confusion can be seen as an inevitable consequence of Wolff's formulation of the issue: "If a thing is to exist there must be something more added to possibility, through which the possible receives its fulfillment. And this fulfillment of the possible is precisely what we call actuality."[78]

Once the problem is posed in this way, once the actual is conceived as the possible plus something, the Wolffian confusion is unavoidable. This was clearly recognized by Kant in his famous discussion concerning the relationship between the one hundred real and the one hundred imaginary thalers, and it forms the very heart of his critique of the Leibniz-Wolff concept of possibility:

It does indeed seem as if we were justified in extending the number of possible things beyond that of the actual, on the ground that something must be added to the possible to constitute the actual. But this alleged process of adding to the possible I refuse to allow. For that which would have to be added to the possible, over and above the possible, would be impossible.[79]

Such was the Kantian critique of the Wolffian formulation, which in all essential respects was anticipated by Lessing. However, although these criticisms of the Wolffian concept of the relationship between possibility and actuality are substantially identical, they draw diametrically opposed conclusions from this insight. For Kant it leads to the denial of the concept of the possible as a more inclusive sphere than the actual; for Lessing it leads to a denial of the actual, as something distinct from the possible. Thus, whereas Kant proceeds to formulate a new conception of possibility, in accordance with the principles of the "critical philosophy," Lessing constructs an idealistic-monistic metaphysics, wherein the world is conceived of as existing within the divine mind.

In the final paragraphs of the fragment, Lessing endeavors to defend his monistic hypothesis against some possible objections. Most philosophers, he argues, insist upon the reality of things outside God in order to emphasize the distinction between the finite and the infinite, between necessary and contingent being. But, reflects Lessing, these distinctions are perfectly reconcilable with the doctrine that the ideas which God has of real things are the real things themselves. As ideas in the divine mind they are distinguishable from God, and their location does not vitiate their contingent status, for "what is contingent outside God is also contingent in God, or God could not have any idea of the contingent outside him."[80]

These lines furnish a graphic illustration of both the influence of Spinoza upon Lessing's thought and of the vast gulf which nevertheless separates their respective philosophical positions. The above passage suggests that Lessing reinterpreted Spinoza's fundamental distinction between "*natura naturans*" and "*natura naturata*" in terms of the distinction between the divine mind and its conceptual content. Thus, rather than finite modes which follow necessarily from the infinite essence of God,[81] created beings, for Lessing, are contingent ideas within the divine understanding. This emphasis upon the divine mind suggests that here, as well as in

The Christianity of Reason, Lessing was still writing from within the Leibnizean tradition, although his criticisms thereof were no doubt sharpened by his study of Spinoza.

It is, therefore, in light of these considerations that the thorny question of Lessing's relationship to Spinoza must ultimately be determined. The most important source in this regard is obviously Friedrich Heinrich Jacobi's *On the Doctrine of Spinoza, in Letters to Moses Mendelssohn* (1785), in which he related a conversation which he had with Lessing in 1780 with the intention of proving to Mendelssohn and the world that Lessing was a Spinozist. Although this conversation took place some fifteen years after Lessing left Breslau, its main themes stand in an intrinsic connection with the fragments just discussed, and, consequently, we shall analyze it within this context.

The substantial accuracy of Jacobi's account is generally accepted[82] and is not called into question here. The real problem concerns the interpretation and evaluation of the report in the light of Jacobi's own presuppositions. It was Jacobi's favorite thesis that all systematic or scientific philosophy leads inevitably to fatalism and atheism[83] and that the philosophy of Spinoza constitutes the ultimate achievement in that direction.[84] However, as an orthodox theist and champion of freedom of the will, he also believed that all such fatalistic world views are false and dangerous and can only be refuted by means of a "*Salto mortale*" or leap of faith beyond the realm of rational demonstrations.[85] It was with this in mind and with the desire of enlisting Lessing's aid against that dreaded evil—which he termed, indifferently, fatalism, atheism, and Spinozism—that Jacobi visited Lessing at Wolfenbüttel in July 1780.[86]

This intent, however, was soon frustrated, for upon being shown Goethe's poem "Prometheus," which combined a vague pantheism with a bitter attack upon the orthodox conception of providence, Lessing shocked Jacobi by expressing his hearty approval: "The point of view from which the poem is written is my point of view. The orthodox conceptions of the Deity are no longer for me; I cannot appreciate them. 'hen kai pan' I know no other."[87]

These remarks could, for Jacobi, only mean Spinozism, and his fears were confirmed by Lessing's hypothetically formulated response to this charge: "If I should name myself after any one, I know no other I should choose,"[88] and later, "There is no other philosophy than the philosophy of Spinoza."[89]

The bulk of the subsequent discussion is ostensibly devoted to the demonstration of Lessing's adherence to the philosophy of Spinoza, but in characteristic fashion Jacobi discloses a good deal more about his own views than about Lessing's. What is revealed, however, is to a large extent consistent with the views expressed in the Breslau fragments, and many of the new theories are based upon Lessing's subsequent study of Leibniz and Bonnet. Thus, only in the very loose sense in which Jacobi used the term, did he succeed in showing Lessing to be a Spinozist. This usage is evident in his "triumphant" conclusion: "Lessing did not believe in any transcendent cause of the world; Lessing is a Spinozist."[90]

Furthermore, Lessing's ironical and half-serious attitude during much of the conversation may be gleaned from his failure to take issue with many of Jacobi's remarks. This is particularly evident in regard to Jacobi's comparison of the philosophies of Leibniz and Spinoza. This comparison was initiated by Lessing's whimsical remark that Leibniz "was himself at heart a Spinozist,"[91] which Jacobi used as the occasion to reiterate Mendelssohn's youthful assertion that Leibniz took his doctrine of the preestablished harmony from Spinoza.[92] In view of what we have previously seen of Lessing's attitude toward the question, his silence at this point must be considered indicative of his lack of complete sincerity in the discussion with Jacobi.

Nevertheless, despite Lessing's lack of complete sincerity and Jacobi's failure to establish his thesis, this document is not without significance for an understanding of Lessing's philosophical views. Primarily, it suggests that Lessing's interest in the thinker about whom the people speak "as of a dead dog"[93] was not a passing fancy, but a permanent aspect of his thought. But more particularly, it provides evidence of Lessing's abiding concern with and appreciation of Spinoza's concept of God and doctrine of universal determinism.

Lessing's denial of the orthodox concept of God and adherence to the "hen kai pan" has been mentioned,[94] but he later elaborated this in a manner more directly reminiscent of Spinoza's doctrine of God as an infinite substance, possessing an infinite number of attributes. This was undertaken in response to Jacobi's defense of teleology, against which Lessing states:

It is one of our human prejudices that we regard thought as the first and foremost thing, and try to derive all else from it; since everything, ideas included, depend upon higher principles. Extension, motion, and thought are obviously grounded in a higher power, which is far from exhausted by them. It must be infinitely more excellent than this or that effect, and so there may be a kind of enjoyment for it which not only surpasses all concepts, but lies altogether outside of concepts.[95]

However, this apparent rapproachment with Spinoza is somewhat mitigated by a later remark of Jacobi's, which once again casts doubt upon the seriousness of Lessing's "confession." According to Jacobi:

> When Lessing wanted to think of a personal God, he represented him as the soul of all, and the totality according to the analogy of an organic body. This soul of all was therefore, as with all other souls in all possible systems, as a soul, only an effect. However, its organic extension cannot be conceived of according to the analogy of the organic parts of this extension. For since this extension does not stand in relation to anything which exists outside of it, nothing can receive or produce it. Therefore, in order to stay alive it must from time to time return, as it were, into itself, and unite in itself death and resurrection with life. But one could depict the inner economy of such a being in many diverse manners.[96]

Such views are obviously far from those of Spinoza and do not seem to be in any way reconcilable with Lessing's other remarks, both here and elsewhere,[97] concerning the nature of God. In any event they make it quite clear that one cannot derive a consistent doctrine of God from the few scattered remarks presented by Jacobi.

The situation, however, is somewhat different in regard to the question of free will. Here Lessing's position is unequivocally deterministic and, in this respect, thoroughly in accord with Spinoza.[98] Thus, in response to Jacobi's lament that fatalism is an inevitable consequence of the denial of teleology, Lessing states: "I desire no free will,"[99] and supports this with a defense of Spinoza's rejection of final causes: "He was, however, far from presenting our miserable manner of acting according to purposes as the highest method, and so putting thought in the highest place."[100] And, finally, we even find Lessing declaring: "I remain an honorable Lutheran and maintain 'the more bestial than human error and blasphemy, that there is no free will,' with which the clear, pure mind of your Spinoza was also satisfied."[101]

Thus, as in the case of the denial of the transcendence of God, so too the denial of free will is here equated by both Jacobi and Lessing with Spinozism. However, the extent to which Lessing's determinism can be attributed to his study of Spinoza remains a moot question. There are clear indications of a deterministic viewpoint in Lessing's earliest writings, which antedate his study of Spinoza,[102] but more important, despite the apparent appreciation of Spinoza's rejection of final causes, we shall see in our subsequent discussion that Lessing adhered to the Leibnizean concept of providence and that his deterministic views are ultimately to be understood in this sense.[103]

Thus, in conclusion, we can see that Lessing denied both the freedom of the will and the transcendence of God, but that in both cases this is the basis of his appreciation rather than the result of the influence of Spinoza. Lessing was never in any technical or doctrinal sense a Spinozist. Nevertheless, as the chief representative of the monistic, deterministic world view to which he adhered, Lessing was willing and able to defend the philosophy of Spinoza and even to claim that it is the best and only philosophy. This was, in all essentials, Lessing's position in 1764, and, so far as may be determined from Jacobi's report of their conversation, it was his opinion in 1780.

Lessing and Spinoza, Religion: If Lessing's philosophical speculations concerning the relationship between the mind and the body, the concept of God and the doctrine of universal determinism were profoundly influenced by his study of Spinoza's *Ethics,* his religious-historical work of this period was no less inspired by the *Theologico-Political Treatise.* His own historical investigations at Breslau provided the material for these studies, but Lessing's method is basically that of Spinoza. This can best be seen from his ambitious, albeit incomplete, attempt in this direction: *Concerning the Manner of the Propagation and Dissemination of the Christian Religion.*[104]

The propagation and rapid growth of the Christian religion, despite adverse circumstances, was traditionally considered to have been miraculous and, thus, one of the basic historical proofs of its truth or divine origin. Although he never explicitly affirms it, Lessing's interest here, just as it was in his earlier treatment of Cardanus, was to discredit the "proof," and this is achieved through the presentation of a satisfactory naturalistic, and purely objective explanation of the phenomenon.[105] His ideal is complete historical objectivity: "Enter upon this investigation, I say to myself, like a noble man. See everything with your own eyes. Disfigure nothing, gloss over nothing. As the consequences flow, so let them flow. Neither check the stream nor divert it."[106]

Lessing begins by methodically subdividing the investigation into three parts. He shall determine (1) the advantage furnished by external circumstances to the rapid spread of Christianity, (2) Christianity's internal means for such a rapid spread, and (3) the strength of the obstacles which it had to surmount.

The first section, which in the extant text consists of little more than a list of subheadings, proposes to discuss the conditions of the "competing" religions: Judaism and paganism, as well as the various philosophical schools. The general conclusion is that they were all in a state of disunity and corruption and, consequently, open to the propagation of a new doctrine.[107]

The question of Christianity's internal resources for its own development is divided into two parts. Lessing first discusses its method of teaching and shows that one of their most successful techniques consisted in the holding back of doctrine in order to arouse curiosity.[108] In the second part he abandons his cynical tone and asserts that the purity of life and character of the early Christians was a major factor in their effectiveness in gaining converts.[109] However, he qualifies this by adding that the invention of prophecies, and the forging of books (which he does not attempt to reconcile with the purity of character) also played an important part.[110]

Finally, Lessing considers the obstacles which the Roman government placed upon the Christian religion. The first of these was, of course, the infamous persecutions, and Lessing goes to great lengths to show both that they were not nearly so severe as is generally thought and that they were not undertaken on religious grounds, but simply because the Christians disobeyed the civil laws by conducting secret nightly assemblies.[111]

Thus, not only did Lessing show that the propagation and spread of the Christian religion required nothing miraculous but also that the situation was actually highly propitious for such an event. This is, in effect, the reductio ad absurdum of the argument from miraculous growth, but Lessing is careful to deny any dangerous consequences therefrom: "If from all that has so far been adduced it should follow that the Christian religion was propagated and disseminated by purely natural means, one should yet be wary of believing that this implies something disadvantageous for the religion itself."[112]

Nevertheless, despite his protestations of innocence, Lessing's intent is again clear: the total rejection of the claim of the divine origin of the Christian religion. Thus, the end result of the Breslau studies, and especially of the study of Spinoza, was a confirmation of the un-Christian, basically deistic standpoint, which we have encountered in the earlier writings. For the author of *On the Reality of Things Outside God* the orthodox concept of revelation was a manifest absurdity, and for the learned historian the growth and spread of the Christian religion was explicable in purely natural terms.

These general tendencies found their most systematic formulation in another brief fragment of this period, *On the Origin of Revealed Religion*,[113] which despite its brevity is one of the most significant of Lessing's early religious-philosophical writings, for it contains in a capsule form all the essentials of his religious beliefs at this time. He begins, appropriately enough, with a description of the basic principles of natural religion: "To acknowledge one God, to seek to form the ideas most worthy of him, to take account of these most worthy ideas in all our actions and thoughts, is the most complete summary of all natural religion."[114]

This classic statement of the deistic emphasis upon the simplicity of religion is highly reminiscent of the religion of Adam, discussed in the *Thoughts on the Moravians*. For Lessing, as for Tindal and Reimarus,[115] the true and sufficient worship of God contains no dogmas and no ceremonies. However, given this primitivistic, ahistorical conception of natural religion, the problem is to explain the origin of revealed religion. Again Lessing's position is fundamentally deistic. He sees this origin in a corruption of the original simplicity of natural religion through the addition of conventional or positive elements, but he differs from the more vehement deists, such as Voltaire or Reimarus, in that he grounds this corruption in a real human need rather than in the deliberate deception of priests and princes.

This need for a positive religion containing conventional elements is caused, for Lessing, by the varying capacities of different individuals to practice the natural religion to which all men are bound. Because of this difference in capacity it is necessary for the sake of social cohesion that people become united about certain things and ideas, and in order to achieve the unity they must attribute to these conventional elements precisely the significance and necessity which the universally acknowledged truths of natural religion possess intrinsically; that is to say: ". . . out of the religion of nature, which was not capable of being universally practised by all men alike, a positive religion had to be constructed, just as out of the law of nature, for the same cause, a positive law had been constructed."[116]

Thus, positive religion is not completely repudiated, but given a relative justification based upon its social utility. However, such a view is far from any real appreciation of the conceptual content of the historical religions. They are all dismissed as purely human inventions whose inner truth consists solely in their indispensability,[117] and in this regard Lessing's "dispute" with the deists concerns only the social function and not the essential nature of positive religion. For Lessing, as well as for Tindal and Reimarus, all positive religion must be judged according to the standard of the evident, universally valid and completely reasonable religion of nature, and hence: "The best revealed or positive religion is that which contains the fewest conventional additions to natural religion, and least hinders the good effects of natural religion. . . ."[118]

Such were, in all essentials, Lessing's religious views during the early 1760's. Revealed religion is presented as a purely natural phenomenon, without any mention of the concept of revelation. It was presupposed that all such religions were merely human inventions, and the attempt was made to find some basis in human nature for their invention. The inevitable result of this procedure was that positive religion in general and the Christian religion in particular were seen as necessary evils, totally devoid of any specific philosophical content, whose sole value consists in their social utility. This formulation is somewhat more extreme than Spinoza's, but it is basically in accord with the standpoint of the *Theologico-Political Treatise*, whose main tenet is that Scripture (for which we may substitute revealed or positive religion) does not teach philosophy, but merely obedience, and consequently, is always accommodated to the opinions and prejudices of the multitudes.[119]

During the subsequent period, from 1765 through 1770, Lessing was occupied with his great aesthetic, dramatic, and critical works —*Laocoon* (1767), *Minna von Barnhelm* (1767) and the *Hamburg Dramaturgy* (1767–69)—and paid scant attention to religious and philosophic questions. However, when he did return to such issues after 1770, it was not only with a greater intensity and interest than he had exhibited previously, but also with a radically different standpoint. Thus, it shall be the task of the balance of this study to analyze and evaluate this new standpoint and to attempt to determine its philosophical presuppositions and historical significance.

CHAPTER 3

Lessing Versus the Theologians

As the survey of the historical background of Lessing's thought has indicated, the question of the truth of the Christian religion was identified throughout the eighteenth century with the question of the facticity of its alleged revelation. For Protestant orthodoxy this facticity was guaranteed by a divinely inspired sacred text. For the conservative rationalism of Locke and Leibniz it was guaranteed partly by the rationality, or at least nonirrationality of the doctrines revealed, and partly by the external evidences, that is, the supernatural credentials provided by the miracles of Jesus, the fulfillment of prophecy, and the miraculous growth of the Church. For neology or post-Wolffian German rational theology, the facticity was guaranteed by the completely rational and morally beneficial character of the revelation, which was viewed as the divinely appointed means for the enlightenment of mankind.

Furthermore, the deistic or naturalistic refutations of Christianity worked within the same framework. Accepting the hypothesis that Christianity is true if the Gospel narratives are accurate, the deists used critical tools to attack the credibility of these accounts, while the more philosophical among them argued against the very possibility or at least the significance of any such historical revelation. Because of the matter of fact, unhistorical manner in which the issue was posed, the alternative constantly arose: either the Christian religion is true, or Jesus and his disciples were deliberate deceivers, or more charitably, deluded fanatics. Defenders of the faith were often content merely to show the unreasonableness of the latter alternative, while the deistic critique (and here Reimarus was the most forceful spokesman) was generally devoted to the malignment of the character and credibility of the Biblical authors and personages.

We have already seen that although he did not disparage the character of Jesus and his disciples, the young Lessing had completely rejected the traditional concept of revelation, and was at one with the deists in the repudiation of the divine origin of the Christian religion. However, in May 1770 Lessing was installed as the ducal librarian at Wolfenbüttel and soon began to exhibit a far more positive attitude toward Christianity. Moreover, whereas his earlier discussions of philosophical and theological questions were largely in the form of unpublished fragments, he now openly entered the theological arena and engaged in what I hope to show was a systematic campaign against the three major contemporary theological positions: orthodoxy, neology, and deism.

The determination of the reasons behind this changed attitude toward Christianity and the evaluation of the standpoint assumed in the theological controversies of this period are the major problems confronting any interpretation of Lessing's mature philosophy of religion, and it is to these questions that I shall devote the balance of this study. The present chapter is concerned with an exposition and analysis of Lessing's position as contained in his correspondence and polemical writings, and Chapter 4 with an attempted reconstruction of the philosophical roots of this position. On the basis of this reconstruction I shall endeavor to interpret Lessing's three major writings of this period: *Ernst and Falk, Nathan the Wise,* and *The Education of the Human Race.*

The first inkling of a fundamental change of attitude is found in a letter to Mendelssohn. After receiving from him a long-awaited copy of a book by the Scottish moral philosopher Adam Ferguson, he wrote to his friend:

> I am now going to make an actual study of Ferguson. I can already see from the table of contents that this is the kind of book which I have missed here, where for the most part I only have books which sooner or later dull my understanding and waste my time. When one does not think for a long time, he ends up not being able to think at all. However, is it really good to contemplate and to concern oneself seriously with truths with which one has lived and, for the sake of peace, must continue to live in constant contradiction? I can already see from afar many such truths in the Englishman.
>
> Among them are some which I have for a long time ceased

to regard as truths. Still, it is not since yesterday that I have been
concerned that while discarding certain prejudices I might have
thrown away a little too much, which I shall have to retrieve. It
is only the fear of dragging all the rubbish back into my house
which has so far hindered me from doing this. It is infinitely
difficult to know when and where one should stop, and for the vast
majority of men the object of their reflection lies at the point at
which they become tired of reflecting.[1]

The importance of this passage has often been noted by
Lessing scholars, and because of it Ferguson has been cited as a
decisive influence on Lessing's thought. However, while there is a
general agreement that the passage is significant, there is a wide
range of opinion concerning its proper interpretation.[2] Nevertheless, the conflicting interpretations are united in the recognition of
the fact that the passage shows Lessing's thought in the process
of transition, and when we view his earlier theological productions,
such as the *Vindication of Hieronymus Cardanus* and *On the Origin
of Revealed Religion*, in the light of his later Wolfenbüttel writings,
we cannot help but conclude that the transition concerned Lessing's
relationship to Christianity and that the truths suggested by Ferguson are of a religious-philosophical nature.[3]

Thus, we may assume that the truths which Lessing lost while
ridding himself of "certain prejudices" and which he desired, at
least in part, to re-affirm are the Christian beliefs which he had
long since repudiated. We have seen in Chapter 2 that Lessing
lost these "truths" through his contact with Bayle, the Enlightenment, and Spinoza. Now, however, he suggests a changed standpoint by expressing the desire to reappropriate part of what he
had previously rejected, but he hesitates because of the fear of
dragging back at the same time "all the rubbish."

This "rubbish" can only refer to the eighteenth-century
Protestant orthodoxy, with its historically grounded, absolutistic
pretensions, made credible by miraculous events, and guaranteed
by an infallible, verbally inspired Scripture. It is unnecessary to
dwell any longer upon Lessing's repudiation of this position. The
whole tenor of his early writings reveals a basic agreement with
deism in regard to revealed religion, if not in regard to the concept of God. But, as the passage seems to suggest, by early 1771
Lessing had become dissatisfied with the naive naturalism which
characterizes deism. Since he was afraid of dragging back "all the

rubbish," he obviously did not wish to become an orthodox Christian, but, as he now apparently saw some philosophical and religious significance in traditional Christian thought, he could no longer accept the deistic position.[4]

Rather than completely repudiating naturalism or deism, however, Lessing came to realize its onesidedness. In that it refutes the absolutistic claims of the Christian revelation, he continued to see in it a negative moment of truth, but since it fails utterly to grasp either the philosophical significance of Christian thought or the needs of the religious consciousness, he realized that it must be transcended or incorporated into a higher standpoint. This recognition of the need for a higher standpoint is suggested by the autobiographical reflection with which he ends the above passage. Here Lessing seems to express for the first time a full consciousness of the task which is to occupy the last decade of his life. He is the one man in a thousand who must continue reflecting beyond the point where one grows weary of reflecting— with the attainment of the negative moment of truth. His problem henceforth will be to find a standpoint in terms of which the positive significance of Christian thought may be appreciated without at the same time vitiating the truth in the deistic and Spinozistic critique of the traditional concept of revelation. *Within the context of eighteenth-century thought this implies the separation of the Christian religion from its historical or factual foundation, and it is precisely this separation which we shall see Lessing propose and defend in his polemical writings.* Moreover, since such a separation entailed a total repudiation of the theology of the Enlightenment, it could only be established through a systematic polemic with this theology, and it is, I believe, in the recognition of this fact that one can see the deepest reason for Lessing's publication of the fragments of Reimarus and active participation in theological controversy, despite its inevitably unpleasant personal consequences.

I

LESSING VERSUS NEOLOGY[5]

Two years after the publication of the above letter, Lessing officially embarked upon his theological campaign, the heart of which lay in the publication, together with his "counter-assertions," of the fragments from Reimarus. This overt offensive was preceded by a series of scholarly historical studies in which Lessing ostensibly defended the orthodox position against the neological tendencies which had come to dominate German theological thought.

The key to Lessing's attitude toward neology can be found in a letter written to his brother Karl early in 1774. The latter, together with Lessing's Berlin friends, Mendelssohn, Nicolai, and the editors of the *Allgemeine deutsche Bibliothek*, was disturbed by the apparent betrayal of the Aufklärung and advocacy of orthodoxy in these historical studies. Lessing responded by proclaiming that he is a champion of true enlightenment and that he believes, as they do, that each individual should be taught to think rationally about religion. He admits that orthodox Christianity, with its absolutistic pretensions, is false and "impure water," but he nevertheless asserts its superiority to the shallow rationalism of the neologists:

> With orthodoxy, thank God, things were fairly well settled. A curtain had been drawn between it and philosophy, behind which each could go his own way without disturbing the other. But what is happening now? They are tearing down this curtain, and under the pretext of making us rational Christians, they are making us very irrational philosophers. I beg of you, my dear brother, inquire more carefully after this point and look less at what our new theologians discard than at what they want to put in its place. We are agreed that the old religious system is false, but I cannot share your conviction that it is a patchwork of bunglers and half philosophers. I know of nothing in the world in which human sagacity has been better displayed and cultivated. The real patchwork of bunglers and half philosophers is the religious system which they now want to set in place of the old, and with far more influence on reason and philosophy than the old ever presumed. And yet you still find fault with me for defending the old? My neighbor's house threatens to collapse upon him. If my neighbor wants to raze it, then I shall sincerely help him. However, he does not want to raze it, but rather to support and underpin it in such a way that my house will be completely ruined. He must desist from this project or I shall concern myself with his collapsing house as if it were my own.[6]

Thus, although orthodox Christianity is false, it is at least honest. It claims to be a divine revelation, but it does not claim to be rationally demonstrable or even fully amenable to human reason. Neology, however, proceeds upon a different basis. It attempts to underpin the collapsing house of Christianity with a new and rational foundation, thereby reconciling what was formerly left separate. As we have seen, this reconciliation involved the emptying of Christianity of all of its traditional content, and its reduction to a practically oriented restatement of natural religion.

Although Lessing's "enlightened" friends were highly pleased by such a procedure, Lessing himself regarded this reduction and consequent dismissal of almost the whole of traditional Christian doctrine as later accretions to, or perversions of "an original, pure and reasonable Christianity," as both dishonest and superficial. The dishonesty lay in the adherence to the fact of revelation (most of the neologists, for example, Sack, Spalding, and Jerusalem, were ministers), despite the rejection of its traditional content and the superficiality in the facile explaining away of all the embarrasing, irrational, or morally offensive aspects of Christian thought.

The philosophical basis for Lessing's dissatisfaction with neology can best be seen by noting its similarity to the very deism which he had outgrown. For the deistic original religion of nature, neology substituted true, simple, and original Christianity, and for the politically motivated formation of positive religions it substituted the historical development of Christian doctrine. In both cases truth was found in the original, primitive state, and only error and distortion in the subsequent development. Lessing, however, had come to realize perhaps under the influence of Ferguson,[7] that one is just as much a fiction as the other, that this purely rational revelation was no more a historical reality than the original religion of nature.

Above all, however, Lessing was concerned with the danger that the neological underpinning of Christianity constituted to his own house. This danger was grounded in the deceptive rationality which tended to obscure its basic fallacy—its adherence to the fact of revelation—and thus to hinder Lessing's great attempt to separate the Christian religion from its historical foundation. Hence, it was probably with neology in mind that Lessing stated in his *Berengarius Turonensis*, a learned historical study ostensibly designed to depict the eleventh-century heretic as a precursor of the Lutheran doctrine of transubstantiation, that "the greater the error, the shorter and straighter is the road to truth. A subtle error, however, can keep us perpetually from the truth, since it is much more difficult for us to recognize it as an error."[8] Moreover, it was with full awareness of this danger that he later wrote to Karl: "I comport myself with my obvious enemies, in order to be better able to be on my guard against my hidden foes."[9]

Lessing's overt polemic with his "hidden foes" began with the publication of two essays vindicating Leibniz against the attacks of Eberhard. The first of these, *Leibniz on Eternal Punishments* (1773), is one of Lessing's most direct confrontations with neology, as well as the clearest manifestation of his knowledge and appreciation of Leibniz—that "great man" of whom he wrote: "If it were up to me [he] would not have written a line in vain."[10] The work takes the form of a commentary on a hitherto unpublished preface of Leibniz to an attack on the doctrine of eternal punishments by the Socinian Ernst Soner. After some introductory remarks concerning Mosheim's mention of this preface and the sad state of Leibniz scholarship in Germany, Lessing presents Leibniz's brief preface.[11] In it Leibniz defends the concept of eternal punishment on the grounds of the infinite continuity of sin. The argument is similar to that of the *Theodicy*, but since it is directed to a particular opponent, it is differently expressed. Soner based his case upon the finitude of sin and the principle that there can be no relationship between the finite and the infinite. Leibniz, in rebuttal, addresses himself to the first point, showing that in asserting the finitude of sin, Soner neglected the one point of view from which it could be considered infinite. This omitted point of view is that of the infinity of number. Neither in themselves nor in relation to their object can sins be regarded as infinite, but, if one considers the future life, the possibility of the infinite continuity of sin and consequently of punishment cannot be denied.

The major portion of Lessing's essay is devoted to a refutation of Eberhard, who, as we have seen, had accused Leibniz of accommodation in order to win universal support for his system. In the course of this refutation, Lessing not only presents a masterful defense of Leibniz's philosophic integrity, but once again provides important clues as to his own philosophical position. Leibniz, he argues, did not endeavor to accommodate his views to the prevailing opinions, but rather sought to find a meaning in these opinions which he could accommodate to his system. Furthermore, he only proceeded in this manner because he firmly believed that no opinion could be generally accepted which was not at least in a certain sense true. Thus, Leibniz would analyze the common opinions until he found their true or "supportable sense." In Lessing's words: "He struck fire from the flint, but he did not conceal his fire in the flint."[12]

Moreover, he continues, it is true that Leibniz only accepted the orthodox doctrines in their "supportable sense," but Eberhard ought not to have added "without really believing in them," for, Lessing declares:

> To be sure he believed in them, that is in the supportable sense which he did not so much add as discover in them. The supportable sense was true, and how could he not believe in the truth? This should not be regarded as either duplicity or vanity. He did nothing more nor less than the ancient philosophers were wont to do with their exoteric lectures. He observed a bit of prudence for which our latest philosophers have become much too wise. He willingly set his own system aside and sought to lead each along the road to truth on which he found him."[13]

Finally, in reaction to Eberhard's charge of hypocrisy, Lessing adds in a similar vein:

> Rather I am convinced, and believe myself able to prove that Leibniz only acquiesced to the common doctrine of damnation, with all of its exoteric grounds, and even strengthened it with new grounds, because he recognized that it better agreed with a great esoteric truth of his own philosophy than the opposing doctrine. To be sure, he did not accept it in the crude and unseemly sense in which so many theologians accept it. But he found that even in this crude and unseemly sense it still possessed more truth than the equally crude and unseemly concepts of the enthusiastic defenders of the restoration.[14]

Even a cursory reading of the previously discussed letter to Karl leads one to realize that in thus defending Leibniz, Lessing was likewise characterizing and defending his own position. Just as his brother and the Berlin group failed to grasp his true meaning, so too Eberhard was totally incapable of grasping Leibniz's esoteric point of view. Eberhard, as we have seen, believed that the doctrine of the best of all possible worlds implied the supposition that all rational creatures eventually reach blessedness and contended that this was also Leibniz's true opinion. Eberhard's contention was largely based on his interpretation of Leibniz's letter to Louis Bourguet, wherein Leibniz suggests that the perfection of the universe may be conceived of as either static or as infinitely increasing. Although Leibniz explicitly states that he sees no way to demonstrate which of these is the case, Eberhard believed that he really advocated the developmental conception, and in view of this could not seriously have maintained the doctrine of eternal punishments.

Lessing refutes this contention by showing that Leibniz, in fact, expressed no such preference for the developmental conception[15] and by demonstrating that, even granting his assumption, Eberhard's inference is invalid. Leibniz, he argues, intended either hypothesis to refer only to the general condition of the totality, while Eberhard unjustifiably applied it to each individual. On this basis there would be no such a thing as sin, and such a doctrine is far from the opinion of Leibniz, who explicitly affirmed that the totality could have all perfections, although individual members were lacking therein.[16]

In these few pages Lessing succeeded in articulating the vast difference between the cosmic contextualism of Leibniz and the superficial utilitarianism of the Wolffian school, of which Eberhard was a member. The Wolffians, we have seen, conceived of the divine purpose as directed primarily to men, and the best of all possible worlds as the happiest possible place for the human race. Such was Eberhard's view, and Lessing shows that his misunderstanding grew out of his attempt to read a similar conception into Leibniz.

Having demolished Eberhard, Lessing proclaims the "great esoteric truth" which he believes to lie at the heart of Leibniz's defense of the doctrine of the eternality of punishment: the proposition that "nothing in the world is isolated, nothing is without consequences, nothing is without eternal consequences."[17] Thus, if punishment is the natural consequence of sin, it too must be eternal, and if perfection is understood in the true Leibnizean fashion, only in reference to the totality, then the eternality of punishment is perfectly reconcilable with the doctrine of eternally increasing perfection. Even on this assumption it is possible that a moral being may not only remain infinitely removed from his goal, but may actually continually regress from it, and, Lessing concludes, it is precisely this possibility which underlies the Leibnizean position.

Finally, Lessing argues that the doctrine of the eternality of punishment is even reconcilable with the view which he shared with Eberhard and the whole Enlightenment: that the only legitimate purpose of punishment, both divine and human, is the moral improvement of the victim. Even granting this the doctrine may be saved:

> Enough that each delay on the path to perfection is in all eternity not to be recouped, and therefore in all eternity is to be punished through itself. For now, granted that the highest Being can only punish for the purpose of improving the punished, granted also that improvement is sooner or later the necessary consequence of punishment; does it therefore follow that punishment can achieve its purpose in any better way than by continuing infinitely? Will it be said: "To be sure, through the living memory which it leaves behind"? As if this living memory were not likewise punishment.[18]

This, however, is not the problem, for even Eberhard accepted eternal punishment in this sense. "Not the eternity of natural punishment is denied, but—what then?—the eternity of Hell.—"[19] Thus, the real issue concerns the understanding of the concept of Hell, and at this point, Lessing turns from a justification of Leibniz to a general attack on neology and an oblique suggestion of his own position. What is this Hell, he asks, "but the totality of these punishments?"[20] The difficulty which leads Eberhard and other rational theologians to deny the eternality of punishment is that Scripture and tradition depict these punishments in corporeal terms, so consequently the eternality of punishment is seen as an eternity of unrelenting physical torment, an "intensive infinity." Such notions, however, Lessing argues, are mere metaphors, designed to inspire moral earnestness and not literal descriptions of fact. The rationalistic critics of the doctrine of eternal punishment have not realized this and, therefore, have confused the image with the thing. Thus, it is not the infinite continuity of punishment, but only the metaphorical, intensive infinity, which, if literally understood, contradicts the goodness and justice of God.[21]

This equation of Hell with the natural consequences of sin implies a relativization and hence complete transformation of the traditional concept, and Lessing explicitly affirms this relativization in his defense of the doctrine of eternal punishment. Rewards and punishments, he states, are certainly positive entities, "but a condition of reward and a condition of punishment are both relative concepts, which remain the same so long as they increase or decrease proportionally."[22]

Thus relativized, Heaven and Hell become reduced to states of mind, and given the nature of man they are not only compatible with, but actually seem to require the notion of eternal punishment (understood as the eternal consciousness of one's imperfections). For, as Lessing so eloquently declares:

> If it be true that the best man still has much evil, and the worst is not without some goodness, then the consequences of evil must follow the former even to Heaven, and the consequences of goodness accompany the latter even in Hell. Each man must find his Hell still in Heaven, and his Heaven still in Hell.[23]

With this reflection we reach the very heart of Lessing's position, and can see the vast gulf which separates him from the rationalism of an Eberhard or his Berlin friends. He had defended with Leibniz the doctrine of the eternality of punishment, but in so doing had completely transformed the concept of Hell with which it was traditionally conjoined. This is a typical example of Lessing's ironical method, already manifested in the *Vindication of Hieronymus Cardanus,* which we shall encounter time and again in his subsequent controversies. Although apparently orthodox in his defense of the doctrine of eternal punishment, his reinterpretation of the concept of Hell shows that his critique of Christianity is actually far more radical than Eberhard's, and it is because of this that some scholars[24] have viewed this essay as a secret attack, disguised as a defense, on Christian doctrine. Such an interpretation, however, completely misses the essential point, which is the superficiality and potential danger which Lessing sees in Eberhard's view. It was this neological procedure—which just as it accepts the concept of revelation and empties it of all its content similarly accepts the concept of Hell and endeavors to remove its embarrassing features—and not Christianity per se, which Lessing desired to undermine.

Thus, Lessing's concern was not so much with the doctrine of eternal punishment as it was with a position which would deny this doctrine by obscuring the source from which it derives its apparently offensive nature. The source of this offensiveness is the traditional concept of Hell, and Lessing clearly realized that Eberhard's critique of the doctrine of eternal punishments presupposes and lends support to that very concept. Hence, he saw in Eberhard's treatise one of those "subtle errors" which greatly retard the cause of truth. Since such errors have the semblance of veracity, they are actually far more dangerous than the gross untruths of orthodoxy, and it was with this in mind that Lessing wrote to his brother:

The Hell which Mr. Eberhard does not want to be eternal does not exist at all, and the one which really does exist is eternal. Is it not therefore better to refute the insipid, meaningless conceptions of the nature of this Hell than to bring forward a good explanation of its finite duration?[25]

Lessing's next publication, *Andreas Wissowatius' Objections Against the Trinity,* is likewise a commentary attached to a Leibnizean text, which he found in the Wolfenbüttel library. The text, *Defense of the Trinity by Means of New Logical Inventions,* was written by Leibniz (c. 1670) at the request of Baron Boineburg, in response to the logical objections to the doctrine of the Trinity raised by the Socinian Michael Wissowatius. After a brief historical introduction, in which he offers a detailed criticism of Jaucourt's chronology,[26] Lessing presents both Wissowatius' objections and Leibniz's replies.[27]

The logical principles by which Leibniz demonstrates the invalidity of Wissowatius' syllogisms are of little concern to Lessing. He merely uses the example of Leibniz's procedure against the Socinians as a vehicle for his own attack on neology. Because of the basic affinity between the Socinian and the neological rationalisms,[28] Lessing saw in Leibniz's polemic the perfect complement to his own. Although neither can be considered Christian in the orthodox sense, both Lessing and Leibniz saw fit to defend the orthodox doctrines against the pretensions of their shallow, rationalistic opponents.[29]

Lessing begins his commentary with a clarification of Leibniz's intent. The latter did not wish to give the doctrine of the Trinity a new philosophical support, but merely to defend it against the charge of irrationality, and, as Lessing points out, this is perfectly consistent with his general attitude toward the mysteries of the Christian religion. Since they are admittedly "above reason," they are not rationally demonstrable, but are nevertheless defensible against any charge of irrationality. Many, however (one is immediately reminded of Eberhard), do not believe that a thinker of Leibniz's stature could seriously uphold the orthodox doctrines, and they therefore accuse him of insincerity.

Against this rather prevalent conception that Leibniz "believed nothing of what he tried to persuade the world to believe,"[30] Lessing suggests that even if this were so, it would not prevent him from forming a judgment on the respective merits of the orthodox and Socinian christologies and that, in fact, his impartiality would enable him to reach a more objective evaluation of the philosophical significance of the two positions.[31] However, Lessing argues, one must not believe that Leibniz's defense of the orthodox doctrine of the Trinity against the Socinian views was insincere, for:

> The whole of his philosophy aroused him against the super-stitious nonsense that a mere creature could be so perfect as to deserve to be named next to the Creator; that he, I will not say may be worshipped with Him, but yet could be regarded by infinitely imperfect beings as if he were somehow less infinitely removed from the Godhead than they. The truths that God and God alone has created the world, that He would not let it be created by any creature, that a creature can create nothing, that even the most perfect creature must be a part of the world and, in comparison to God, no more considerable a part than the smallest mite; these truths, or rather this single truth (for one cannot be thought with-out the other), is the soul of his philosophy. Thus, can one still be surprised that he rejected a religious concept directly conflicting with this truth, a truth which is the foundation of all natural religion and which must necessarily be the indubitable foundation of any revealed religion not wearing the testimony of its founder on its face? Can one still doubt that he wholeheartedly rejected that concept, that he wholeheartedly preferred the common doctrine, which can stand without harm beside any truth of reason because it contradicts none of them and can justifiably claim that it has not been correctly understood if it seems to do so?[32]

Thus, Lessing saw that the source of Leibniz's dissatisfaction with the Socinian doctrine was its unphilosophical confusion of the categories of the finite and the infinite, a dissatisfaction similar to that which Lessing himself felt toward neology. The Socinian com-bination of the denial of the divinity of Christ with his veneration, and even worship, is the same type of inconsistent compromise with rationalism which neology attempted in regard to the relation between reason and revelation. Both are superficial and ultimately contradictory, halfway positions, and in calling attention to Leibniz's attack upon the former, Lessing is underlining the basis of his quarrel with the latter.

Lessing, however, was not yet finished with this "modern theology." What is implicit in the beginning becomes explicit at the end. One may wish to say, he reflects, that Leibniz proceeded justly against the Socinians, but that in actuality he is equally far from orthodoxy: "in short, of the whole thing he believed nothing."[33] This provides Lessing with the perfect occasion for a direct attack upon the neological confusion of faith and reason which lies at the heart of his opposition to the movement, and once again Lessing combines a defense of Leibniz with an attack upon neology:

> He believed! If only I still knew what is meant by this word. I must confess that in the mouths of so many of our modern theologians it has become a true mystery. In the past twenty or thirty years these men have made such great strides in the knowledge of religion that when I turn from them to an old dogmatist I seem to be in an entirely different world. They have at hand so many compelling reasons for belief, so many incontrovertible proofs of the truth of the Christian religion, that I can never cease to wonder how anyone can be so shortsighted as to hold the belief in these truths to be a supernatural effect of grace.[34]

Thus, Lessing ends on a note of irony and succeeds in suggesting that the neological (and especially Eberhard's) critique of Leibniz presupposes the superficial rationalism which he so vehemently opposed. If true Christianity, the neologists seem to reason, is completely rational and demonstrable, its alleged "mysteries" being merely later accretions, then such an eminently rational thinker as Leibniz could certainly not adhere to these mysteries and his profession of faith must be explicable as hypocrisy. This was the view which Lessing endeavored to confute in his two essays on Leibniz, and in so doing he also confuted the presupposition on which it was based.

A discussion of Lessing's critique of neology would not be complete without mention of his "counter-assertions" to the first fragment of Reimarus, *On the Decrying of Reason in the Pulpit.* Although Lessing's publication of the fragments, together with his "counter-assertions," belongs to the second stage of his polemical campaign, his reflections upon this fragment refer directly to neology, and, in fact, constitute his most explicit, published attack on this movement. Reimarus, it will be remembered, had censured the clergy for their admonitions against the use of reason in religion and had proposed a completely objective examination of all religious questions as the only way to provide one's faith with a rational foundation. In response to this Lessing reflects upon the radically changed conditions since the time of Reimarus (a change no doubt brought about by the advent of neology). Now, rather than decrying reason, preachers are continually emphasizing the "inner bond between faith and reason,"[35] with a rather dubious result:

> Faith has become reason, strengthened by miracles and testimony, and reason has become an argumentative faith. The entire revealed religion is nothing but a renewed sanction of the religion of reason. Either it contains no mysteries at all, or if there are such, it is of no concern whether the Christian connects them with this or that concept, or even none at all.[36]

This brings Lessing to the heart of his quarrel with neology. What, he asks, is a revelation which reveals nothing? Is it enough to keep the name and reject the thing? Does the acceptance of the mere name entitle a man to call himself a Christian? Against this inconsistent and superficial compromise, Lessing asserts that the concept of revelation, the very concept which he had long since rejected, implies "a certain captivity under the obedience of faith."[37] This, however, is the point which neologists overlooked, with the result that in their attempt to make Christianity appear reasonable, they have completely distorted its true significance and succeeded only in creating an ungainly hybrid, which is neither philosophically sound nor religiously meaningful.[38]

The subsequent discussion is reminiscent of Lessing's earlier critique of Cramer's scheme of religious education. Reimarus' recommended rational instruction in the principles of religion is shown to anticipate and be subject to the same difficulties as the neological position. Since an incomprehensible element is an essential ingredient in any revelation, there can be no immediate transition (such as Reimarus proposed, and neology actually carried out) between natural and revealed religion. Or, as Lessing expresses it: "Revealed religion does not in the least presuppose a rational religion, but rather includes it in itself . . . since it contains all the truths which the latter teaches, and only supports them with a different kind of proof."[39]

In this passage Lessing presents his own, original alternative to the neological rationalism and expresses, in nuce, the basic principles of *The Education of the Human Race*. Although this aspect of Lessing's thought cannot be examined at this time, we can clearly discern his negative intent. This is nothing less than the total repudiation of the confusion between reason and revelation, which is implicit in the neological conception of an immediate transition between the two. This confusion tends to obscure the essentially mysterious or suprarational character of a divine revelation, thereby lending a deceptive veneer of credibility to the factual claims of the Christian revelation. As already seen, Lessing regarded such subtle errors as infinitely more dangerous than the obvious untruths of orthodoxy, and, thus, he saw that their repudiation was a necessary preliminary to his attempt to establish the Christian religion upon a new foundation.

II

LESSING AND REIMARUS

This attempt finds its first clear expression in the "counterassertions" to the fragments of Reimarus. Here Lessing discloses the fruits of the reflections which took him beyond the point where Reimarus and the entire Aufklärung had become tired of reflecting. The fragments contained a bitter attack on the Christian concept of revelation and on the claims of the Old and the New Testament to contain such a revelation. Thus, their publication provided Lessing with the ideal means for decisively repudiating this concept and for showing that the doctrines of the Christian religion can be understood and accepted apart from it. The basic outline of Lessing's position is presented in the form of editorial comments on the general implications of the whole series of fragments. He begins by asserting that the believing Christian has nothing to fear from their publication. The theologian may be dismayed to see his system demolished and his carefully constructed historical proofs of the Christian religion utterly repudiated:

> But what are this man's hypotheses, explanations, and proofs to the Christian? To him this Christianity, which he feels to be so true and in which he feels so blessed, exists forever. When the paralytic experiences the beneficial shocks of the electric sparks, what does he care whether Nollet, or Franklin, or neither of them is right.[40]

Thus, all the difficulties raised by Reimarus, all the discrepancies in the accounts of the resurrection, which cast doubt upon the verbal inspiration and infallibility of the Biblical text, are of no essential concern to the religious consciousness. For, as Lessing expresses it:

> The letter is not the spirit, and the Bible is not religion. Hence, objections to the letter and to the Bible are not likewise objections to the spirit and to religion.

For the Bible obviously contains more than belongs to religion, and it is a mere hypothesis, that it must be equally infallible in these extras. Moreover, religion existed before the Bible. Christianity existed before the evangelists and apostles had written. A long time passed before the first of them began to write, and a very considerable time before the entire canon was completed. Thus, although much may still depend upon these writings, it is inconceivable that the whole truth of the religion could depend upon them. If there was a time when it was already widespread, and when it had possessed many souls, and when, nevertheless, not a single letter of what has come down to us was yet written, then it must be possible that all that the evangelists and apostles had written could be lost, and the religion taught by them still continue to exist. The religion is not true because the evangelists and apostles taught it, but they taught it because it is true. The written traditions must be explained according to their inner truth, and no written tradition can give it any inner truth if it has none.[41]

This, Lessing suggests, is the attitude one may assume even if Reimarus' objections are unanswerable, that is, even if the factual claims of the Christian religion are insupportable and the Biblical accounts of these alleged facts hopelessly contradictory. In short, this is the standpoint from which Christianity may be appreciated and vindicated irrespective of its historical foundation. *Thus, for the first time in the eighteenth century the question of the facticity of the Christian revelation was held to be irrelevant for the truth of the Christian religion.* This religion contains an intrinsic truth, immediately grasped by the believer, and this truth retains its validity whether or not the various accounts of the resurrection agree, and in fact, whether or not Jesus of Nazareth actually arose from the tomb after three days.

In the subsequent discussion Lessing applies this general principle to the specific fragments. In each case he affirms his basic agreement with the facts brought forth by Reimarus, but completely rejects the interpretation which Reimarus gave to these facts. Thus, the negative moment of truth in the naturalistic critique of the historicity of the Christian revelation is admitted, and at the same time transcended. All of Reimarus' allegations may be substantially correct, but the Christian religion nevertheless retains its intrinsic truth.

Lessing's reply to the first fragment, which we have already discussed, is essentially directed against neology, and is not directly relevant to the present discussion. However, his response to the second fragment, *Impossibility of a Revelation Which All Men Can Believe on Rational Grounds,* provides an excellent example of his procedure. Reimarus had here argued against the possibility of a reasoned acceptance of a historical revelation becoming the basis of a universal religion. He showed in great detail that only a small portion of the human race could ever become aware of such a revelation and that an even smaller portion could ever have the learning necessary to evaluate its pretensions and arrive at a reasoned belief. Lessing begins by accepting Reimarus' conclusion. A universally acceptable revelation is indeed impossible. But this does not preclude the possibility of a partial revelation, directed to those people—the Jews—who have a special aptitude for religion. Such a procedure, Lessing reflects, is quite reasonable, for barring the possibility of a universally acceptable revelation, an omniscient and benevolent Deity must necessarily choose that method of communication and instruction which would reach the widest possible audience in the shortest possible time.[42]

Lessing's method here is similar to that which we have already encountered in his treatment of Eberhard. The possibility of revelation is apparently justified in the face of Reimarus' attacks, but only at the cost of the complete transformation of the traditional concept. Thus, it is no longer the supernatural revelation which first gives the "chosen people" the superior aptitude for religion, but this very aptitude, as a purely natural, human characteristic, is the source of that heightened state of the religious consciousness, which orthodoxy erroneously ascribes to a supernatural revelation.[43]

Finally, Lessing agrees with Reimarus' contention that the doctrine that the acceptance of a supernatural revelation is necessary for the salvation of those who have no knowledge of it is intolerable. However, he denies that this was either the teaching of Christ or the universally recognized doctrine of the Christian Church. The fault lies with Reimarus, for "he took everything maintained by a certain system of Christianity, in certain symbolic books, for the only true, actual Christianity."[44] In short, the latter committed the unpardonable error of confusing the doctrines of Lutheran orthodoxy with those of true Christianity, and the reader is left to draw the obvious inference that the teachings of this Church not only do not represent but stand in essential conflict with the true spirit of the Christian religion. Thus, in his reply to Reimarus, Lessing shows that the concept of revelation may be "saved," if it is understood in terms of a purely human capacity for religion, and the Christian religion upheld, if it is sharply distinguished from the teachings of the Lutheran or any other particular sect.

The third fragment, *The Passage of the Israelites Through the Red Sea,* is treated in a somewhat lighter vein. Lessing reflects that all the difficulties which Reimarus found in the account had been noticed previously, but never presented with such force.[45] Then, he proposes three possible answers to these difficulties. The first is that the narrator may have been in error concerning the number of Israelites who crossed the Red Sea. A far smaller number, say 6000, instead of 600,000 would make the account far more credible. Lessing points out with a touch of irony that this solution is unacceptable to orthodoxy, because it implies the abandonment of the doctrine of verbal inspiration. How could a divinely inspired author make a mistake in arithmetic?[46] Lessing next suggests a possible rationalistic explanation of the type common in the Wolffian school. This tour de force involves the hypothesis of a strong wind, which kept the waters back long enough for the Israelites to cross, and which changed direction as soon as the Egyptians arrived.[47] This, of course, is not meant seriously, but simply to suggest the absurd lengths to which theologians were willing to go to defend the doctrine of the infallibility of Scripture. Finally, he suggests the view which he believes to be the most suitable for the orthodox position: the frank acceptance of the miraculous nature of the event, without any attempted rationalization. Although it involves the acceptance of a manifest absurdity, such a standpoint at least has the virtue of honesty and removes orthodoxy beyond the pale of philosophic refutation.

In *That the Books of the Old Testament Were Not Written to Reveal a Religion,* Reimarus had argued that since the Old Testament contains no doctrine of immortality, it cannot possibly be accepted as the revelation of a "soul-saving religion." In his reply Lessing admits with Reimarus that the Old Testament does not contain any doctrine of immortality, and he even goes a step further and points out that until the time of the captivity, the Hebrews, except for certain enlightened individuals, did not even possess the true concept of the unity of God. Rather than a Supreme Being and Lord of the universe, they merely worshipped Jehovah as a national deity. However, Lessing adds, such considerations are completely irrelevant to the question of the divine origin of the Old Testament. If the concept of God contained therein were the basis upon which the divinity of a book is to be decided, then the holy books of the

Brahmans would undoubtedly have a claim superior to that of the Hebrew Scriptures.[48] Moreover, the Brahmans also claim to have received a divine revelation, but this is only natural:

> For although the human understanding only develops very gradually, and truths which now seem obvious to the common man were once very hard to conceive and must therefore have seemed like immediate inspirations from God, which was the only manner in which they could then have been accepted, there have nevertheless been certain privileged souls in all times and places who by means of their own powers were able to transcend the intellectual level of their contemporaries, hastening to the greater light, and who could not really communicate, yet could at least relate their feelings to others.[49]

Thus, since many of the basic principles of natural religion are found in the sacred books of the Brahmans, but are not admitted as proof of the divine origin of these books, so, too, the absence of these principles can be no proof of the lack of such an origin. A divine revelation, argues Lessing, following Spinoza, is addressed to the historical condition of its recipients, and its concepts must be commensurate with their level of understanding. A religion which teaches merely temporal rewards and punishments is surely not the Christian religion, but, asks Lessing: "If the Christian religion could first appear only at a certain time, in a certain place, does it therefore follow that all previous times, and all other places had no soul-saving religion?"[50]

With this Lessing completely repudiates one of the fundamental axioms of the Enlightenment: that the truth of any revealed religion is to be judged, at least in part, by its conformity to a hypothesized natural religion. It was, as we have seen, generally agreed that any divine revelation must contain clear concepts of the unity, goodness, omnipotence, and wisdom of God, the immortality of the soul, and the absolutely just distribution of future rewards and punishments. It may, as in fact Christianity does, contain additional "positive precepts," but a clear presentation of the basic principles of natural religion was nevertheless universally maintained as a minimal condition which it must fulfill. This criterion had been applied by the apologists in defense of the divine origin of the New Testament, and by Bayle and the deists before Reimarus, to cast doubt upon the authenticity of the Hebrew Scriptures. However, by citing the examples of the Brahmans, Lessing showed that an honest adherence to this critical procedure will by no means prove favorable to Christianity, and as an alternative he proposes a historical and naturalistic conception of revelation. Rather than the miraculous communication at a particular moment in history of absolute and saving truth (which would, of course, have to include the basic principles of natural religion), revelation is now viewed as a historical process, wherein different degrees of insight are produced in various historical communities, each sufficient for the needs of that community.

Understood in this sense, any particular revelation loses its decisive significance, and any historical religion its claim to absolute truth. Each is merely a partial adumbration of the truth, more or less obscurely expressed, depending upon the level of development of its followers. From this standpoint, which is that of *The Education of the Human Race*—the first fifty-three paragraphs of which Lessing appended to this discussion—the historical question concerning the facticity of any particular revelation completely loses its relevance. A given religion must now be considered simply as a cultural phenomenon, representing a particular stage in the development of the religious consciousness and, as such, may be evaluated and appreciated in its own terms. Such was the manner in which Lessing came to understand the Christian religion, and it was upon this basis that he affirmed his allegiance to it in his subsequent controversies.

Thus, once again we can see the same dialectic at work. Lessing begins by maintaining the orthodox position against rationalistic objections, and ends by so transforming the orthodox doctrine that the result is more radical than the objections themselves. Lessing defends the revealed character of the Old Testament, but in so doing undermines and relativizes the very concept of revelation upon which its authoritative character was traditionally based.

Lessing's treatment of the fifth fragment, *On the Resurrection Narrative*, is more straightforward, but perfectly consistent with his basic principles. Commenting upon Reimarus' almost exhaustive analysis of the discrepancies between the Gospel narratives of the resurrection, he notes that the evangelists were not themselves eyewitnesses and that consequently a distinction must be made between contradictions among the actual witnesses and contradictions among the evangelists. Contradictions among the former group are only to be expected, for, as experience shows, various witnesses to the same event often give widely disparate accounts, and even the same individual may describe the same event in different ways at different times. Such natural contradictions in the eyewitnesses are sufficient to account for the discrepancies in the Gospel narratives, and thus these narratives may retain their basic credibility despite Reimarus' objections.[51] However, as Lessing observes, this credibility is only retained at the cost of the doctrine of infallibility. Such infallibility, implying absolute unanimity on every point in a series of documents composed over a period of forty years, would require a continuous miracle. In support of such a claim it would be necessary to remove all ten contradictions disclosed by Reimarus, and, Lessing adds, to do so in a far more satisfactory manner than is to be found in the ordinary harmonies.[52] Thus, as in the case of the concept of revelation, the credibility of the Gospel narratives is "saved," but only at the cost of reducing them to purely human historical documents, subject to the normal amount of errors and discrepancies.

III

REACTIONS TO THE FRAGMENTS

The expected refutations of the fragments were not long in coming. The first published response was a pamphlet entitled *On the Evidence of the Proofs for the Truth of the Christian Religion*, by Johann David Schumann, the director of the Hanover Lyceum. This work, which appeared in September 1777, was a standard orthodox defense of the Christian religion against Reimarus' attack. Completely ignoring Lessing's "counter-assertions," Schumann defended the verbal infallibility of Scripture, and, basing his argument upon Origen's discussion of the "proof of the spirit and the power" (*Contra Celsum* 1, 2), reaffirmed the traditional historical proofs of the truth of the Christian religion.

Lessing's reply, *On the Proof of the Spirit and of Power*, is the most influential of his polemical writings. It contains the clearest formulation of his rejection of all historical proofs of the Christian religion, but it also endeavors to show that the truth of this religion, considered as a body of doctrine and ethic, may be evaluated independently of all such historical considerations.

He begins with the distinction between fulfilled prophecies and miracles actually experienced and historical reports thereof. The former may have given immediate certainty of the truth of the Christian religion to the actual witnesses. At that time, Lessing admits, the proof of the spirit and the power may still have retained its strength. But now, after the cessation of miracles, no such immediate certainty is available, and we are left with nothing but historical narratives of these events.

However, despite this fact many theologians continue to offer historical arguments for the truth of the Christian religion, and it is precisely this procedure, adhered to by both enlightened and orthodox theologians, which is the real object of Lessing's attack. If the proof of the spirit and the power is no longer valid, and if no historical certainty is strong enough to replace it, he asks: "How is it to be expected of me that the same inconceivable truths which sixteen to eighteen hundred years ago people believed on the strongest inducement, should be believed by me to be equally valid on an infinitely lesser inducement?"[53]

Both the distinction between the different degrees of certainty obtainable from rational demonstration, direct experience, and testimony, and the awareness of the radically different situation vis-à-vis the New Testament miracles, of early and contemporary Christianity, were commonplaces of Enlightenment thought. Lessing recognized and acknowledged the general acceptance of these distinctions, but he also saw, and herein lies the heart of his complaint, that the Enlightenment did not really grasp the full significance of its own insights. Thus, Lessing asserts, no one actually claims that the reports of historians can yield the same degree of certainty as rational demonstrations or even immediate certainty. What is claimed, however, is: "that the reports which we have of these prophecies and miracles are as reliable as historical truths ever can be. And then it is added that although historical truths cannot be demonstrated: nevertheless we must believe them as firmly as truths that have been demonstrated."[54]

This passage, which in addition to being a general indictment of eighteenth-century apologetics may very well contain a specific reference to Charles Bonnet,[55] expresses Lessing's basic attitude toward the problem. He is willing to grant, purely for the sake of argument, that the historical facts brought forth in support of the Christian religion are as reliable as historical facts can be, but he rejects the inference which theologians are wont to draw from this. As historical facts they can never be anything more than probable and, as such, do not offer an adequate basis upon which to ground one's religious convictions. These convictions must be apodictically certain and cannot be grounded in any merely probable arguments. Or, as Lessing succinctly expresses it: "Accidental truths of history can never become the proof of necessary truths of reason."[56]

This argument, formulated in Leibnizean terms, constitutes in the words of Gottfried Fittbogen, "the complete elimination of the historical from religion."[57] In essential agreement with Spinoza,[58] Lessing sharply delineates the radical gulf between the acceptance of a historical narrative and true religious conviction, and it is precisely this gulf which he calls "the broad, ugly ditch which I cannot get across."[59] Thus, he can grant orthodoxy's contention that there is solid historical evidence for the resurrection, that Christ called himself the Son of God, that he was held to be such by his disciples, and even that the Scripture which asserts this is infallible. All this may (for the sake of argument) be accepted as historically certain, but Lessing complains:

> To jump with that historical truth to a quite different class of truths, and to demand of me that I should form all my metaphysical and moral ideas accordingly; to expect me to alter all my fundamental ideas of the nature of the Godhead because I cannot set any credible testimony against the resurrection of Christ: if that is not a metabasis eis allo genos, then I do not know what Aristotle meant by his phrase.[60]

This, in all essentials, is Lessing's polemic against the historical proofs of the Christian religion, and, as we have repeatedly seen, he is here in perfect accord with Spinoza and the deists.[61] However, Lessing differs from both in that he endeavors to combine the rejection of the historical foundation of Christianity with the acceptance of the actual content of Christian doctrine. This positive aspect of Lessing's attitude toward Christianity is suggested by the final, and generally neglected paragraphs of the work. After denying that any historical propositions can oblige him to accept the doctrines of the Christian religion, he asks rhetorically what can, in fact, bind him, and replies:

> Nothing but these teachings themselves. Eighteen hundred years ago they were so new, so alien, so foreign to the entire mass of truths recognized in that age, that nothing less than miracles and fulfilled prophecies were required if the multitude were to attend to them at all.[62]

With this we reach the positive standpoint of the "counter-assertions" to the fragments of Reimarus and *The Education of the Human Race*. These alleged miracles served as the occasions for the reception of these wonderful new truths of which we now possess the fruits. Thus, even if these miracles are not genuine, even if, as Reimarus and many of the deists contend, they were the products of deliberate deception, these truths—the Christian doctrines—have an intrinsic value which is independent of their origin. Lessing closes with a graphic example clearly illustrating this point. Suppose, he suggests, there were a great and useful mathematical truth which had been arrived at by means of an obvious error:

> Should I deny this truth? Should I refuse to use this truth? Would I be on that account an ungrateful reviler of the discoverer, if I were unwilling to prove from his insight in other respects, indeed did not consider it capable of proof, that the fallacy through which he stumbled upon the truth, could not be a fallacy.[63]

The next voice to be heard in the controversy was that of the Wolfenbüttel superintendent, Johann Heinrich Ress, who in December 1777 published anonymously his *Defense of the History of the Resurrection of Jesus Christ*. Like Schumann, Ress directed his attack solely to the fragments, completely ignoring Lessing's "counter-assertions." His particular concern with the fifth fragment, in refutation of which he composed a rather crude dialogue wherein the champion of orthodoxy (advocating the verbal inspiration of the Gospel narratives) completely overwhelms the weak-minded spokesman for the fragmentist. The result of this exercise, however, was nothing more than a standard harmony of the very type which Lessing had ridiculed in his "counter-assertions."[64]

It was only natural that Lessing should be irked by such a production, which in addition to its dubious literary merit, completely missed the point he was trying to make. His whole purpose in publishing the fragments was to demonstrate the irrelevance of all factual, historical considerations to the question of the truth of the Christian religion and, thus, to raise the entire debate to a higher level. This attempt, however, was momentarily thwarted by Schumann and Ress who, by endeavoring to defend the factual foundations of Christianity against the attacks of Reimarus, returned the debate to the superficial level which it had occupied previously.

The result of his displeasure was *A Rejoinder*, a work whose bitter tone has often been attributed to the personal tragedy which Lessing underwent during its composition.[65] The bulk of this fairly lengthy polemic is devoted to a detailed demolition of Ress's harmony, showing that in each case he failed to reconcile the contradictions disclosed in the fragments. However, the really significant portion of the work is the discussion which Lessing prefaced to these textual considerations. It is here that he directly attacks the doctrine of verbal inspiration and reaffirms the opposition between religious truth and historical fact.

He begins with a precise statement of his independent position vis-à-vis Reimarus and Ress:

> My anonymous author declared that an additional reason for not believing the resurrection of Christ is that the accounts of the evangelists contradict one another.
>
> I replied: the resurrection of Christ may still be true, even if the accounts of the evangelists contradict one another.
>
> Now comes a third who says: the resurrection of Christ is to be believed absolutely, because the accounts of the evangelists do not contradict one another.[66]

After thus delineating the situation, Lessing reaffirms the substantial accuracy of Reimarus' findings. Most of the contradictions which he discloses are real contradictions, but this justifies neither the negative inferences which he draws therefrom nor the bitter attack of Ress. Merely because the sacred historians disagree in regard to many details of the resurrection narrative is no reason to doubt the credibility of the substantial portions in which they do agree. Such a procedure would be manifestly absurd in regard to profane historians, and what is absurd in the one case is equally so in the other.[67]

This argument is virtually identical with that of Lessing's earlier essay, *Concerning the Manner of the Propagation and Dissemination of the Christian Religion*. The former work discusses the "miraculous" growth of the early Church, and the present piece is concerned with the resurrection narrative, but both contend that sacred history must be judged by precisely the same standards as profane history and that it is only on this basis that it can be understood. Since the Bible is the joint product of several authors writing at different times and in different places, some difference in detail is inevitable and does not even destroy the possibility of divine inspiration. Moreover, not only are all such attempts to reconcile the various discrepancies in the Biblical accounts utterly fruitless, but the forced and tortured interpretations of the orthodox theologians completely destroy the meaning of the text,[68] and it is this which prompts Lessing to ask: "If Livy, and Dionysius and Polybius and Tacitus are now so frankly and generously treated by us, that we do not place them on the rack with every syllable; why not also Matthew and Mark and Luke and John?"[69]

However, despite the manifest absurdities in which it involved them, orthodox theologians continued both to defend the doctrine of verbal inspiration and to construct elaborate harmonies in order to reconcile the "apparent" contradictions in the Biblical accounts. This endeavor was grounded in the prevalent tendency to equate the acceptance of the Christian religion with the acceptance of certain historical facts (concerning the life, death, and resurrection of Jesus of Nazareth). Within this context the infallibility of Scripture furnished an absolute guarantee of the truth of these facts and functioned as the ultimate foundation of the religion built upon them. Hence, for the orthodox mentality of the eighteenth century, to question the veracity of the most insignificant Biblical assertion was to undermine the very foundation of the Christian religion. For Lessing, however, the question of the truth of the Christian religion is sharply distinguished from the question of its alleged facts and, thus, not only is the insupportable hypothesis of infallibility rejected as superfluous, but the way is actually opened for the objective, historical study of these facts, that is, for the treatment of the evangelists as "merely human historians."[70]

This argument stands in an intrinsic connection with *On the Proof of the Spirit and of Power*, and Lessing suggests the analogy between the adherence to the doctrine of verbal inspiration and the acceptance of miracles. Both are products of the same confusion of the Christian religion with its historical foundation, and just as an infallible Scripture was shown to be unnecessary, so too, Lessing argues, there is no longer any need of miracles to prove the truth of the Christian religion. This is adequately proven by the "ever continuing miracle of the religion itself."[71] Moreover, he continues, the miracles performed by Jesus and his disciples were the scaffolding and not the building itself, and as the scaffolding is removed once the building is complete, so too, now that Christianity is complete or at least established, the events through which it was founded lose their decisive significance. This was Lessing's basic theological conviction, and he concludes the present discussion by giving it poignant expression: "When will they cease wanting to hang nothing less than the whole of eternity on a spider's thread!

—No, the scholastic dogmatics never inflicted such deep wounds upon religion as historical exegesis now inflicts upon it daily.[72]

IV
GOEZE'S ATTACK

With the advent of Johann Melchior Goeze, pastor of the Lutheran Church of St. Catherine of Hamburg, the polemic entered a new stage. Goeze was the first directly to attack Lessing rather than the fragments themselves. He regarded the former's ambiguous "counter-assertions" as a greater danger to Christianity than the overt blasphemy of the latter. He began his onslaught with a newspaper article on December 17, 1777. This was followed on January 30, 1778, with a glowing review of Ress's work, and soon after by six other pieces, all bitterly attacking Lessing. In April Goeze added a preface and published the entire series in book form: *Something Preliminary Against Herr Hofrat Lessing's Direct and Indirect Malevolent Attacks on Our Most Holy Religion, and on Its Single Foundation, the Bible.*

Goeze's standpoint was that of the strictest orthodoxy. He believed in the divine inspiration and infallibility of each letter in the Bible and in the absolute truth of the Augsburg Confession. As such, he constituted the perfect opponent, representing everything which Lessing desired to overcome. But, unfortunately, because of his highly antagonistic attitude, which soon came to be shared by Lessing, the controversy rapidly degenerated into an exchange of scurrilous personal attacks having little philosophical or theological significance. In his first attack, however, Goeze's attitude is somewhat subdued. He does not mention Lessing by name, and apart from a few vindictive comments in regard to the publication of the fragments, he is content to state the orthodox opposition to Lessing's position as contained in the "counter-assertions."

After a preliminary sally against Lessing's "theater logic,"[73] Goeze directs his main concern to Lessing's general answer to the fragments. From his rigidly orthodox standpoint he rejects Lessing's views in toto and proposes a point by point refutation. Commenting on the passage he proclaims:

> In the entire passage I do not find a single proposition which in the context in which it stands, I can regard as correct. To be sure, the editor regards everything therein as genuine axioms, but some of them still require a very strong proof, while the remainder, and these constitute the majority, are demonstrably false.[74]

The ensuing discussion may be seen as the definitive expression of Goeze's position, and it formed the starting point for all of Lessing's counterarguments. Lessing had based his contention that the fragments were of no danger to the believing Christian on the distinction between the letter and the spirit and the Bible and religion. In opposition to this Goeze declares emphatically: "The letter is the spirit, and the Bible is religion, and for the same reason for which Jesus said: the words which I speak are spirit and life."[75] Goeze supports this contention by means of a distinction between objective and subjective religion.[76] The former includes all those doctrines which a man must know and accept as true, and the latter consists of the state of mind and behavior of the individual in relation to God. Since the doctrines contained in Scripture constitute religion considered objectively, Goeze can quite confidently conclude that in this sense the Bible is religion.

Moreover, on the basis of his distinction between the letter and the spirit, Lessing had argued that objections against the one are not *eo ipso* objections against the other. However, since Goeze has just demonstrated the falsity of this distinction, he can readily deny the consequences drawn from it. Thus, in the sense in which the letter is the spirit and the Bible is religion, objections against the one are necessarily objections against the other.[77]

Lessing had further maintained that "the Bible obviously contains more than belongs to religion," and against this Goeze reasons somewhat pedantically that if this is so, then it must also contain religion, and therefore Lessing had contradicted himself. In addition, Lessing had deduced from this that "it is a mere hypothesis, that it must be equally infallible in these extras," and in reply Goeze passionately proclaims his orthodox convictions: "No," declares the Herr Pastor, "this is not an hypothesis, but incontrovertible truth."[78] In defense of this view Goeze proclaims the impossibility of separating the essential and inessential and claiming that only the former is divinely inspired. To deny the infallibility of part, he argues, is to cast doubt upon the infallibility of all.[79]

In the fifth through the eighth propositions Lessing had argued from the temporal priority of the Christian religion to the Bible, to the dispensability of the Bible for the continuance of this religion. Since Christianity existed before the Bible, Lessing had declared, the whole truth of the Christian religion cannot depend upon it, and since it had influenced and affected so many souls before a word of the New Testament was written down, it is conceivable that if everything which the evangelists and apostles wrote were lost, the Christian religion could still exist.

For Goeze, the champion of orthodoxy and staunch defender of the "book religion," such an assertion was utterly nonsensical, and a large portion of his later polemics are devoted to this point. In this instance he is content to proclaim arrogantly Lessing's argument a mere sophism. Although Christianity existed and spread before the collection of books which later became known as the New Testament were written, one cannot say that Christianity existed before its doctrines were preached, and he concludes triumphantly:

> The whole of the Christian religion rests upon the teachings and deeds of Christ, as upon its immediate ground. But where can we now learn about these teachings and deeds except from the writings of the evangelists and apostles? Therefore, if the latter were lost, the former must certainly be lost also.[80]

Lessing's last two propositions were to the effect that the Christian religion is not true because the evangelists and apostles taught it, but that they taught it because it is true, and consequently, that the written tradition must be explained solely on the basis of its intrinsic truth. This was, of course, an expression of Lessing's endeavor to drive a wedge between religious truth and historical fact, and Goeze again counters this with a restatement of the orthodox position. Since the evangelists and apostles were inspired by the Holy Ghost, the Christian religion *is* true because they taught it, or more properly, because God, speaking through them taught it.[81] In regard to the question of inner truth, Goeze simply asks: where but from Scripture can the inner truth of the Christian religion be obtained?[82]

In his subsequent polemics, which are contained in the balance of the *Something Preliminary*, and in a second series of three installments entitled *Lessing's Weaknesses*, Goeze added little to this basic attack. He comments on each of Lessing's writings as they appear, criticizes his style as a "theater logic," intended to dazzle rather than convince, repeatedly classes him with Bahrdt, Basedow, and Semler, as an archenemy of Christianity, and generally impugns his character. But he is never able to achieve the slightest appreciation of Lessing's standpoint. Largely on the basis of Lessing's statement in *On the Proof of the Spirit and of Power* that his reason rebels against the proposition that God had a son of like essence with himself, Goeze believed that Lessing was a disguised naturalist, and in his later contributions to the controversy he repeatedly demands that Lessing proclaim what he understands by the Christian religion. Only then, Goeze asserts, will he return to the basic point of contention, which is, as he defines it: "Could the Christian religion endure, even if the Bible was completely lost, if it had been lost for a long time, if it had never been?"[83]

All this is of great historical or biographical, but of relatively little philosophical or theological significance. What Goeze had to say in this respect, he said in his first attack. Between such a self-assured dogmatism and Lessing's free search after truth, there could be no real dialogue, but merely a continual, and increasingly bitter reiteration of the same points. However, although he had nothing to add, Goeze did succeed, in the third article of his *Lessing's Weaknesses,* in giving classic expression to the standpoint of eighteenth-century Protestant orthodoxy, an expression which one should keep constantly in mind when evaluating Lessing's polemic against this position. "In no article of faith," he declares, "does one find a greater agreement between Catholic, Lutheran, Reformed, Socinian, etc., than in this: that the Bible was inspired by God through the Holy Ghost, and therefore everything which it contains, whether it be history or doctrine, is the indubitable truth."[84]

And finally, commenting on the critical treatment of the Bible by Bahrdt, Semler, and Reimarus: "And what is the result of all this clamor? None other than that your Bible is the most absurd and untrustworthy book and that you are fools to recognize it as the indubitable basis of your faith and life and to ground your hope for eternity upon it."[85]

V

LESSING'S COUNTER ATTACK

Lessing responded to this attack with three short pieces: *A Parable, A Small Request,* and *A Challenge.* The first two were composed in January in reply to Goeze's first article, and the third, which is much more bitter in tone, was written in February, after Goeze's second and more vindictive piece. All three were published together in March.[86]

The *Parable,* which in Lessing's words was "not the worst thing that I have written,"[87] is an allegorical description of the contemporary theological situation. The Christian religion is depicted as a king's palace of inestimable size and of singular architecture.

Although this architecture conflicted with all the acceptable canons of style, the palace was nevertheless pleasing and convenient. Outwardly it appeared somewhat bewildering, but the inside was full of light and well ordered. The strangeness of its outward appearance was due to the presence of very widely scattered windows and very many doors and gates of all sizes and shapes. Because of this odd arrangement people were perplexed as to how so much light could penetrate through so few windows into so many rooms, and it is with true religious feeling that Lessing explains the brightness of the rooms in terms of the light they receive from above and justifies the presence of many small doors, rather than a few main entrances, as enabling all who are called into the palace to enter through the shortest and surest way. However, in the course of time numerous controversies arose among various connoisseurs of architecture. Each claimed to possess the ground plan of the original architect, written in a language now lost, and consequently each desired to remodel the building according to his interpretation of these plans. There were, nevertheless, a very few who were not at all concerned with the plans, but were content to acknowledge that the most beneficial wisdom fills the entire palace and that from this source nothing but beauty and wisdom can spread over the entire land. But one night when the controversy over the ground plan was not so much settled as slumbering, the watchman was heard shouting: "Fire! The palace is on Fire!" And each connoisseur dashed into the street with his own plan, but instead of hurrying to save the palace each endeavored to show the others through his plan the place where the palace might most readily burn and where the fire might best be approached. If it were up to these industrious squabblers, Lessing reflects, the palace would readily have burnt down had there been a real fire, but, fortunately, the frightened watchman had merely mistaken a northern light for a conflagration.

In view of what we have already seen of Lessing's polemical position, this document requires little intepretation. It is simply a very powerful, poetic restatement of the distinction between the letter and the spirit, the Bible and religion, between Christianity and the historical facts (ground plan) upon which it is based. The Christian religion is seen to possess an inner truth and beauty (suggested by the description of the palace as filled with light from above) which is independent of its outward appearance and historical origin. Thus, the lesson which is obviously intended to be drawn is that the theologians, and especially Goeze, should concern themselves solely with the inner truth of the Christian religion and not squabble over the various interpretations of the ground plan, that is, with the fruitless attempt to reconcile the various discrepancies in the Gospel narratives.

The *Request* is Lessing's demand for fair treatment from Goeze. The latter had accused him of deliberately attempting to undermine Christianity through the publication of the fragments. Lessing justifies his action by drawing the analogy between a librarian and a pastor, and a botanist and a shepherd. The librarian and the botanist are permitted to engage in an impartial search for truth, regardless of the outcome, while it is the duty of the pastor and the shepherd to protect their flocks from any harm which may accrue from these researches. Thus, Lessing, the librarian, can ask of Goeze, the pastor to "censure me at least less severely for having been honest enough to rescue from oblivion and bring to light not only some very un-Christian fragments but also a very Christian work of Berengarius.[88]

Furthermore, Lessing declares, Goeze had deliberately falsified his position, and he requests a retraction. Lessing's actual words implied that the Christian religion remained intact in the hearts of believers, even if the objections against the literal truth of the Bible cannot be met, but Goeze had interpreted this to mean that none of the objections against the Bible could in fact be answered.[89] Finally, against Goeze's narrow orthodoxy, which rendered him incapable of distinguishing between the letter and the spirit, Lessing comments upon the evolutionary character of the Christian religion, in relation to which the various sects, including the Lutheran, are merely stages to be surpassed:

> Christianity proceeds on its eternal gradual pace, and eclipses do not bring the planets from their orbits. But the sects of Christianity are its phases, which can only endure through the stagnation of all nature, when sun and planet and observer all remain at the same point. God protect us from this frightful stagnation![90]

In the *Challenge*, written after the appearance of Goeze's second article, Lessing openly declares war. "I will," he writes to Goeze, "positively not be decried by you as the man who intends less good for the Lutheran Church than you."[91] And in a passage which has profoundly influenced the historical understanding of the Reformation,[92] he expresses his desire to have Luther himself as judge:

> Oh that he could do it, he whom I should most like to have as my judge!—Thou, Luther!—Great, misunderstood man! And by none less understood, than by the shortsighted, obstinate people, who with your slippers in their hand and an affected noisy zeal saunter along the road which thou prepared!—Thou hast released us from the yoke of tradition: who will release us from the more intolerable yoke of the letter? Who will finally bring us a Christianity, such as thou would'st now teach; as Christ himself would'st teach! Who——[93]

Finally, Lessing concludes with a passionate challenge:

> Write, Herr Pastor, and let your supporters write, as much as you will: I shall also write. If in the least thing which concerns me or my anonymous author I leave your writing unanswered when you are wrong, it will mean that I am incapable of holding a pen.[94]

Together with these three works, Lessing also published his *Axioms, If There Be Any in Such Things.* The title was suggested by Goeze's ironical reference to the "axioms" in the counterassertions" to the fragments, and Lessing takes the opportunity to formulate a point by point refutation of Goeze's first article. Except for the question if there could be religion before revelation, which Lessing regards as a mere screen,[95] he systematically answers all of Goeze's objections. Depicting himself as "an amateur in theology and not a theologian,"[96] he displays considerable erudition in the field of Patristics in providing a historical foundation for his position. The themes are identical with those of the "counterassertions," but they are presented in a different and, it is claimed, more logical order.[97]

This new arrangement begins with the proposition that the Bible obviously contains more than belongs to religion. By thus placing it first, Lessing intends to suggest that it serves as the fundamental premise of his argument. It is the principle in terms of which the distinction between the letter and the spirit, and the Bible and religion, or more fundamentally, between religious truth and historical narrative is to be established. Goeze had accepted this statement in qualified form, that is, if it was meant only to distinguish between what is essential to religion and what serves

merely to explain and corroborate these essential principles. To
this Lessing ironically replies that Goeze refuses to allow him to
declare about the most trivial passages what other good Lutheran
theologians have affirmed about whole books of the Bible, that is,
that they are dispensable,[98] and further:

> One must be at least a Rabbi or a homilete in order to dig up a
> bare possibility or a quibble, by means of which the Haijemin of
> Ana, the Krethi and Plethi of David, the cloak which Paul forgot
> at Troas, and a hundred other such things, could be brought into
> any relation with religion.[99]

Thus, far from being a disadvantage, as Goeze had feared,
the proposition is of the utmost advantage to religion. Only such
a view enables one to regard the Bible as a significant and meaningful document rather than as the depository of secret and incomprehensible mystical lore, and upon this basis Lessing feels
justified in stating categorically: "Therefore the proposition, that
the Bible contains more than belongs to religion, is true without
qualification."[100]

Granted this, the second proposition: that it is a mere hypothesis that the Bible is equally infallible in these "extras," follows
directly. Goeze, however, had countered this with a dilemma:
either these "extras" are inspired by God or they are not. If so, they
are likewise infallible, and if not, then the essentials also lose their
credibility. Lessing first answers this with an analogous dilemma
designed to illustrate the absurdity of Goeze's argument, but the
essence of his response is directed to the assertion that the divine
authority of the essentials is irrevocably linked with that of the
"extras." In regard to this he asks: "Has then a revealed truth no
inner marks at all? Has its immediately divine origin left no trace
on or in it, except the historical truth, which it has in common
with so many petty narratives."[101]

Implicit in this rhetorical question was Lessing's basic distinction between historical and religious conviction. He clearly
saw that Goeze's insistence upon the absolute infallibility of the
entire Bible was grounded in the failure to recognize this distinction, and he once again calls attention to the inner marks of divinity
in order to raise the question of the truth of the Christian religion
above the historical or factual level.

Lessing's third proposition, wherein he explicitly delineates the distinction between the letter and the spirit, the Bible, and religion, stands in an intrinsic connection with the first two. If it is true, he argues, that the Bible contains more than is necessary to religion, who can prevent one from ascribing to that totality, merely insofar as it is a book, the name "letter" and reserving the name "spirit" for the inner core, or religious content thereof. Moreover, he continues, this application could even be acceptable to those who accept the doctrine of the inner testimony of the Holy Spirit. Since this testimony can only manifest itself in those places in the Bible which more or less relate to our spiritual development, what can be more appropriate than to call only those places the spirit of the Bible?[102]

Given this distinction, Lessing's fourth proposition—that objections against the letter and the Bible are not thereby objections against the spirit and religion—follows as a matter of course. Although this proposition does not require any comment, it should be kept in mind that it constituted Lessing's basic theological justification for the publication of the fragments.

The fifth through eighth propositions, which are here repeated in their original order, form a unit expressing the historical side of Lessing's argument. The basic fact upon which he builds his case is the temporal priority of the Christian religion to the formation of the New Testament. It is, he argues in effect, an indisputable fact that the Christian religion not only existed for a considerable length of time before any of the evangelists or apostles began to write, but that it had become a widespread and powerful movement long before the entire canon was formulated. From this historically demonstrable preexistence of the Christian religion, Lessing argues against the Protestant thesis of the absolute dependence upon the Bible (Luther's sola Scriptura), and by way of corroborative support, rather than sincere conviction, often alludes to the Catholic concept of oral tradition, as an alternative vehicle for the transmission of religious truth.

In opposing Lessing, Goeze was forced to accept his historical analysis, but attempted to deny the consequences which Lessing drew therefrom. Thus, Goeze distinguished between the truth of the Christian religion and our conviction of this truth. The former, he argued, exists partly in itself, that is, in its agreement with the attributes and will of God, and partly upon the historical certainty of the facts concerning its origin, while the latter rests merely upon Scripture. In response Lessing asks why the truth of the Christian religion must rest on two such disparate grounds? Does not each ground entail its own conviction? In what connection do these two types of conviction stand to one another? And finally: "Why should I only believe things—which I accept because of their agreement with the will and attributes of God—because other things connected with them in time and space are historically proven?"[103]

This is precisely the *metabasis eis allo genos* for which he had previously criticized Schumann, and Lessing proceeds to emphasize this point without using the term. Thus, he continues, it may very well be true that the Bible can "prove" all the facts upon which the Christian religion is said to be partly grounded. Books are able to prove facts, so there is no reason why the Bible should not offer proof of these. But, he adds: "Enough that the Christian doctrines are not all founded upon facts."[104] The remainder, according to Goeze's own admission, are grounded in their inner truth, and how, Lessing asks, "can the inner truth of any proposition depend on the authority of the book in which it has been propounded?"[105]

Goeze had also posed for Lessing the question of whether, if the Gospels had never been written or had not remained extant, a trace of the deeds and teachings of Christ would still remain in the world? This was, of course, intended as a question which could only receive a negative answer, but Lessing's reply is both passionate and suggestive. "God forbid," he proclaims: "I should ever think so little of the teachings of Christ, as to venture to give this question the straightforward answer no! No! I would not utter this no, though an angel from heaven proclaimed it, much less when a Lutheran pastor would put it in my mouth."[106]

Moreover, as he proceeds to show, this refusal has a philosophical justification, for "everything which happens in the world leaves traces behind, even though man cannot always detect them."[107] Should then the teachings of the Christian religion be an exception to this rule? Must, he asks, the word of God first be changed into a dead letter before it can become efficacious? In the face of the absurdity of this contention, Lessing again appeals to oral tradition. Not only, he suggests, is oral tradition a possible means for the communication of religious truth, but it actually was the chief means employed by the early Church and the source of the bulk of the Apostles Creed.[108]

Lessing concludes the historical phase of his argument with another fable.[109] There was once, he relates, a Lutheran field preacher and family who, after a shipwreck of which they were the only survivors, found themselves on a beautiful island. Since the island supplied all the necessities of life the preacher and his family decided to remain there. The only book which they managed to salvage from the wreck was a copy of Luther's *Shorter Catechism*, but through this book the preacher managed to teach his children the rudiments of the Christian religion, and when they grew up they similarly taught their children. This process continued until one day, many generations later, another Lutheran preacher arrived on the island and found to his amazement that despite the lack of a Bible and with only the battered copy of the Catechism, which no one knew how to read, the inhabitants reiterated good orthodox Lutheran doctrine, albeit in a somewhat antiquated German.

After relating this little fable Lessing asks Goeze whether or not these good people, who although they had never even heard of the Bible were nevertheless familiar with the essentials of Lutheran doctrine, could be considered Christians. Goeze, he confidently proclaims, must necessarily say no, because they had no Bible, and by answering in the negative, he will manifest the absurdity of his position.[110]

As one might suspect Goeze greeted this fable with cries of derision and "theater logic," and there is some truth in the charge. When Lessing became a theologian or "amateur in theology" he never ceased being a dramatist, and this must be kept in mind if one is to understand his theological polemic. Self-confessedly not a systematic thinker, he often plays with ideas, such as that of the oral tradition, simply because they offer interesting dramatic alternatives to the views which he is attacking,[111] and it is largely because of this, as well as the fact that many of his profound ideas are clothed in metaphor, that he has so often been misunderstood.

In the last two axioms Lessing presents the philosophical basis of his opposition to orthodoxy, and the issue is shown to rest ultimately on the concept of truth. The Christian religion, he had written, is not true because the apostles and evangelists taught it, but rather they taught it because it is true. In opposition to this, Goeze had asserted that since the apostles and evangelists were inspired by God the Christian religion is true because they, as spokesmen of God, taught it. Now Lessing, in defense of his basic principle, goes one step further and proclaims: "Even what God teaches is not true because God teaches it, but God teaches it because it is true."[112]

This passage strongly suggests that Lessing grasped the nominalistic presupposition of the orthodox position, and that, following Leibniz, he rejected the ultimate arbitrariness implicit in this view. Truth cannot be grounded in fiat, either human or divine, but, rather, the divine fiat must be grounded in the pre-existent truth. This, it will be remembered, was precisely the argument of Leibniz in his critique of Descartes, wherein he affirmed the priority of the divine intellect to the will, and we here find Lessing advancing the same argument against Goeze and his allies: ". . . what a charming concept these gentlemen have of the will of God!" he remarks, ". . . according to their view, God could will something merely because he wills it."[113]

This nominalism, implicit in the orthodox theological system, accounts for its absolutistic pretensions, and more directly, it explains the demand for complete reliance upon the Bible. This demand is predicated upon the belief that the Bible is the literal word of God—that it is true precisely because God revealed it. Furthermore, it is this very nominalism which determined the matter of fact manner in which the eighteenth century approached the question of the truth of the Christian religion. Given the presupposition that to be "true" a positive religion must be the revealed word of God and, further, that a divine decree is true precisely because it is divine, then the only question which remains is whether or not a certain religion is *in fact* a decree of God.

Thus, it is against this implicit nominalism, with its arbitrary authoritarianism and external proofs that Lessing emphasizes his concept of "inner truth." If the Christian or any other religion is not true because God, as a matter of fact, revealed it at a certain moment in history, then the question of facticity becomes irrelevant. This, in essence, was the argument of the *Parable*, and Lessing gives the same point an even more explicit formulation in his last axiom: "The written traditions must be explained according to their inner truth, and no written traditions can give [a religion] any inner truth if it has none."[114]

In response to this Goeze had asked where we derive our knowledge of this inner truth, and then, answering his own question, asserted that such knowledge could only come from the writings of the evangelists and apostles. To Goeze's question Lessing replied quite simply: "From itself. Indeed, it is on that account that it is called the inner truth, that truth which stands in need of no external confirmation."[115]

Furthermore, as Lessing proceeds to show, this very question betrays a confusion of the inner truth with the historical knowledge thereof, and by way of illustration he suggests the analogy between Goeze's position, and one who accepts a geometrical theorem, not because he grasps its demonstration, but because it is found in Euclid. "That it is found in Euclid," Lessing writes, "may well be a strong prejudice in favor of its truth. However, it is one thing to believe the truth because of prejudice, and quite another to believe it on its own account."[116]

Thus, just as the miracles discussed in *On the Proof of the Spirit and of Power*, so too, the actual writings of the evangelists and apostles, served, for Lessing, merely as the occasion for the communication of this inner truth, and it is upon this basis that he can defend the oral tradition as a historically prior and equally valid mode of communication. Although both the oral and written traditions have served as vehicles for the spread of Christian doctrine, neither is the ground of the truth of this doctrine, and it is for this reason that Lessing proclaims:

> But if the written tradition of the Christian religion neither can, nor ought to give it inner truth; then it is not from it that the Christian religion has its inner truth. But if it does not derive its truth from this tradition, then it does not depend upon it. But if it does not depend upon it; then it can persist without it. That is all I want.[117]

This, in brief, is Lessing's argument against Goeze for the separability of the Christian religion from its Biblical and historical foundation. He sincerely desired to defend the Christian religion, and its inner truth, to the extent to which it is defensible, but he saw that this could only be done by raising the question above the contemporary level. Thus, he concludes:

> With me the Christian religion remains the same: it is only that I want to separate religion from the history of religion. It is only that I refuse to regard the historical knowledge of its origin and development; and a conviction of this knowledge, which positively no historical truth can yield, as indispensable. It is only that I consider objections made against the history of religion as irrelevant; whether they can be answered or not.[118]

With the end of the *Axioms*, Lessing's polemic with Goeze reached its logical culmination. In his "counterassertions" to the fragments Lessing had articulated his distinction between the Christian religion and its historical foundation (which includes the Bible, viewed as the divinely authorized documentation of this foundation). He had argued that the former possessed an inner truth, immediately grasped, that is, felt by the believer, irrespective of all possible objections which could be raised against its historical foundation. Goeze had attacked this view, defending the orthodox position, which involved an absolute reliance upon the Bible as the literal word of God, and, finally, in the *Axioms* Lessing reaffirmed his earlier position, answered Goeze's objections, and suggested some of the erroneous presuppositions upon which they were based.

The subsequent controversy, which consisted of eleven issues of the famous *Anti-Goeze*, and a continuing series of *Lessing's Weaknesses*, contains nothing more than an increasingly bitter reiteration of the same points. This was finally ended by a ducal order, forbidding any further attacks on Lessing's part, but before this could be put into effect, Lessing published one last polemical writing, *The Necessary Answer to a Very Unnecessary Question of Herr Haupt Pastor Goeze in Hamburg*. Here, in response to Goeze's persistent question as to what he understood by the Christian religion, Lessing gave the evasive historical reply that he understood this religion to mean all those doctrines which are contained in the symbolic books of the first four centuries and that this was to include the Apostles and Athanasian creeds. This shifted the debate to the historical level, and in his final theological studies, which remained unpublished during his lifetime, Lessing endeavored to show that the Christian religion, thus understood as a body of doctrine, existed long before the formation of the canon of the New Testament and that in primitive Christianity the "Regula fidei" and not the Bible was the ultimate spiritual authority. These fragmentary writings, which were directed against Goeze's more learned lieutenants, especially Christian Walch, display a remarkable erudition and suggest the seriousness with which Lessing approached these problems. However, since they add nothing to the general position already delineated, they can be omitted in the present discussion.

CHAPTER 4

Lessing's Philosophy of Religion, and Its Leibnizean Roots

□

I

THE PROBLEM

The preceding analysis of Lessing's polemical writings has attempted to show that his apparently contradictory attitudes in regard to the various theological tendencies of his age were all manifestations of a consistent standpoint. Against neology, naturalism, and orthodoxy alike he endeavored to separate the question of the truth of the Christian religion, considered as a body of doctrine and ethic, from the question of the facticity of its alleged revelation. It was in virtue of this endeavor that he championed the orthodox fideism against the seductive and superficial rationalism of neology, and it formed the basis of his independent position vis-à-vis Reimarus' critique and the orthodox defense of this facticity.

It has been suggested that the bracketing of the question of the facticity of revelation, the separation of religion from the history of religion, was ultimately grounded in a rejection of the traditional concept of revelation. This rejection, it was further maintained, was a logical consequence of Lessing's monistic metaphysics, which antedated but was profoundly enriched by his study of Spinoza. For the author of *The Christianity of Reason* and *On the Reality of Things Outside God*, and most explicitly, for the Lessing who confessed to Jacobi: "The orthodox conceptions of the Deity are no longer for me; I cannot appreciate them. 'hen kai pan'! I know no other," the decisive manifestation in history of a transcendent God is an utter absurdity. Thus, we concluded that Lessing's original rejection of traditional Christianity was to a large extent based upon his "Spinozistic" presuppositions, although we also saw that

121

Lessing was by no means an orthodox follower of Spinoza and could not in any doctrinaire sense be called a Spinozist.

The denial of the possibility of a historical revelation originally led the young Lessing to formulate an essentially deistic conception of the origin of positive religion. Stripped of divine origin, the "revelations" were viewed as merely human inventions, possessing a certain social and political usefulness, but adding nothing to the universally recognized verities of natural religion. However, as we have already seen, by 1771 Lessing's attitude toward the Christian religion had undergone a profound change. This change cannot, of course, be regarded as a religious conversion. He still rejected the concept of revelation, and his correspondence, the ironical tone of his polemical writings, and a late fragment, *The Religion of Christ*,[1] wherein he distinguishes between the religion which Christ practiced as a man and the Christian religion, built upon the assumption of his divinity, all make it abundantly clear that Lessing never became a Christian in any usual understanding of the term. Nevertheless, it is also true that with the recognition of the separability of the question of the truth of the Christian religion from the historical claims associated with it, Lessing was able to find an "acceptable sense" in traditional Christian doctrine, to justify an objective, historical approach to the Bible and to raise the whole question of religious truth beyond the level attained by the Enlightenment.

This was accomplished through the concept of "inner truth," the interpretation of which provides the key to Lessing's mature philosophy of religion. It was, Lessing argued, precisely because the Christian religion possesses such an "inner truth," binding even upon the will of God, that it may be evaluated and appreciated independently of all factual, historical considerations. In response to the orthodox views of Schumann, Ress, and Goeze, Lessing went to great lengths to distinguish between this "inner truth" and the historical knowledge thereof, and to show that the Gospel narratives and the miracles of Jesus and the apostles served merely as occasions for the communication of this "inner truth," and not as the ground of its validity. When Christianity first entered the world as an unknown Jewish sect, these miracles, and later the Bible itself, provided the means for the propagation of the great truths which it contained, but now that Christianity had established itself, such external aids are no longer necessary for the recognition of these truths and the religion maintains its "inner truth" even if these miracles and narratives were products of deception (as Reimarus claimed). In support of this thesis, which is based upon the sharp distinction between the logical question of truth or validity and the historical, psychological question of origin or awareness, Lessing often resorted to mathematical analogies, but the clearest expression of this standpoint is contained in his famous assertion that "accidental truths of history can never become the proof of necessary truths of reason."

This assertion, as well as the whole tenor of the argument, strongly suggests the Leibnizean background of Lessing's thought. Just as Leibniz had argued against Locke that the senses, that is, experience, never provide anything but examples or particular truths and consequently that necessary truths, which are innate and which include the principles of natural theology, can be suggested but never established by or derived from experience,[2] so too, Lessing proclaimed that religious truth can be suggested or occasioned, but never legitimized, by historical events.[3] Thus, the Christian religion is not true because of the contingent fact that the evangelists and apostles happened to teach it, but they taught it because they recognized its "inner truth." Understood in this sense, the "inner truth" of the Christian religion must be seen in analogy with Leibniz's innate principles, as a truth of reason, and the distinction between "inner truth" and historical event as the theological application of the Leibnizean distinction between "truths of reason" and "truths of fact." Moreover, such an application is itself not without foundation in Leibniz, who in regard to the idea of God, admits that the proper concept may first have been suggested by revelation (which thus functions as an occasion), but that the inclination to receive this concept is grounded in the innate, and hence necessary principles in the human soul.[4]

However, far from resolving the issue, this recognition of the rational or nonempirical character of Lessing's concept of "inner truth" serves only to sharpen it. The Christian religion in which Lessing professed to find such an "inner truth," that is, those doctrines contained in the symbolic books of the first four centuries, is obviously not such a self-consistent, rationally demonstrable body of necessary truths as the analogy with Leibniz's "truths of reason" might tend to suggest.[5] This analogy serves to distinguish it from empirical, historical truths, but it does not indicate its specific content. In *On the Proof of the Spirit and of Power*, Lessing explicitly referred to these truths as inconceivable, and his whole

He drew from Leibniz

critique of neology was directed against the superficially rationalistic tendency to reduce the content of the Christian revelation to a reaffirmation of natural religion. Moreover, in response to Reimarus he also affirmed that a certain irrational element—a subjection of the understanding to the obedience of faith—is an essential ingredient in any revealed religion, and, finally, in the "counterassertions" to the fourth fragment, he declared that revelation is accommodated to the condition of its recipients and, that its truth cannot be judged in terms of its conformity to a purely rational, natural religion.

There is no definite "true" religion

Thus, our analysis of Lessing's concept of "inner truth" seems to have led to the recognition of a basic contradiction in his thought. Arguing on the basis of the Leibnizean epistemology, Lessing rigidly distinguishes between religious and historical truth, thereby suggesting the rational, universally valid character of the former. However, the objective historian and close student of Christian doctrine emphasizes that this truth cannot be identified with the wholly rational natural religion of deism or neology and, that, since such truth is first manifested in history as revealed and as immediately grasped—felt—rather than rationally comprehended by the believer, it must be clothed in an obscure and authoritarian form.

If Lessing is not to be dismissed as a mere "occasional thinker," if his treatment of the Christian religion and, in fact, his whole religious-philosophical authorship are to be taken seriously, then this apparent contradiction must be resolved. To resolve it we must first determine (1) the nature and significance of the (in some sense rational) content, which he claimed to have found within traditional Christianity and (2) the relation between this content and the positive, authoritarian form in which it confronts the believer.

II
THE SOLUTION

These questions may be answered and the apparent contradictions resolved by means of an analysis of Lessing's adaptation and reinterpretation of some of the main principles of the Leibnizean philosophy. This adaptation, which led Lessing to formulate a new notion of religious truth and a new conception of the relation between religion and history, was made possible by the publication of the new editions of Leibniz's work by Raspe in 1765, which included the *New Essays,* and by Dutens in 1768. These editions, it

will be noted, were published in the years immediately preceding
Lessing's arrival at Wolfenbüttel, and his acquaintance with them
thus helps to explain his decisive change in standpoint at this time.

The second, and simpler question, which I shall discuss first,
is readily resolvable in terms of Leibniz's doctrine of "small perceptions," as delineated in the *New Essays*, and, thus, this doctrine
provides an important clue for the interpretation of Lessing's
philosophy of religion.[6] One of the many uses to which Leibniz
put this doctrine was to counter Locke's argument that ideas, or
truths, such as the law of contradiction and the main principles of
mathematics, metaphysics, and morality (all supposedly expressing
necessary, universally valid truths) cannot be regarded as innate
because a large portion of the human race has no awareness of
them. Against this Leibniz alleges that such ideas and truths are
often within the soul in an obscure, even unconscious form, as
inclination, propensities, dispositions, or habits, rather than as
clearly apprehended principles or actions.[7] Moreover, as he later
shows in regard to practical principles, although they may at first
only be obscurely felt, as if by instinct, they may eventually be
comprehended and demonstrated as rational, universally valid
truths.[8] This conception involves a special application of the
principle of continuity,[9] so that there is no longer a radical opposition, as with Descartes, Spinoza, and again with Kant, between
sense or feeling and reason, but only a difference in the degree of
clarity with which the same fundamentally rational content is
apprehended. Thus, the obscure or prerational, that is, feeling,
is seen to contain an implicitly rational content, or, in Leibniz's
language, "there are innate truths which we find in us in two ways,
by insight, and by instinct."[10]

Now, this enclosure of an intrinsically rational content in an
obscure authoritarian form is precisely what we find in Lessing's
mature concept of a revealed religion. This is clearly suggested by
his statement in the "counterassertions" to the fourth fragment of
Reimarus that the human understanding can only develop very
slowly and that truths which are readily comprehended by the
common man could originally only be apprehended as immediate
and mysterious revelations of the Deity. This view no doubt lay
behind his emphasis, against Goeze, on the validity of the feeling
of the simple believing Christian, but it found its clearest expression in the remark that revealed religion does not presuppose
natural, but rather includes it within itself, that it contains all the

truths found in the latter and merely supports them with a different type of proof, that is, authority and feeling rather than reason. Disregarding the term "natural religion," which the whole previous discussion indicates cannot refer to the hypothetical construction of neology and deism but rather simply suggests a rational content of some sort, we can find in this passage all the ingredients of Lessing's conception of the relation between reason and revelation, and further we can see its close parallel to the above quotation from Leibniz. Just as there is one rational truth apprehended in two manners, so too there is one religious truth, which may be grasped either through immediate feeling, that is, implicit belief, or rational thought.[11]

This, however, still leaves unresolved the far more difficult question of the actual rational content of revealed religion, a content which so far we have only determined cannot be equated with the principles of natural religion, as commonly understood by the Enlightenment. Nevertheless, we believe that here again Lessing derived his inspiration from Leibniz and that the clue to his position, and hence the key to the interpretation of his conception of the "inner truth" of the Christian religion, is to be found in his defense of Leibniz's sincerity against Eberhard's attack.

Lessing, it will be recalled, had argued that Leibniz did not, as Eberhard maintained, accommodate his views to the orthodox, but on the contrary, never accepted an opinion unless he was convinced that it was in a certain sense true, and finding that acceptable sense he endeavored to reconcile it with his own philosophy. Thus, as Lessing expressed it: "He struck fire from the flint, but he did not conceal his fire in the flint." Upon this basis Lessing further held that although Eberhard was right in maintaining that Leibniz only accepted these doctrines—such as eternal punishments—in their "supportable sense," he was nevertheless wrong in denying Leibniz's sincerity in thus accepting them. He concluded by pointing out that not only is such a procedure perfectly legitimate but it is substantially identical with the exoteric method of the ancient philosophers, who like Leibniz set their own system aside in order to lead the individual to the truth along the path on which they found him.

These reflections on Leibniz's method, the importance of which for Lessing's own views have long been recognized by scholars,[12] demonstrate his profound understanding of and sympathy with the Leibnizean concept of truth. It is this tendency, so characteristic of

Leibniz, to find an element of truth in diverse standpoints, which fascinated Lessing, and which he so fruitfully applied to the problem of religious truth. In addition to the passage just mentioned, Jacobi's report of his conversation with Lessing can also attest to this interest. According to Jacobi, Lessing had declared:

> Leibniz's concept of truth was of such a nature, that he could not bear to have too narrow limits set to it. Many of his assertions have flowed from this manner of thinking; and it is often hard, even with great acuteness, to discover his real intent. It is for this reason that I esteem him so highly; I mean: because of his grand manner of thinking, and not because of this or that opinion which he seemed to hold, or even actually held.[13]

Lessing's abiding concern with the Leibnizean philosophy in general, and with his "grand manner of thinking" in particular, is further evidenced by some scattered fragments in his literary remains. These fragments, which contain a sketch of Leibniz's life, together with brief passages from his works, a few scattered comments, and the beginning of a translation of the *New Essays*, were first published by Karl Lessing, under the title of "Leibnizesterei" in 1795 in his biography of his brother.[14] These brief fragments, which are probably only a small portion of the material which Lessing actually collected for his proposed life of Leibniz,[15] have received scant attention from scholars, but they nevertheless provide valuable clues in regard to Lessing's understanding of and adherence to the Leibnizean philosophy.

The first of these which is relevant is a passage from a letter of Leibniz to Bierling[16] (November 19, 1709), repudiating Locke's critique of innate ideas and maintaining, as he does in the *New Essays*, that innate ideas or principles are required to explain the possibility of necessary truths. Lessing's special attention to this passage provides additional evidence of the Leibnizean basis of his distinction between religious and historical truth.

The majority, however, of the extant passages from Leibniz concern themselves precisely with the "grand manner of thinking" —with Leibniz's statements concerning the reconciliation of diverse standpoints. One of these, taken from the *New Essays*, contains Theophilus' advertisement of the "advantages" of the Leibnizean philosophy and stresses its success at reconciliation: "This system appears to unite Plato and Democritus, Aristotle and Descartes, the scholastics with the moderns, theology and ethics with reason.

it could unite the religions by taking elements of truth from each

It seems to take the best from all sides, and then it goes much farther than any has yet gone."[17]

Another, and even more suggestive passage, consists of brief excerpts from, and a German summary of, some of the content of Leibniz's letter to Remond, of January 10, 1714,[18] wherein he relates his youthful reconciliation of the scholastic doctrine of substantial forms with the new materialism. The important element, however, is not the specific reconciliation, but the passage immediately preceding and justifying it: "I have found that the majority of the sects are right in a good part of what they affirm, but not so much in what they deny."[19] Although this precise quote is not found in the extant portion of Lessing's selection from Leibniz, the portion of the letter in which it is contained is discussed, and since this is one of Leibniz's most explicit statements of the basis of his "grand manner of thinking," there can be little doubt that it influenced Lessing and, as I shall try to show, provides the key to the understanding of his conception of religious truth.

However, before the precise nature of Lessing's debt to Leibniz can be demonstrated in detail, it will be necessary to attempt a brief analysis of the relationship between Leibniz's "grand manner of thinking" and the basic principles of his philosophy. This tendency to find a measure of truth in diverse standpoints serves, more than anything else, to distinguish his philosophy from that of such rationalists as Descartes, Spinoza, and Wolff, and it is thus vital to see that the tendency is not the result of a shallow eclecticism, but is grounded in his deepest philosophical insight—the universal harmony.

In the *New Essays*, which was Lessing's main source, this universal harmony, or the intrinsic connection of all parts of the universe, is explained in terms of the doctrine of small perceptions. These small perceptions, Leibniz argues, are the ground of the connection which each being has with the rest of the universe. It is by virtue of them that "the present is big with the future and laden with the past," that "all things conspire," and consequently it is because of the universal interconnection of all things "that in the least of substances eyes as penetrating as those of God could read the whole course of the things in the universe."[20]

The immediate epistemological consequence of this grandiose conception is the orientation of knowledge toward the ideal as realized in the divine mind.[21] This universal and completely rational context, this total interconnection of all things, by virtue of which the whole course of the universe may be discerned in the most insignificant event, is only accessible to an infinite intellect. Since the finite understanding does not have "eyes as discerning as those of God," it must proceed from condition to condition and, thus, is incapable of the infinite analysis necessary to achieve an adequate knowledge of the totality.[22] In Leibniz's own words:

> . . . it belongs only to the supreme Reason, whom nothing escapes, distinctly to comprehend all the infinite and to see all the reasons and all the consequences. All that we can do in regard to infinites is to know them confusedly, and to know at least distinctly that they are such.[23]

However, although the finite mind is incapable of such absolute and adequate knowledge, it is not thereby utterly removed from the source of truth. Rather, and this constitutes one of Leibniz's main philosophical insights, there are various levels of knowledge, each possessing a partial or relative truth, but each falling short of the ideal of infinite analysis.[24] The first level is that of ordinary experience, which man shares with the higher animals. There is, he argues, a connection between the perceptions of animals and of men, insofar as they remain "empirics," which has some resemblance to reason, but this connection is grounded only in the memory of facts or effects and not in the knowledge of causes.[25] Although Leibniz thus grants a certain relative validity to the lowest level of cognition, he sharply contrasts it with rational knowledge, which depends upon necessary or eternal truths. Furthermore, at least two levels may be distinguished within the domain of finite rational knowledge. The first is that of mathematical physics, wherein phenomena are explained in terms of scientific laws. At this level the mind grasps intelligible connections, but it is only the connections between phenomena, which themselves must be explained in terms of a higher standpoint.[26] This higher standpoint is the monadological or philosophical level, at which the mind achieves a confused idea of the ultimate nature of things. It is able to see *that* the universe forms one thoroughgoing context, that it is the best of all possible worlds, and that the laws of physics are based upon the fitness of things. But being finite, it is incapable of grasping the details of this plan.[27]

The possibility of such partial or relative knowledge at various standpoints is grounded in the very structure of the monadological scheme. The Leibnizean universe consists of an infinite number of simple substances or monads. These monads do not interact, but because of the preestablished harmony according to which the supreme wisdom has ordered them, each has relations which express all the rest, and thus, each is "a perpetual living mirror of the universe."[28] Leibniz generally illustrates this intermonadological relationship by means of the analogy of a city, which while remaining identical, yet appears different when viewed from various perspectives. Thus, he argues, although each of the infinite number of simple substances represents the universe from a particular point of view, and hence differs from all others, all of these diverse points of view are merely aspects of one and the same universe as seen from the particular perspective of each monad.[29] Moreover, since each of these substances or points of view expresses, albeit confusedly, all that occurs within the universe, past, present, and future, it can be said that each bears within it a certain resemblance to an infinite perception, and consequently to the divine wisdom.[30]

With this the conception of partial or relative knowledge is given a metaphysical foundation. Just as each monad represents the universe from a particular point of view, so too, each standpoint or level of knowledge can be viewed as a more or less obscure imitation of the divine understanding. As he explains in his correspondence with Arnauld, this representative function, understood as the expression of a multiplicity (the universal context) in a unity (in a particular perspectival adumbration), constitutes the essential activity of all monads. But when, in a rational monad, this representation is accompanied by self-consciousness or apperception, it becomes thought.[31] Thus, rational thought is viewed as the highest expression of a universal process, wherein the prerational levels retain their relative validity as more or less obscure representations of the ultimate truth.[32] At the rational level this multiplicity of perspectives may take the form of conflicting philosophical or theological positions, so that when Leibniz asserts that "the majority of the sects are right in a good part of what they affirm, but not so much in what they deny," he is merely reflecting the basic principles of his philosophy. Translated into monadological language, this means simply that each sect is a confused expression of the ultimate truth and consequently contains a relative truth, but, since it is merely one among a number of possible perspectives, it is wrong in denying the validity of opposing standpoints.

Lessing and the Leibnizean Perspectivalism: Lessing's documented concern with Leibniz's perspectivalism and the concept of truth which it implies was surely not developed without any consideration of its metaphysical basis. In his earliest philosophical work, *The Christianity of Reason,* Lessing engaged in monadologically oriented speculations, wherein the various simple substances were ranked in a continuous series according to the clearness of the consciousness of their perfections. However, a much later and more relevant evidence of this concern is contained in a brief fragment, *That Man Could Have More Than Five Senses.*[33] This work, which is generally dated at about the time of the publication of the fragments,[34] also suggests the influence of Bonnet[35] and thus provides the most concrete example of the manner in which Lessing understood and reinterpreted the key Leibnizean insights.[36]

Lessing begins (Section 1) with an essentially Leibnizean definition of the soul as a simple substance, which is capable of an infinite number of representations. However (Section 2), qua finite, it is incapable of receiving them all at once, but only gradually in an infinite succession of time.[37] Moreover, since (Section 3) the soul receives its perceptions successively, there must be an order and a measure in which it receives them, and (Section 4) this order and measure is provided by the senses. Upon this basis Lessing speculates (Sections 5–6) about the possibility of the future attainment of new senses.[38] Since (Section 6) nature never makes a leap (the Leibnizean principle of continuity) the soul must have gone through all of the preceding stages of development before it attained its present condition. Thus, before possessing five senses, it must have had each one singly, and then two, etc., in all possible combinations. Furthermore (Sections 7–8), if it so developed in the past, there is nothing to prevent the possibility of the acquisition of further senses in the future.

In support of this contention, Lessing presents an extremely vague and schematic discussion of the nature of the senses. He begins by defining matter (Section 9) as that which sets limits, and argues that since the senses determine the limits of the representations of the soul, the senses are therefore matter. From this he concludes (Section 11) that since the soul receives all its representation through the senses, it must always be connected with a material body.[39] Furthermore, since (Section 13) the whole material world is animated even in its smallest parts,[40] each atom of matter can serve the soul as a sense, and thus the number of senses which the human race may in time acquire depends solely

(Section 15) upon the number of "homogeneous substances"[41] which the material world contains. Although (Section 16) this number is obviously many more than five (thereby insuring the possibility of additional senses) it cannot (Section 19) be infinite.

In view of these speculations, Lessing argues (Sections 17–22) for the possibility of the future intellectual development of the race. This development, which will be achieved through the acquisition of new senses, will make accessible new levels of insight or perspectives of truth totally beyond the ken of mankind at its present stage of development. Lessing illustrates this fanciful conception of the intellectual advance of the soul through the acquisition of new senses with the suggestion (Section 17) of the possibility of the eventual development of organs capable of perceiving the phenomena of magnetism and electricity. In order to indicate the radically new vistas of knowledge which such acquisitions would provide, he compares our present knowledge of these phenomena with the knowledge of optics possessed by Saunderson, the blind mathematician, who was made famous by Diderot's *The Letter on the Blind,* and concludes that if we ever come to possess organs for the perception of electricity or magnetism: "A whole new world, full of the most splendid phenomena, will arise, a world of which we can now form as little a notion as he (Saunderson) could form of light and color."[42]

This curious fragment, to which a brief statement affirming the doctrine of metempsychosis[43] was attached, is quite typical of Lessing. Like his other metaphysical forays it is more of an occasional piece than a systematic statement of his philosophical position. However, despite its somewhat whimsical nature, it is not totally without significance. As we shall see in an analysis of *The Education of the Human Race,* Lessing seems to have seriously entertained the doctrine of metempsychosis, and the general argument of the work provides concrete evidence of his concern with the Leibnizean concepts of representation and development and also contains some hints of the way in which he endeavored to adapt and reinterpret these concepts.

This reinterpretation is considerable; for although the fragment suggests an extensive knowledge of Leibniz, it is far from an uncritical reiteration of Leibnizean principles. We have already seen that Lessing rejected the doctrine of the preestablished harmony, which underlies Leibniz's formulation of the theory of representation, and the adoption of Bonnet's sensationalistic standpoint is perfectly consistent with that rejection. The result is that instead of the Leibnizean monad, which represents the universe from a particular point of view, "in agreement with its organs,"[44] Lessing posits a simple substance, which perceives the universe *through* these organs, but whose representations are, as with Leibniz, limited and ordered according to the condition of the organism to which they belong. Furthermore, the development, or intellectual progress of the soul, which Leibniz understood as a gradual clarification of its perceptions, is now viewed, purely quantitatively, as the simple acquisition of new senses, each of which yields a new level of insight.

Although such a scheme is obviously crude and in many ways un-Leibnizean, it does seem to provide a new foundation for the perspectival-developmental conception of truth. Since the perceptions of each simple substance are determined by the condition of its sense organs, it may be said to perceive the universe according to the perspective disclosed by these organs. Thus, visual, auditory, and tactile phenomena, etc., may each be said to "represent" the universe from a particular point of view, and each type of perception to contain a partial or relative truth, which may be judged and appreciated in its own terms. Since each perspective contains only a partial truth, that is, nature seen from the point of view of that sense organ, no single perspective may be proclaimed as the absolute or whole truth, and the possibility of the future development of more adequate or inclusive perspectives must be admitted. Thus, as with Leibniz, the recognition of the relative truth of each perspective or standpoint is combined with the belief in eventual progress to higher standpoints, and, as we shall see, it is precisely this dual conception which underlies the basic argument of *The Education of the Human Race.*

Thus, in light of (1) Lessing's reflections upon Leibniz, especially in his polemic with Eberhard, (2) the similarity of his own treatment of religious questions to that which he ascribes to Leibniz, (3) the nature of the passages which he selected from the Leibnizean corpus, and finally (4) the obvious attempt to reconcile this theme with the naturalistic speculations of Bonnet, *it is the contention of this study that Lessing's adaptation of the Leibnizean perspectivalism, albeit in a radically revised form, provides the key to his concept of the rational content or "inner truth" of the Christian religion.*

As a partial, perspectival adumbration of this ultimate truth—

that truth as seen from a particular, historically determined point of view—the Christian religion may be said to possess a rational kernel, and it was by virtue of this that Lessing was able to acknowledge its relative truth, and to reaffirm a good deal of what he had previously rejected as mere prejudice. Furthermore, since in keeping with the dialetic manifested in the polemical writings, this was only accomplished at the cost of its claim to absolute validity, we can see that Lessing achieved this without dragging back in "all the rubbish." Christianity, thus understood, is no longer the absolute, universally binding word of God, but merely one of the many paths along which the human race has striven to understand the Divine, and its relative "validity" no more mitigates the similarly partial truth content of other religions, than the "validity" of the perception of the universe from the standpoint of vision mitigates the "validity" of a purely tactile perception.

One of the more fruitful results of this theological application of the Leibnizean perspectivalism is that it provides a positive philosophical foundation for the doctrine of toleration, an ideal which Lessing shared with the entire Enlightenment. Prior to Lessing, this doctrine was defended by Bayle, Locke, and others, largely in terms of the finitude of knowledge, the innocence of error, and "the rights of the erring conscience." With Lessing, however, the concept of human finitude undergoes a subtle but significant change. Now the emphasis is no longer on the fact that no faith possesses the absolute truth, or that if one does, human reason is incapable of determining which one, but rather upon the reflection that each possesses a partial or relative truth. Since each religion possesses a relative, and none the absolute truth, each is worthy of respect. On this basis they can coexist in a harmonious relationship, as mutually respected members of one universal family, and this was precisely the theme of *Nathan the Wise*.

From this standpoint the various positive religions are no longer conceived of as merely politically necessitated, conventional additions to or distortions of an original and purely rational religion of nature, but rather as the necessary forms which the religious consciousness assumes in the course of its development. A purely rational religion, although not that which was postulated by deism or neology, was for Lessing the ultimate truth. *However, rather than the original religion of mankind, of which the positive religions are subsequent distortions, it is now seen as an ideal toward which the human race may strive, but which can never completely realize.* To return to the Leibnizean metaphor, the city as viewed directly from its center, understood absolutely, and not perspectivally. Thus, just as for Leibniz such total insight is seen as an infinite task, never realizable by the finite mind, so too, Lessing can write in his most oft-quoted lines:

It is not the truth which a man possesses, or believes that he possesses, but the earnest effort which he puts forth to reach the truth, which constitutes the worth of a man. For it is not by the possession, but by the search after truth that he enlarges his power, wherein alone consists his ever-increasing perfection. Possession makes one content, indolent, proud—

If God held enclosed in His right hand all truth, and in His left hand the ever-active striving after truth, although with the condition that I must forever err, and said to me: choose! I would humbly fall before His left hand and say: Father give! The pure truth is for Thee alone.[45]

III
THE EXEMPLIFICATION

Despite the evidence in regard to Lessing's concern with the Leibnizean perspectivalism, and the light which it sheds upon his polemical activities, the assertion that this conception (in the form in which Lessing understood it) underlies his whole philosophy of religion may, so stated, seem somewhat arbitrary and inconclusive. Thus, the main task of the balance of this study will be to show in concrete terms that this conception finds its concrete exemplification in, and furnishes the key to, the interpretation of the major works of Lessing's last years: *Ernst and Falk, Nathan the Wise,* and, above all, *The Education of the Human Race.*

Ernst and Falk, Conversations for Freemasons: This work consists of five dialogues which discuss "the true ontology of free-masonry."[46] These dialogues, which contain the major expression of Lessing's political philosophy, are divided into two parts. The first three, published in 1778, are concerned with the essence of freemasonry and the task of its adherents, while the latter two, published in 1780, without Lessing's consent, are largely devoted to the history and present condition of the order of which Lessing himself was a member.[47] These latter dialogues contain many bitter reflections on the sad state of contemporary freemasonry, but only the first group, is of general philosophical interest.

The two characters are Falk (Lessing), a sharp and sceptical Mason, and Ernst, an inquiring young friend. Ernst is eager to learn as much as possible about the order, but Falk repeatedly responds to his friend's queries in an elliptical manner, which leaves him more confused than ever. Thus, to Ernst's straightforward question whether he is a member, Falk replies: "I believe that I am."[48] This evasive answer is incomprehensible to Ernst, for whom membership in the order is simply a question of fact, and Falk is forced to clarify his meaning. "I believe that I am a Freemason, not so much because I have been accepted by elder Masons in a lawful lodge, but because I comprehend and know, what and why freemasonry is, when and where it has been, how and by what means it is advanced or hindered."[49]

Thus, just as he had previously done with Christianity, Lessing here raises the question of the nature of freemasonry above the factual level. Just as little as the belief in certain historical facts makes one a Christian, does membership in a particular lodge make one a Freemason, for "freemasonry is nothing arbitrary, nothing superfluous, but something necessary, that is grounded in the essence of man, and of civil society. Hence, one could just as well have come upon it through his own reflection, as be brought to it through instruction."[50]

Consequently, the peculiar rites and symbols of the order do not constitute the essence of freemasonry. "Freemasonry has always existed,"[51] and the true Mason is distinguished not by his ceremonial customs, but by his deeds. But what are these deeds which uniquely characterize the freemason? They are not, Falk argues, the ordinary works of charity and civic responsibility. The Freemason may and should perform such works, but he does not do so qua Freemason. Rather, asserts Falk at the end of the first dialogue, "the true deeds of the Freemason aim at making everything, which one generally regards as good deeds, superfluous."[52]

This paradoxical response sets the stage for the second dialogue, which contains much of the philosophical significance of the work. After some preliminary remarks on the cohesion found among a society of ants, the discussion turns abruptly to human society. Falk's (Lessing's) conception of a civil state is thoroughly within the Lockean, liberal tradition. The state is a humanly devised means for the promotion of human happiness and not some super-personal entity, existing as an end in itself:

> The states unify men so that in and through this union, each single man can all the better and more surely enjoy his portion of happiness. The total happiness of all the members is the happiness of the

state. Apart from this there is none. Any other happiness of the state, by which a single member suffers and must suffer, be it ever so little, is nothing but a cloak for tyranny.[53]

However, and this is the important point, the state as a purely human institution is by nature imperfect. Even in the best possible state the ideal of complete unity is not realizable. Some disunity is an inevitable concommitance of all attempts to unify mankind.[54] This is Falk's (Lessing's) thesis, and he proceeds to corroborate it at different levels. The first is that of international relations. Granting the invention of the best possible constitution, mankind would still be divided into different states, and each state would naturally pursue its own interest.[55] Furthermore, continues Falk, echoing Montesquieu, many of these states would have different climates and consequently different needs, and thus different customs, morals, and even religions: "Men would even then still be Jews and Christians and Turks and the like."[56]

Finally, Falk endeavors to suggest that this disunity would still be found even within each state. A completely classless society is rejected as an impossibility. Different social strata, both intellectually and financially determined, are inevitable. Hence, even if all the possessions of a state were originally divided equally among all the inhabitants, this equality would never last more than two generations. One would know how to make better use of his property than another. One would have to divide his property among more descendants than another. In short, even in the best possible society there would still be rich and poor.[57]

Yet despite this impressive catalogue of inevitable imperfections, civil society is still recognized as a positive good, as the only effective means for the unification of mankind.[58] The ensuing disadvantages, of which religious diversity is one, are to be lamented, but they are necessary evils, grounded in the very nature of things, and do not diminish the positive value of the degree of unity achievable through civil society. For, as Ernst so eloquently expresses it: ". . . men are only unified through separation! Only through increasing separation is this unity preserved!"[59]

But what is the source of this inevitable disunity which Lessing finds manifested at all levels of human affairs? If our previous analysis is correct it can be nothing but the very perspectivalism which Lessing borrowed from Leibniz. Only such a concept can explain the strong emphasis upon the inevitability of diversity. It is because each individual and each society have only finite, partial perspectives of the absolute truth (which as Lessing reminds us, is for God alone) that they inevitably clash, and it is because this diversity of perspectives is an ultimate "ontological fact" and not a contingent circumstance that it cannot be removed by any possible social or political system. Thus, it is in virtue of his perspectival conception of truth that Lessing differs from so many eighteenth-century thinkers in regarding a universal religion, a world state, and a classless society as unrealizable ideals, rather than as the inevitable result of increased enlightenment.

Furthermore, the analogy between the above delineation of the inevitable imperfection of civil society and the major outlines of the Leibnizean theodicy are readily apparent. Just as for Leibniz, metaphysical evil, grounded in the original imperfection of finite being, is a necessary ingredient in the best of all possible worlds,[60] so too for Lessing, disunity and conflict (social evil) is a necessary aspect of the best of all possible societies. Owing to the respective purposes of their works, Leibniz minimizes and Lessing emphasizes this evil, but the fundamental insight is identical. In both cases this evil is seen not as something arbitrary, which can be removed by a better constitution or plan of creation, but as an ultimate and irreducible aspect of reality.

This perspectivalism not only characterizes for Lessing the human condition, but it also determines the ethical task, which is precisely the minimization of this diversity.[61] This conception was first formulated in *The Testament of John*, a brief dialogue which Lessing appended to *On the Proof of the Spirit and of Power*. There Lessing pleaded that the testament of the dying evangelist, which consisted solely in the call for mutual love, should unite all those whom the Gospel of John, that is, theological doctrines, may separate.[62] Thus, diversity of religious beliefs was recognized as inevitable, and love was postulated as a means for the unification on the ethical plane of those who were divided in their beliefs. In *Ernst and Falk* this same ideal is suggested in a somewhat broader and more secular context. Here it is recognized that men are separated not only by religion but also by cultural, socio-economic, and political factors, and the ethical realm is defined as that level on which men confront one another not as Jew and Christian, Frenchman and German, employer and employee, but simply as men.

However, such a transcultural and transnational ethical order, such a unity of love amid a diversity of beliefs and customs, cannot by its very nature be furthered by individual states or particular civil laws. Rather, as Lessing clearly recognizes, the advancement of such an ideal requires an "Opus supererogatum," and with this in mind, Falk expresses his desire "that there may be men in each state, who are above the prejudices of their nation, and who know precisely where patriotism ceases to be a virtue."[63] And later: "It is greatly to be wished, that there may be men in each state who do not accept the prejudices of their native religion; men who do not believe that everything is necessarily good and true which this religion recognizes as such."[64]

Such men, as the third dialogue suggests, are the Freemasons. It is this striving for universal brotherhood which constitutes their peculiar task, and it is the achievement of this brotherhood, which is the good deed that renders all other good deeds, that is, the ordinary social virtues, superfluous. However, since diversity is grounded in the very nature of things and can thus be minimized but not eradicated, this ethical ideal of a universal brotherhood, just as the speculative ideal of absolute truth, remains for Lessing an infinite task.

Nathan the Wise: When prevented by the authorities from continuing his controversy with Goeze, Lessing returned to his first love, the stage, for the expression of his religious-philosophical views. The result was *Nathan the Wise*, a poetic drama in which Lessing graphically depicts his conception of the nature of positive religion and of religious truth, his ideal of tolerance, and an essentially Leibnizean conception of divine providence.

The heart of the play, around which the dramatic structure is more or less superimposed, is the famous parable of the rings, which Lessing borrowed from Boccaccio[65] and modified to suit his own purposes.[66] It is here that he returns to the problem of the relationship of the three major religions: Judaism, Christianity, and Islam, which he had already treated in his youthful work on Cardanus, and the contrast between the youthful and the mature treatment of this theme sheds a good deal of light on the development of Lessing's thought.

Since the scene is located in the very center of the drama (Act III, Scene 7), some knowledge of the preceding development of the plot is necessary for its proper understanding. The situation which ultimately leads to the parable scene is based upon the financial difficulties of Saladin, the enlightened sultan. Through his treasurer, Al-Hafi (also Nathan's friend), he hears of a rich and wise Jew (Nathan) who would seem to be the one possible source of the necessary revenue. However, anxious to protect his friend, Al-Hafi tells Saladin that since Nathan is wise as well as rich, he does not lend money. Thus, Saladin is confronted with the problem of inducing Nathan to provide the requisite sum. As a noble and enlightened ruler, he refuses to resort to force, but being in desperate straits he is not above trickery. Hence, he decides to embarrass Nathan into lending him the money, and with this in mind he summons Nathan to the palace and asks him which of the three religions he prefers.[67]

Nathan's initial, straightforward response: "Sultan, I am a Jew," fails to satisfy Saladin. As a typical spokesman of eighteenth-century rational theology, he firmly believes that "—Of these three/ Religions only one can be/ The true one," and consequently that the question can be settled by an impartial examination of the evidence, both internal and external. In light of these presuppositions, he says to Nathan:

> A man like you will not consent to stay
> Where'er the accident of birth has cast him;
> Or if he stays, 'twill be of 's own election
> As insight, reason, choice of best things, prompt him.
> Come, then, impart to me your insight: let me hear
> The moving reasons: since for this high quest
> Time was not granted me. Tell me the choice,
> Tell me the grounds—of course, in confidence—
> Which fixed the choice, that I may make it mine.[68]

As the entire previous analysis of Lessing's position endeavored to show, it was precisely such a formulation of the problem of religious truth which he found repugnant.[69] This either/or approach presupposes the very concept of revelation which he long rejected. It presupposes that one faith is in fact true, that is, God given, and the others completely false, that is, human inventions. In his early work on Cardanus, Lessing was content to treat the question in a sceptical fashion, suggesting that none of the spokesmen could "prove" the truth of their respective creeds and even that Christianity gets somewhat the worst of the argument. At that stage Lessing's standpoint was essentially deistic. None of the religions could really substantiate their claims, and hence all were "false." Now, however, in virtue of his perspectival conception of truth, he views the problem in a somewhat different light. Instead of dismissing all of the religions as false, he endeavors to suggest that each is true to the extent to which it provides a means whereby the individual can relate himself to God, and each is false to the extent to which it absolutizes itself as the only means for achieving this relationship.

The new standpoint is suggested in the next scene (6) which depicts Nathan soliloquizing upon the proper strategy to adopt in response to Saladin's demand. Acutely conscious of his precarious position as a Jew in a Mohammedan court, he reflects:

> Hm! Hm! Marvellous! What's to happen now?
> What does the Sultan want? I came prepared
> For money, and he asks for truth—for truth!
> And wants it paid in ready cash, as though
> The truth were coinage.[70] Yea, even as if
> It were old coinage that was told by weight.
> That might pass, truly! But such new-coined pieces
> That owe the die their value, must be counted.[71]

The meaning of this passage is clear. Religious truth cannot be measured in straightforward, factual terms. Such standards may be applied to some types of truth—mathematical, scientific, or historical—but not to the question of which is the true religion. Here a new criterion is required. Rather than a mechanical, external comparison of the various religions (as with the new coins which are evaluated in accordance with an external stamp), one must consider their intrinsic qualities (their weight), or in the language of the Goeze controversy, their "inner truth." Since such considerations do not lend themselves to a concise either/or formulation, and since Nathan is prudent enough to recognize the danger inherent in his situation, he decides to answer Saladin with a parable.

The ensuing parable scene may be divided into roughly four parts. The basic narrative follows the main lines of Boccaccio's version. Once, in the ancient East, Nathan relates, there lived a man who received "from the hand of his most dear beloved" a beautiful ring of inestimable value, which had the magic power to render the wearer, provided he trusted therein, beloved before God and man.[72] The ring was kept within the family from generation to generation, each bearer bequeathing it to his favorite son, who thereby automatically became the head of the house. Finally, it was given to a father who had three sons whom he loved equally, and since he could not choose between them he promised the ring to each. As the hour of death drew near the father became perplexed and, not wishing to disappoint any of his sons, had two exact replicas made and gave one ring to each son. However, scarcely had the father died, than each son claimed in virtue of his ring to be the head of the house, and all three quarreled bitterly. But since the three rings were identical in appearance, the true ring was not provable, almost, adds Nathan after a pause, as unprovable as the true creed is now.[73]

Thus, following Boccaccio, and in essential agreement with his earlier treatment of the subject, the first portion of the parable ends in complete scepticism, and Nathan admits that this narrative was not intended to decide the question of the true religion, so much as to excuse him from the task.[74] However, this evasive answer does not satisfy Saladin any more than Nathan's straightforward assertion that he is a Jew. The three religions, he remarks, are not like the three rings, but rather easily distinguishable, not only in regard to doctrine, but even in matters of prescribed food and clothing.

Saladin's reflections on the external differences of the various religions bring Nathan to the second portion of the narrative, and it is here that we receive the first inkling of the parable's true relevance to the problem of the relationship of the various positive religions. Despite their external differences, Nathan remarks, all three religions are identical in regard to their foundation. All three base their claims upon historical tradition, either written or oral. And, adds Nathan, reflecting Lessing's attitude toward historical truth: "History must be received on faith implicitly."[75] Moreover, he concludes, since acceptance of historical facts requires an implicit faith, in whom can we better put this faith than in those of our own blood and in the tradition in which we were raised?[76]

Lessing has here given poetic expression to his basic conviction: the irrelevance of the historical as a foundation for religious truth, and this irrelevance is one of the main themes of the parable. Just as the sons receive the rings "from the hand of his most dear beloved," so also do the followers of the positive religions receive their creed, and as little as the fact of derivation serves to establish the authenticity of the rings does it confirm the truth of religion. However, a religion thus accepted out of mere piety or respect rather than rational demonstration *eo ipso* loses all pretensions of absoluteness. It may very well serve the individual as an adequate means for the attainment of "blessedness," but it cannot pretend to be the only means. Other individuals stand in precisely the same relation to their faiths, and their piety is equally sincere, and their claims equally valid.

After this brief, interpretive digression, which for the first time pleases Saladin, Nathan returns to the parable. The three sons appealed to the law to settle their dispute. Each one swore before the judge that he had received the ring immediately from his father's hand and thus deserves to enjoy its privileges. In addition, each contended that the father could not be false toward him, and hence that his brothers must be deliberate deceivers, deserving of punishment.[77] With this the parallel to the religious situation becomes perfectly explicit. For just as each brother, so too, each religion bases its claim to be the true faith on the fact that it received its creed "from the hand of his most dear beloved," that is, from an authoritative tradition, and ultimately from God, and it is in virtue of this that each claims divine sanction and views the other two religions as products of deliberate deception.

Such, suggests Lessing, is the inevitable result of the absolutistic either/or conception of religious truth, implicit in the attempt to ground religion upon historical fact, and this view is expressed in the judge's verdict which ends the third section of the parable. After originally denying the possibility of deciding between the rival claims without the testimony of the father, the judge suddenly recalls the magic power allegedly inherent in the true ring. In view of the impossibility of deciding between the various historical claims, the internal criteria must determine the issue. Hence, the judge proclaims that whichsoever of the brothers is best loved by the other two shall be declared the possessor of the genuine ring. However, as the judge remarks, none of the brothers is in fact loved by the other two, but, rather, each is intent solely upon his own claims, and loves only himself. Thus, in lieu of any decisive evidence to the contrary, the judge arrives at the only possible conclusion. Since none of the rings has demonstrated the magic power to make its wearer beloved before man and God, all three are false. The genuine ring was probably lost, and in order to placate his sons the father had three replacements made.[78]

The verdict, however, is only provisional. The three positive religions are not absolutely false, but only so to the extent to which they promote disunity and conflict, that is, to the extent to which they claim to be absolutely and uniquely true. Since as a matter of fact, the three religions, just as the three rings, had led to nothing but increasing conflict and mutual distrust, they must, on the basis of the present evidence, be considered false. However, this is not to imply that the negative judgment is final, for if the followers of each religion view their creed as relative and not mutually exclusive expressions of absolute truth, and if on this basis each follower places his confidence in his religion thus understood, then they all shall manifest the magic power of making their adherents beloved before God and man.

Such was Lessing's belief,[79] and such is the meaning of the judge's counsel which constitutes the fourth and final section of the parable. After deciding on the basis of the evidence at hand, against the genuineness of the three rings, the judge suggests that the brothers accept the situation precisely as it stands. Each should believe his ring to be the true one, and each should strive, through the exercise of mutual love and true piety, to demonstrate its magical powers. Then, concludes the judge:

> *And when in days to come the magic powers*
> *Of these fair rings among your children's children*
> *Brighten the world, I call you once again,*
> *After a thousand thousand years are lapsed,*
> *Before this seat of judgment. On that day*
> *A wiser man shall sit on it and speak.*
> *Depart! So spake the modest Judge.*[80]

Thus ends the parable of the rings, and it is only in this concluding section that its full significance becomes manifest. The key point is that the power of the genuine ring and the true religion is no longer conceived of as something magical, that is, positive, which automatically bestows its efficacy upon its wearer or follower, but that this efficacy must be produced by the activity of the individual. Thus, the realization of the power of the genuine ring or the true religion becomes not a gift but a task, not a fact but a result to be achieved. Moreover, since this task is universal, it is equally binding upon adherents of all faiths, and it provides the unifying standpoint from which the relatively unessential differences of the various religions can be overcome. This standpoint constitutes the realm of pure humanity, wherein men confront one another simply as men, and not as Christians or Jews, and it is with this in mind that Nathan earlier admonished the Templar for his bigotry:

Are Jew and Christian rather Jew and Christian
Than men? Ah, had I found in you one more
Whom it suffices to be called a Man![81]

Within the drama Nathan, and to a lesser extent Saladin, are the ideal representatives of this realm. Like the Freemason they have risen above the prejudices of their religion and no longer arrogantly view it as the only road to God. In sharp contrast to them stands the bigoted patriarch, probably modeled after Goeze, who, in reply to the Templar's query about the fate of a Jew who brings up a baptized Christian in his own faith (which Nathan actually did with his adopted daughter Recha), can only reply to every description of the Jew's virtue: "It matters not! The Jew must burn."[82]

However, although men such as Nathan and Saladin may be said to be above the prejudices of their religion in the sense of the Freemason, and thus able to love men as men, they have not totally rejected their traditional faith. Rather than the complete repudiation of all revealed religion, the parable advocates a changed attitude toward one's own faith.[83] It is thus that Nathan can say to Saladin, just as Mendelssohn had said to Lavater: "I am a Jew," and at the same time emphasize to the Templar, the underlying basis of their common humanity. Each ring and each religion retains its relative significance. Each is capable of rendering its believers (those who trust therein) beloved before God and man. But in each case this latent magical power or "inner truth" must be brought out through human effort, and not simply received in an immediate manner.

Thus, the conception which underlies the parable of the rings is that of a genuine religious pluralism, united by the common bond of universal humanity. Saladin suggests this when he remarks to the Templar: "I never have desired/ That one bark grow on all trees of the wood,"[84] but its fullest expression is only to be found in the whole course of the drama, wherein Jew, Christian, and Moslem eventually make the symbolic discovery that they are all members of the same family. In the last analysis this discovery is the main theme of the drama. It is another expression of the ethical ideal of unity in diversity, which we have already seen in *The Testament of John* and *Ernst and Falk,* and consequently another demonstration of the seriousness with which Lessing took the Leibnizean perspectivalism.

This parable certainly provides the central theme of the play, but it does not exhaust its philosophical and religious significance. Also worthy of mention is the concept of providence which governs the entire course of the drama. This concept is not directly relevant to the problem of religious truth, but it is vital for an understanding of *The Education of the Human Race*, and it furnishes further evidence of the Leibnizean basis of Lessing's thought.

As we have already seen, the Leibnizean doctrine of providence is formulated in terms of the preestablished harmony between nature and grace. God, as the supreme architect, or director of the laws of nature, is at the same time the supreme monarch or omniscient governor of the kingdom of ends. As a result the great moral purposes which prevail in the best of all possible worlds are all achieved by purely natural means. Thus, rather than a radical opposition between the natural and the supernatural order, whereby the former disrupts and rectifies the latter, the supernatural, that is, the divine purpose, is seen to have its true exemplification in the natural order.

Now this very conception of a benign providence, according to which everything is determined for the best, is one of the cardinal principles of Lessing's theory of the drama[85] and finds its concrete manifestation in the plot of *Nathan the Wise*. The whole structure of the play is intended to exhibit the guiding hand of providence, leading all events by purely natural means to an inevitably happy issue.[86] Since all of the main characters are basically good, the good dramatist, just as the beneficent Creator, must show that they are ultimately rewarded, and it is precisely this popular moralizing which is generally considered to be the play's major flaw. Thus, it was apparently by chance—by a remarkable physical resemblance to his long lost brother—that Saladin spares the captured Templar, and it is by mere coincidence that the Templar, thus reprieved, happens to be on hand at the precise moment when Recha is trapped in the fire. These and other apparently fortuitous events conspire to produce the happy discovery that Recha is actually the Templar's sister and that both are, in fact, children of Saladin's brother.[87]

It is this same providential scheme, so typical of the Aufklärung, which Nathan suggests is the true explanation of Recha's fortunate rescue. In her highly excited state she was convinced that her savior was not a man but an angel who swept her out of the flames on his white wings,[88] and Nathan endeavors to convince her that she was saved by an actual flesh and blood knight, wearing a white cloak, and not by an angel. Nevertheless, Nathan reflects, because the event was wrought by purely natural means, it is not any less a miracle, that is, the result of a benign providence, for:

> *Chief miracle it is*
> *That the true miracles become to us*
> *So commonplace, so everyday. Without*
> *This universal miracle could it be*
> *That thinking men should use the word like children,*
> *Who only gape and stare upon what's strange,*
> *And think what's newest is most wonderful.*[89]

Thus, the greatest miracle, the true manifestation of providence, is found not in the irregular and inexplicable events, but in the everyday course of affairs which are governed by purely natural laws, and it is here that we can see the true significance of Lessing's denial of free will in his conversation with Jacobi. Lessing is indeed a determinist. All of the events of the play are seen to follow inevitably from the divine plan. It is beyond the power of any character to change its outcome, and Nathan's wisdom is itself shown to be rooted in his recognition of and submission to this fact.[90] However, this rigid determinism involves, like Leibniz's, a "happy" or wise and not like Spinoza's, a blind or logical necessity. Everything in the universe happens necessarily, but everything happens necessarily for the best.[91]

This thought, which is implicit in the whole structure of the play, found its clearest expression in Lessing's introduction to his edition of the philosophical writings of Karl Wilhelm Jerusalem (1776), in which in defense of the determinism of his departed friend, he writes:

> What do we lose if freedom be denied us? Something—if it is anything—which we do not need; something which we need neither for our activity here, nor our happiness hereafter; something whose possession must make us far more anxious and disturbed than its absence could ever do. Compulsion and necessity in accordance with which the idea of the best works, how much more welcome they are to me than that bare capacity of being able to act in different ways under different circumstances. I thank the Creator that I must do the best.[92]

The Education of the Human Race: This work is the culmination and the keystone of Lessing's philosophy of religion. It is here that all of the various aspects of his thought, which we have discussed previously, find their decisive expression. Here the Leibnizean perspectivalism and principle of development are joined with Spinoza's conception of the accommodation of revelation to the standpoint of its recipients and used to interpret the history of religion. The result is that the various positive religions, and more specifically Judaism and Christianity, are seen as necessary stages in the development of the moral and religious consciousness, or to use Lessing's metaphor, as means chosen by providence for the education of the human race.

Even apart from the exclusion of Mohammedanism, this developmental treatment of the relation between the positive religions stands in marked contrast to the static conception of the parable of the rings and at first glance seems to be in no way reconcilable with it. However, if one keeps in mind the literary "exoteric" nature and predominantly polemical orientation of the latter work, the contradiction becomes more apparent than real. In *Nathan the Wise*, Lessing endeavored to give dramatic form to the ideal of mutual love and respect among those who differ in their religious beliefs. This was accomplished by pointing to the similar and equally unjustifiable positive, that is, historical, claims of the three faiths, and by demanding, in light of this, that each surrender its absolutistic pretensions and learn to recognize that, above and beyond the inevitable divergence of belief, all men are united by a common bond of humanity. *The Education of the Human Race*, however, is an "esoteric" speculative treatment of the history of religion, wherein Lessing analyzes the intellectual content of Judaism and Christianity and endeavors to show that their differences must be understood in light of the fact that they represent successive stages in the development of the religious consciousness of the race.

The underlying conception of the work, the analogy between revelation and education, and the developmental conception of revelation which it implies, has its roots in Patristic thought, especially in regard to the critique of the Gnostic rejection of the Old Testament.[93] But Lessing understood this conception in a far more radical manner than did the Church Fathers. The basic theme of the work was already suggested in the "counterassertions" to the fourth fragment of Reimarus, to which the first fifty-three paragraphs of *The Education of the Human Race* were appended. This is generally ignored by commentators, but is nevertheless of great significance. There, it will be remembered, Lessing countered Reimarus' attack on the revealed character of the Old Testament with a relativistic conception of revealed religion, whereby each revelation is seen as a historically conditioned accommodation to the community to which it is addressed. Thus, it was argued that the lack of a doctrine of immortality, and even of the true conception of the unity of God, does not militate against the revealed character of the Old Testament. Since it was addressed to a rude people, at a primitive stage of development, it obviously could not contain such sublime conceptions. Hence, it must be evaluated in its own terms, in relation to the intellectual condition of its recipients, and not judged unhistorically, according to a purely rational standard of natural religion. The first fifty-three paragraphs of *The Education of the Human Race* develop this theme in relation to ancient Judaism, while the balance, which only became known in 1780 with the publication of the complete text, treats Christianity in a similar vein and suggests the advent of a third stage of education or progress, an "Eternal Gospel,"[94] which shall signify the maturity of the human race.

As we have already suggested, this conception of accommodation is in all probability taken from Spinoza, but Lessing radically transformed its meaning. Whereas for Spinoza the accommodation of a revelation or prophecy to the condition of its recipients implies that it is purely a product of the imagination, useful for fostering obedience, but utterly devoid of philosophical significance,[95] for Lessing it means that each historically conditioned revelation contains a relative perfection or partial truth. Such a transformation is only to be understood in terms of Lessing's adaptation and historicization of the Leibnizean perspectivalism and conception of the levels of knowledge. For Leibniz, as we have already seen, there is a basic continuity, rather than a radical opposition between the products of reason and imagination, and it is upon this basis that Lessing can argue that each positive religion, just as each level of knowledge, from sense perception to monadological speculation, contains a relative or partial truth. Each religion expresses the ultimate truth (which is for God alone) with the degree of clarity and distinctness appropriate to its level of development.[96] Thus, although succeeding religions represent higher levels of insight, each subordinate stage nevertheless retains its intrinsic worth as the legitimate expression of the religious consciousness at that level of development. This general historical standpoint, with its combination of a belief in

progress and a recognition of the uniqueness and relative significance of each stage, was already formulated by Herder, who was
likewise influenced by Leibniz,[97] but Lessing was the first to apply
it specifically to the history of religion, and it provides the ultimate
basis of his positive attitude toward the content of the Christian
doctrine.

Although *The Education of the Human Race* was published
anonymously, Lessing prefaced the work with some brief editorial
comments, which already suggest its main theme. "Why," he asks
in his assumed role as editor,

> are we not more willing to see in all positive religions simply the
> process by which alone human understanding in every place can
> develop and must still further develop, instead of either ridiculing
> or becoming angry with them? In the best world there is nothing
> that deserves this scorn, this indignation we show. Are the religions
> alone to deserve it? Is God to have part in everything except our
> mistakes?[98]

This rhetorical question contains the essence of Lessing's conception of revealed religion in both its negative and positive aspects.
Insofar as they are based upon historical facts and claim the possession of absolute truth these religions must be dismissed as errors.
However, they are not, as Reimarus and the deists contend, harmful
abberations, but rather the necessary means through which the
human understanding develops, which being finite, must view the
universe from a particular limited perspective, and consequently,
cannot achieve absolute knowledge.

Furthermore, the above passage also helps to answer the
much debated question as to the nature of Lessing's understanding
of revelation. Does it signify, as it did for Clement, an actual
transcendent educational act on the part of the Deity, or is the
whole analogy between revelation and education nothing more
than an "exoteric hull" for a purely naturalistic conception of intellectual development?[99] The latter view is, as we shall see, strongly
suggested by much of the argument of the work and was already
implicit in Lessing's "counterassertions" to the first fragment of
Reimarus, where he argued that the revelation to the Jews must
be understood in terms of their superior propensity for religion.
However, in view of the previous discussion of Lessing's monism,
as well as the explicit statement in the above passage that positive
religions are both human errors and divinely ordained means of

enlightenment, we can conclude that the question thus formulated is illegitimate. Lessing certainly rejected the notion of the decisive manifestation in history of a transcendent God, but from his monistic standpoint, with its immanentistic conception of providence, as seen in *Nathan the Wise*, one can no longer speak of an ultimate opposition between human and divine activity. Thus, we can conclude that Lessing viewed the history of religion, much as Hegel viewed world history,[100] as the result of *both* human forces and providential divine direction, and it is precisely this which provides the "esoteric" justification for Lessing's use of the concept of revelation.

The first five sections provide an introduction to the entire work. Lessing begins (Section 1) by drawing the analogy between education and revelation, which he shall subsequently use to interpret the history of religion. The former, he argues (Section 2), is nothing more than a revelation made to the individual, and the latter an education which has come and still continues to come to the whole human race. Although, Lessing surmises (Section 3), this analogy may or may not be of service to pedagogy, it is undoubtably of great value to theology. This value is suggested in the next two paragraphs where Lessing shows: (1) that it provides a basis for understanding the relation between reason and revelation, and (2) that it explains the occurrence of different and conflicting revelations at different points in history.

The first point is resolved by means of an analysis of the nature of education. Since, Lessing reasons (Section 4), education never gives man anything which he might not have derived from "within himself," but merely gives it to him more quickly and easily, so too, if the analogy is to hold, revelation gives to the race nothing which human reason, left to itself, might not also have attained; although it has given, and significantly continues to give to it, the most important of these things more quickly. The second point is explained in terms of the accommodation hypothesis, which is a logical consequence of the analogy between education and revelation. For, it is argued (Section 5), just as education is directed toward the level of the student, so also, God, who is now viewed as the divine educator, orders his revelations in accordance with the developing intellectual capacities of the race.

Aside from the accommodation hypothesis, which is naturally central to the whole work, the most significant aspect of this section is the conception of education which it implies. This conception is the Platonic,[101] which underlies all of modern rationalism, and which found its decisive expression in Leibniz's theory of innate ideas.[102] Since from this standpoint knowledge is not seen as something acquired from without but rather as something derived from within the innate capacities of the mind, experience in general and education in particular are viewed not as external sources of knowledge, but as occasions or stimulants for the reflection upon the knowledge which lies "within." We have already seen that such a conception is implicit in Lessing's whole treatment of the "inner truth" of the Christian religion (especially in his assertion that the Gospel narratives and miracles served as the "occasions" for the reception of this truth and not as the ground of its veracity), and now we can see that Lessing's concept of revelation is perfectly consistent with this standpoint and can likewise be viewed as an "occasion" in the Platonic sense.

Lessing begins his historical sketch with the hypothetical postulation (Section 6) of an original primitive monotheism. This conception is obviously inconsistent with the developmental scheme and is hardly to be taken seriously. It does, however, furnish a convenient starting point. Since (Section 7) the human race was in its infancy, such a sublime conception could not long endure. Thus, the original concept of the unity of God disintegrated, and polytheism and idolatry naturally arose. This disintegration necessitated (Section 8) a new impetus for the religious education of mankind, and consequently God chose the Hebrews as the crudest and most despised race to be his special instruments of education.

The religious development of the ancient Hebrew nation is thus the subject matter of the remainder of the first part (Sections 9–53). In addition to justifying his accommodation hypothesis, Lessing's intent is to suggest that within the Hebrew religion there occurred an increasingly clearer consciousness of the content of the revelation contained in the Old Testament, so that what was at first merely dimly perceived and blindly accepted became at last rationally comprehended: "Revelation had guided their reason, and now, all at once, reason gave clearness to their revelation."[103] Eventually, however, when the content of the Old Testament had been rationally assimilated and its historically determined limitations recognized, the child outgrew his primer, and the human race stood in need of a new revelation (Section 53) to raise it to a higher level of insight.

Lessing illustrates this development both in regard to the

speculative, that is, the concept of God, and to the moral consciousness of the nation. The Hebrews first conceived of God (Section 11) simply as "the God of their fathers," and later, because of the miraculous manner in which they were delivered from their bondage in Egypt, they began (Section 12) to consider him the mightiest of natural gods. Finally, as they became increasingly aware of his omnipotence, they formed (Section 13) a rudimentary conception of "the One," although this was still (Section 14) far below "the true transcendental conception of the One," and even (Section 20) below the level of insight achieved by other, more advanced nations. It was only later, under the influence of the Persians, that the Hebrews arrived at a more sublime conception of the Deity. Instead of contrasting him with the miserable idols of their neighbors (Section 35), they henceforth began to measure him against "the Being of all Beings," which was worshipped by the more philosophical Persians. Thus instructed, the Jews returned (Section 38) to their primer, the Old Testament, and found that these more sublime conceptions were actually contained therein, although they had previously failed to recognize them.

This latter passage stands in an intrinsic connection with the assertion that revealed religion does not presuppose natural, but rather, includes it within itself, which, we have previously suggested, is to be understood in terms of Leibniz's doctrine of "small perceptions." Lessing's key point is that these philosophical insights concerning the nature of God are in fact contained, albeit in an obscure form, in the Old Testament and constitute its "inner truth." Thus, the religious education of the Hebrews is not to be conceived of as the acquisition of new insights, but as the gradual clarification of what was implicitly there all along. It is in virtue of this fact, that Lessing ventures (Section 40) an explanation of the transformation of the Hebrew nation after the return from exile:

> Thus enlightened respecting the treasures which they had possessed without knowing it, they returned and became quite another people, whose first care was to give permanence to this enlightenment amongst themselves. Soon apostasy and idolatry among them were out of the question, for it is possible to be faithless to a national deity, but never to God after he has once been recognized.[104]

The case, however, is somewhat different with regard to the moral consciousness and the correlative concept of immortality.

Originally (Section 16), such a rude people were only capable of a moral education adapted to the age of children, that is, an education by means of sensible rewards and punishments. Here too, Lessing argues (Section 17), the analogy between education and revelation holds good, and thus:

> . . . God could give to his people no other religion, no other law than one through obedience to which they might hope to be happy, or through disobedience to which they must fear to be unhappy. For as yet they envisaged nothing beyond this life. They knew of no immortality of the soul; they yearned after no life to come. But now to reveal these things, when their reason was so little prepared for them, what would it have been but the same fault in the divine rule as is committed by the vain schoolmaster who chooses to hurry his pupil too rapidly and boast of his progress, rather than thoroughly to ground him?[105]

Thus, as we have seen, Lessing admits the lack of the doctrine of immortality in the Old Testament and justifies it in terms of the accommodation hypothesis. The absence of this doctrine in these writings proves nothing against their divine character.[106] Moses was indeed sent by God, even though the sanctions of the law extended only to this life. For, asserts Lessing (Section 23), in words which seem to echo those of Spinoza: "He was surely sent only to the Israelitish people, to the Israelitish people *of that time*, and his commission was perfectly adapted to the knowledge, capacities, inclinations of the *then existing* Israelitish people, . . ."[107]

As a result, when the Jews eventually became acquainted with this doctrine under the influence of the Persians and the Greeks, they found that it did not correspond with their Scriptures in the same way that the doctrine of God's unity and attributes had done. The latter was contained therein in an obscure form,[108] but the former is totally absent. Thus, unlike a strict monotheism, the doctrine of immortality and the higher conception of morality which it implied could never become the faith of the entire people, but it was (Section 43) and continued to be only the creed of a certain segment (the Pharisees), who were more susceptible to extraneous influences. Hence, with the suggestion of this limitation, the religion of the Hebrews reached its logical culmination, and fulfilled its historically determined function.[109] Subsequent attempts to read these higher insights into the Hebrew Scripture only resulted (Section 50) in the superstitious, hairsplitting understanding of the rabbis, and hence Lessing concludes (Section 53): "A better instructor must come and tear the exhausted primer from the child's hand—Christ came!"[110]

Thus, the transition, marked by the advent of Christ, from Judaism to Christianity was not simply a linear development from an obscure to a clearer comprehension of certain fundamental truths, such as is found within Judaism itself, but rather, a qualitative leap to a new and higher perspective.[111] The attainment of this new perspective, from which the doctrines of immortality and future rewards and punishments can be clearly recognized, required a new revelation, and this was provided by Christ, who became "the first *reliable, practical* teacher of the immortality of the soul."[112]

This superior reliability of Christ's teachings, Lessing suggests (Section 59), was based upon the fulfilled prophecies and apparent miracles. However, he adds, perfectly in keeping with his general position, the facticity of these miracles, and the person of Christ himself, are now irrelevant to the truth of his teachings. The person and the alleged miracles of Christ provided the original occasion for the reception of these doctrines, which we now possess and can appreciate purely in their own terms.[113]

Hence, it was largely in virtue of its teaching the doctrine of the immortality of the soul that the New Testament became the second and better primer for the human race. Moreover, Lessing reflects, if this one great truth is found therein mixed with other, somewhat less enlightening and useful doctrines, that is, the teachings of the evangelists and apostles, this is not only perfectly natural but also advantageous. These subordinate truths are themselves not without significance, and have in fact (Section 63) been "a new directing impulse for human reason." Then, commenting upon the cultural significance of the books of the New Testament, Lessing concludes (Section 65) in a manner reminiscent of the previously discussed letter to Karl: "For seventeen hundred years past they have occupied human reason more than all other books, and enlightened it more, were it even only through the light which human reason itself put into them."[114]

This passage contains the grounds of Lessing's positive appreciation of the Bible, and consequently of his conservative attitude toward Christian doctrine. Although a purely human document, the New Testament has nevertheless been the chief source and stimulant of ethical and religious thought in Western civilization, and it is in light of this that he offers his advice to the Aufklärung from the superior standpoint of the philosophy of history. It was, and still is to a great extent necessary, he argues (Section 67), that each people should for a time recognize this book as a direct revelation from God, and an ultimate authority, and the non plus ultra of their knowledge. Given this purely natural state of affairs, he admonishes (Section 68) the enlightened theologians and philosophers, "you who are cleverer than the rest," who have outgrown this naïve standpoint, not to communicate their insight to their "weaker classmates," who are not yet ready for it, but rather (Section 69) to return to their primer and see "whether that which you take only for variations of method, for superfluous verbiage in the teaching, is not perhaps something more."[115]

This advice seems to suggest an analogy between the contemporary theological situation and that of the Jews during the Captivity. In both instances the immediate relationship to the text (implicit faith) was outgrown, and a new and deeper understanding, based upon philosophical comprehension, became possible. With this deeper understanding one is liberated from adherence to the letter, and it is thus here that we can see the roots of Lessing's argument against Goeze that the Christian religion could very well continue to exist if the Bible were completely lost, for, he argues (Section 72):

> As we by this time can dispense with the Old Testament for the doctrine of the unity of God, and as we are also gradually beginning to be less dependent on the New Testament for the doctrine of the immortality of the soul: might there not be mirrored in this book also other truths of the same kind which we are to gaze at in awe as revelations, just until reason learns to deduce them from its other demonstrated truths and to connect them with them?[116]

As examples of such a philosophical understanding of revealed doctrines, Lessing treats the Trinity (Section 73), original sin (Section 74) and the justification through Christ (Section 75), three doctrines which were generally rejected by neology. Lessing's method is thoroughly in accord with that which he ascribed to Leibniz, and thus furnishes additional evidence of his conscious application of the Leibnizean perspectivalism to religious doctrines. This is best illustrated by his philosophical reinterpretation of the doctrine of the Trinity. Although in regard to content this re-interpretation is very close to his youthful treatment of this subject in *The Christianity of Reason*, the manner in which he here formulates it suggests his more mature standpoint. May not, he asks, this doctrine, after innumerable waverings, have finally brought human reason to the recognition that the unity of God cannot be conceived in the same manner as finite things, that the unity of an infinite being must be a "transcendental unity, which does not exclude a sort of plurality?" This plurality, Lessing argues, is grounded in the divine self-consciousness. As an infinite being, God must have a perfect conception of himself, which qua perfect, must contain all his attributes, including his necessary reality, and as such this conception is not an empty representation, but a true double. Moreover, Lessing concludes, those who wanted to communicate this conception to the popular intelligence could hardly have done better than to call such a double the Son, whom God begets from eternity.

After a similar but briefer treatment of original sin and the justification through Christ, Lessing attempts (Section 76) to justify this procedure, and what was merely implicit in the discussion of Judaism here receives an explicit formulation. Such a free speculative treatment of the mysteries of the Christian religion is allowable, Lessing argues, because the term mystery meant something different to the early Christians than it does now,[117] but more important, because "the development of revealed truths into truths of reason, is absolutely necessary, if the human race is to be assisted by them." Furthermore, such a development is possible because although when revealed these doctrines were certainly not truths of reason, they were revealed "in order to become such."[118]

Lessing illustrates this conception of the relation between reason and revelation by means of the analogy of an arithmetic teacher who foretells the result in order to guide the reckoning of his students. If, he reflects, the students were simply content with the result, that is, with revealed truths as immediately apprehended, authoritative decrees, they would never learn to compute for themselves, and thus thwart the teacher's intention in giving them this help. But, he also seems to suggest, if they were totally without such a guide, they might never begin to reflect. The latter point is made explicit in the following paragraph, which contains in capsule form all of the ambiguities inherent in Lessing's conception of revealed religion:

And why should not we too, by means of a religion whose historical truth, if you will, looks dubious, be led in a similar way to closer and better conceptions of the divine Being, of our own nature, of our relation to God, which human reason would never have reached on its own?[119]

With this we are once again on Leibnizean ground. This whole discussion (Sections 76–77) of the relation between reason and revelation closely parallels Leibniz's analysis of the relation between "small perceptions" and rational insight. Just as these "small perceptions" were seen by Leibniz as both obscure presentiments of and guides to the development of a fully self-conscious reason,[120] so too, Lessing viewed revelation, which from this point of view clearly refers to the religious instinct or propensity of man, both as an anticipation of and a stimulant for the development of rational insight. It is an anticipation because it contains within itself an implicitly rational content, which is destined to be disclosed, and it is a stimulant because, as the analogy with the arithmetical result and the whole tenor of the last paragraph suggests, it provides the occasion which first leads reason to consider this content.

Moreover, this understanding of Lessing's concept of revelation is the only one which can fully reconcile the apparent contradiction between Sections 4 and 77, which has been greatly emphasized by recent scholars.[121] The conception of revelation as an occasion, understood in the Platonic-Leibnizean sense, underlies both passages. In Section 4 Lessing argues that revelation gives man nothing which reason cannot arrive at by itself, but simply gives it to him more quickly and more easily, and in Section 77 he contends that without this aid human reason might never have come to recognize the profound religious truths which it has in fact discovered in Christian doctrine. From the Platonic-Leibnizean standpoint, this latter assertion in no way contradicts the former, but simply emphasizes the necessary function of the occasion which leads human reason to recognize these essentially rational truths. Qua rational, they are not derived from without, and in this sense education, that is, revelation, does not give man anything which he could not get from himself. However, since it does provide the occasion which first enabled man to recognize the truths which lie "within," it is perfectly legitimate to argue that without this education or revelation human reason might never have actually come to recognize them, just as the slave boy might never have come to recognize the geometrical truths which he apprehended under the prodding of Socrates. The former assertion (Section 4) is concerned with the logical structure of these truths, and the latter (Section 77) with the psychological conditions necessary for their apprehension.

Thus, we find the same basic conception underlying Lessing's treatment of both Judaism and Christianity. In both instances he endeavors to show that whereas originally revelation, that is, the religious instinct, serves as a guide to reason, it is the eventual destiny of reason, thus educated, to give clarity to the revelation which first stimulated it. Seen in this light, the development of revealed into rational truths is nothing more than the clarification of an implicitly rational content, which was first merely accepted on authority.

However, and this is the decisive point for the understanding of Lessing's perspectival approach to religious truth, the rational content of both revelations is itself seen to be historically conditioned. Each is only a perspectival adumbration of the ultimate truth, although the Christian revelation thus clarified is seen to contain a higher level of insight, and hence occupies a more adequate perspective than the Jewish. The Old Testament, it was stated, was intended for a primitive people at the lowest stage of development. It contained only an obscure suggestion of the unity of God and no concept of immortality, nor consequently of the moral dignity of man. The New Testament, on the other hand, reflects a more developed stage of the religious consciousness. It not only clearly proclaims the immortality of the soul, and hence provides some indication of the moral dignity of man, but also, through the doctrine of the Trinity, suggests that the unity of God must be understood as "a transcendental unity, which does not exclude a sort of plurality." Nevertheless, although this implies a new and more adequate perspective, a qualitative advance, the rational content of the Christian revelation cannot be equated with the ultimate truth. Just as every primer is only for a certain age, so too, Christianity itself is not the final goal of human development, but merely a preliminary stage which shall one day be transcended. This is the theme of the final section of *The Education of the Human Race*, which Lessing begins (Section 85) with the confident words:

> It will come! it will assuredly come! the time of the perfecting, when man, the more convinced his understanding feels about an ever better future, will nevertheless not need to borrow motives for his actions from this future; for he will do right because it *is*

right, not because arbitrary rewards are set upon it, which formerly were intended simply to fix and strengthen his unsteady gaze in recognizing the inner, better, rewards of well-doing.[122]

Thus, in anticipation of the Kantian ethic, Lessing finds the goal of human development in the achievement of moral autonomy, and this implies for Lessing a fresh advance beyond the standpoint of Christianity. No longer will men require the promise of either temporal or future rewards and punishments in order to live the moral life, but they will come to love and practice virtue for its own sake. The trend of the previous discussion leads one to expect that, together with this development of the moral consciousness, Lessing would provide a similar suggestion of the development of a more adequate conception of God, and the reason why he fails to do so must, I believe, be found in his "Spinozism," which he never publicly acknowledged. If, as he had previously suggested, each of the preceding stages of development express a progressively higher conception of the unity of God, it would appear logical that at the final stage, with the attainment of the intellectual maturity of the race, the full concept of this unity would be achieved, and from what we have already seen of Lessing's concept of God, this could only mean the unity of God and the world.

However, as is evident from his advice to return to the writings of the New Testament and from his whole defense of the "inner truth" of the Christian religion, Lessing obviously did not believe that this new and higher standpoint had yet been reached. Nevertheless, despite his recognition (Section 91) of its distant futurity, Lessing's firm belief in providence and his adherence to the concept of development convinced him of the eventual advent of the age of the "Eternal Gospel." And thus, in a poignant restatement of Herder's philosophy of history, which also suggests the Leibnizean perspectivalism, he proclaims (Section 92) to providence:

> Thou hast on thine eternal way so much that thou must concern thyself with, so much to attend to! And what if it were as good as proved that the great, slow wheel, which brings mankind nearer to its perfection, is only set in motion by smaller, faster wheels, each of which contributes its own individual part to the whole?[123]

Finally, in order to carry the parallelism between ontogeny and phylogeny, between the development of the individual and that of the race, which is implicit in the entire work, to its logical conclusion, Lessing ends with the affirmation of the doctrine of metempsychosis. If, as Lessing believes (Section 93) to be the case, every individual must travel along the same path in which the race reaches its goal, and since it is impossible that in the same lifetime one can be both "a sensual Jew and a spiritual Christian," the logic of the situation dictates (Section 94) that each individual must appear more than once upon the earth. This doctrine is here presented (Section 95) merely as a hypothesis, but it was no doubt one of Lessing's most cherished beliefs.[124] Furthermore, the inclusion of this doctrine suggests that he envisioned a third stage in development of the concept of immortality, just as he had in regard to the concept of God and the ground of moral obligation. At the first stage of the education of the human race, characterized by the revelation of the Old Testament, the concept was completely lacking, or was at best seen in relation to the immortality of the Hebrew nation. In the New Testament, which marked the second stage of development, a concept of personal immortality was attained, but this was viewed as an eternity of unrelenting rewards and punishments in some transcendent realm. Finally, with the third stage in the education of the race, the concept will be grasped in its true form, as implying an infinity of rebirths on earth. This latter parallelism is not explicitly affirmed in *The Education of the Human Race*, but it seems to be a reasonable inference from the whole tenor of the argument and is perfectly consistent with Lessing's other reflections on the subject.

Thus, if viewed in the light of some of Lessing's fragmentary metaphysical forays, the last paragraphs of *The Education of the Human Race* seem to suggest obliquely that the future development of humanity will lead to the general acceptance of something suspiciously like his own monistic Weltanschauung, with its rationalistic ethic and doctrine of metempsychosis. If the law of development manifested in the previous history of religion continues to hold, this would be the content of the "Eternal Gospel" which Lessing believed destined to supercede Christianity and usher in the time of the intellectual and moral maturity of the race. However, since the advent of this period lies in the distant future, and its outlines are as yet only dimly discernable by Lessing himself,[125] he could in all sincerity recommend to his contemporaries that they return to the New Testament with the firm conviction that the content of this "second great primer" for the human race had not yet been exhausted.

Conclusion

Having completed our discussion of the major writings of Lessing's last period, we can return to the problem delineated at the beginning of the previous chapter. There, it will be recalled, it was stated that the analysis of Lessing's concept of "inner truth" of the Christian religion had led us to the recognition of an apparent contradiction in his thought. On the one hand Lessing sharply distinguishes between religious and historical truth, thereby suggesting the rational and necessary character of the former as opposed to the empirical, contingent nature of the latter ("accidental truths of history can never become the proof of necessary truths of reason"), while on the other hand he emphasizes the incomprehensible aspect of those doctrines in which he claimed to find such a rational "inner truth" ("a certain captivity under the obedience of faith belongs to the essence of the concept of a revelation"). It was then suggested that the reconciliation of this apparent contradiction would require the determination of (1) the nature of the rational content which Lessing found within Christian doctrine, and (2) the relationship between this content and the authoritarian, prerational form in which it was first apprehended. The answers to these questions and the reconciliation of the apparent contradiction were then asserted to be found in Lessing's adaptation and reinterpretation of certain Leibnizean insights. However, although we were able to document Lessing's concern with these Leibnizean themes, what was there stated dogmatically only received its full justification in light of the analysis of the last three writings, and especially *The Education of the Human Race*.

162

It is only here that we find the full exemplification of Lessing's perspectival approach to religious truth, for we can now see that the perspective occupied by each religion is determined by its historical place within the ever-continuing development of the human race. Each religion, understood on the analogy with the monad, is a self-contained whole whose "inner truth," that is, its implicitly rational content, is itself conditioned or limited by the historical place which it occupies. Every positive religion, just as every primer, is only for a certain age, and the clarity with which it reflects the ultimate truth, which is for God alone, depends upon the level of intellectual development of its followers. Thus, we can see how Lessing could claim to find a rational content within the traditional mysteries of the Christian religion, and at the same time refuse to equate this content with the natural religion of deism and neology, that is, to reduce revealed religion to a reaffirmation of natural religion. On the contrary, Lessing endeavored to defend the implicitly rational content of those very doctrines, such as the Trinity, original sin, and the justification through Christ, which neology rejected. These are no longer seen, with neology, as the irrational and immoral accretions of a superstitious age, but as obscure historically conditioned expressions of the ultimate nature of things, as the ways in which the human mind at a particular stage in its development attempted to relate itself to the Divine. It is because there is such significance in these Christian mysteries that Lessing can argue for the "inner truth" of the Christian religion, and it is because this truth, as conceived by Lessing, is not ultimate but merely expresses a perspective or level of development which must some day be transcended, that he stands totally beyond the viewpoint of orthodox Christianity. From the relativistic standpoint the apparent contradiction between the emphasis on both the rational and incomprehensible aspects of the "inner truth" of the Christian religion completely vanishes. Since the doctrines of this religion *do* contain a perspectival adumbration of the ultimate truth they may be seen to have an implicitly rational content, but since they are *only inadequate, historically conditioned expressions of this truth* and not the ultimate truth itself, they inevitably contain elements of obscurity and incomprehensibility, which are merely the necessary concomitants of all finite and limited knowledge.

Moreover, we are now in a position to appreciate more fully the profound consistency of Lessing's mature treatment of Christianity. Although he never pretended to be a systematic philosopher,

true, innate religion is rational, but incomprehensible, & must someday be transcended.

and he explicitly rejected the appellation "theologian," all of the theological and many of his religious assertions of the Wolfenbüttel period may be seen to follow directly from this one central intuition, which was only made possible by the publication of the Dutens and Raspe editions of Leibniz's works. It was this intuition which took Lessing beyond the point where Reimarus and the entire Enlightenment had become tired of reflecting, that is, beyond the question of the facticity of the Christian revelation. The Christian religion is false in the sense that it is neither the absolute revealed word of God nor the ultimate stage in the development of the religious consciousness. Yet it is not, as Lessing's "enlightened" friends believed, a patchwork of bunglers, but rather one of the most important manifestations of the human spirit, which contains many significant, albeit obscure, historically conditioned insights. These insights, both moral and metaphysical, constitute its "inner truth," and since these truths are not grounded in the facticity of the alleged revelation, since the Christian religion is not true because the evangelists and apostles taught it, but they taught it because it is true, these truths retain their validity despite all the objections which historical criticism may bring against the divine origin of the Christian religion. Furthermore, we can now acknowledge the sincerity of Lessing's defense of the Christian religion. These positive assertions do not, as many interpreters have claimed, constitute a "Scheintheologie," or a merely exoteric disguise for a radically anti-Christian attitude, but are on the whole genuine expressions of a philosophical conviction, and it is because of this that we can say of him precisely what he affirmed of Leibniz. He (Lessing) only accepted these truths in their "supportable sense," but he nevertheless sincerely accepted them in this sense. "He struck fire from the flint, but he did not conceal his fire in the flint."

Finally, we can see that it is just this which determines Lessing's unique place within the religious philosophy of the Enlightenment and justifies Karl Aner's claim that he was the first rationalist.[1] From the superior vantage point of the philosophy of history, he stood aloof from all the theological parties of his age. He alone, before Kant and the subsequent German idealists, separated the question of the truth of the Christian religion from the question of the facticity of the Christian revelation, and consequently he alone was able to deny that facticity, and the concept of a transcendent revelation which it implies, without at the same time rejecting the traditional concept of this alleged revelation.

The result, as we have already seen, was a new conception of religious truth and a new understanding of the relation between religion and history. The historical is no longer viewed with neology and orthodoxy as the ground of the validity of religious truth, but rather is seen to provide the occasion for the realization of this truth and the place of its fulfillment. Although religious truth is not verified, it is conditioned by and only becomes manifest in history.[2]

It is this new conception of the relation between religion and history which, in the final analysis, constitutes Lessing's major contribution to the development of religious thought. First, it dealt the final death blow to both the unhistorical, either/or approach to religious truth of the Enlightenment and to the old orthodox doctrine of verbal inspiration. Second, it anticipated many of the teachings of German idealism concerning the historical development of religion and the speculative content of Christian doctrine. This is especially evident in Hegel, who likewise viewed the various religions as stages in the development of the religious consciousness and who, in his *Introduction* to the *Lectures on the Philosophy of Religion,* criticized the "theology of reason" in almost the same terms as Lessing criticized the earlier neological movement, arguing that its characteristic tendency to empty the Christian revelation of all of its traditional content reflects a complete lack of comprehension of the philosophical significance of this content.[3] Third, although the concrete results of Lessing's own religious-historical studies, for example, *New Hypothesis Concerning the Evangelists Regarded as Merely Human Historians,* were negligible, the same conception of the relation between religion and history which inspired these studies, also helped to pave the way for the objective, historical investigation of the Bible and the history of the early Church, which played such a large role in the intellectual life of nineteenth-century Germany. Here Lessing's role was crucial, for it was only after men came to see that the truth of the Christian religion does not depend upon the literal truth of the Biblical accounts of its origin and development that they could approach these accounts in a truly scientific manner. Finally, it must be noted that the sharpness with which Lessing depicted this basic opposition between religious and historical truth has provided the starting point for all subsequent treatments of the subject. Here his influence may be discerned in thinkers as diverse as Fichte, who in the spirit of Lessing as well as Kant proclaimed: "Only the metaphysical, and in no wise the historical, brings salvation,"[4] and Kierkegaard, who through his reading of Lessing was brought to realize the paradoxical nature of Christianity's claim to base an individual's eternal happiness upon a historical event, and Bultmann, whose program of demythologization can perhaps be seen as the logical outcome of Lessing's distinction between the letter and the spirit, the Bible and religion.[5]

Notes

CHAPTER 1

1. Immanuel Kant, *What is Enlightenment*, English translation by Lewis White Beck in *Kant on History* (Indianapolis, 1963), p. 3, edited by L. W. Beck.

2. Ernst Cassirer, *The Philosophy of the Enlightenment*, English translation by F. C. A. Koelln and J. Pettegrove (Boston, 1955), pp. 137–41, and also a similar discussion, in relation to the Cambridge Platonists who in turn exercised a tremendous influence upon the English Enlightenment, in his *The Platonic Renaissance in England*, English translation by J. Pettegrove (Austin, Texas, 1953), Chapters II and IV.

3. This brief delineation of the main feature of Protestant orthodoxy is largely based upon A. C. McGiffert's *Protestant Thought Before Kant*, Harper Torchbook Edition (New York, 1961), Chapter VIII, and Emanuel Hirsch, *Geschichte der neuern evangelischen Theologie* (Gütersloh, 1960), Vol. I, Book I, Chapter 2. I have not discussed Catholic theology in this context because its scholastic orientation and practical effect was substantially similar to Protestantism, and since my major concern is with a discussion of the Enlightenment in Protestant countries—England and Germany—which formed the immediate background of Lessing's thought.

4. Leslie Stephen, *History of English Thought in the Eighteenth Century*, second edition (London, 1881), pp. 77–79. My entire discussion of the relationship between seventeenth-century theology and deism is based upon Stephen's account.

5. John Locke, *Essay Concerning Human Understanding* (New York, 1959), edited by A. C. Fraser, Dover edition, Book IV, Chapter 17, Section 23, p. 412.

6. *Ibid.*, p. 413.

7. *Ibid.*, p. 416.

8. Locke's matter-of-fact manner of considering the accreditation of a doctrine through miracles is aptly illustrated by this passage from the *Discourse*. "For example, Jesus of Nazareth professes himself sent from

God; he with a word calms a tempest at sea. This one looks on as a miracle, and consequently cannot but receive his doctrine." *Works,* ninth edition (London, 1794), Vol. VIII, p. 259.

9. This is essentially a restatement of John Tillotson's argument in terms of the epistemological position developed in the *Essay.* In his famous sermon, "The Trial of the Spirits," *Works* (London, 1751), Vol. II, pp. 29–51, Tillotson maintains, p. 36, that "no argument is sufficient to prove a doctrine or revelation to be from God, which is not clearer and stronger than the difficulties and objections against it, because assent is grounded upon evidence, and the strongest and clearest evidence always carries."

10. Locke, *op. cit.,* pp. 418–19.

11. *Ibid.,* p. 423.

12. *Ibid.*

13. John Locke, "Reasonableness of Christianity as Delivered in the Scriptures," *Works,* Vol. VI, pp. 4-5.

14. *Ibid.,* p. 15.

15. *Ibid.,* p. 17.

16. *Ibid.,* p. 105.

17. Since he does not suggest any possible objections from the orthodox standpoint, Locke must feel that his account is justified in that respect by its scriptural basis.

18. Locke, *op. cit.,* p. 132.

19. *Ibid.,* p. 133.

20. *Ibid.,* p. 135.

21. *Ibid.,* p. 137.

22. *Ibid.,* pp. 142–43.

23. *Ibid.,* p. 148.

24. *Ibid.*

25. *Ibid.,* p. 151.

26. *Ibid.,* p. 145.

27. *Ibid.,* p. 146.

28. Clarke's theological position is developed in his Boyle Lectures of 1704 and 1705, *A Discourse Concerning the Being and Attributes of God,* and *A Discourse Concerning the Unchangeable Obligations of Natural Religion, and the Truth and Certainty of the Christian Revelation.* In Clarke this problem of the necessity and content of revelation is heightened by his confident, a priori demonstration of the basic principles of natural religion and morality. Foster's main work is *The Usefulness, Truth and Excellency of the Christian Revelation* (1731), which constitutes the most consistent statement of the rationalist conception of Christianity. He begins by explicitly accepting the supremacy and universality of natural religion and admits that the chief function of revelation is the restoration of natural religion and that reason is the ultimate standard by which revelation itself must be judged (p. 4). However,

granting this, he nevertheless endeavors to prove that revelation may be "useful in enforcing truth already discoverable by reason" and may lay down some rules for the advancement of virtue. In support of this contention, Foster appeals to everyday experience, showing that although reason is capable of grasping all necessary truths, which may be a supreme guide for life, in fact it has not done so (p. 12). Foster's historical importance lies in the fact that he was one of the main channels through which this theological position was transmitted to Germany.

29. Leslie Stephen, *op. cit.*, p. 125.

30. Samuel Clarke, *A Discourse Concerning the Unchangeable Obligations of Natural Religion, and the Truth and Certainty of the Christian Revelation,* third edition (London, 1711), p. 239.

31. A notable exception to this is David Hume's *Essay on Miracles* (1748), which deals a death blow to the attempt to find evidential value in miracles. Aside from the essay, Hume's religious writings fall outside of the reason-revelation polemic and are not treated in this study. Another significant critical work which deserves mention is Conyers Middleton's *Free Inquiry into the Miraculous Powers Which Are Supposed to Have Subsisted in the Christian Church* (1749). This work attempts to treat the history of the early Church in a strictly naturalistic manner and clearly anticipates Lessing, who may in fact have been influenced by it.

32. Leslie Stephen offers a detailed treatment of the controversy, *op. cit.*, Chapter IV, pp. 186–274.

33. John Toland, *Christianity not Mysterious,* second edition (London, 1702), Preface XXV–XXVI.

34. *Ibid.*, p. 16.

35. See, for instance, p. 12, where he asserts: "So that all our knowledge is in effect, nothing else but the Perception of the Agreement or Disagreement of our Ideas. . . ."

36. Toland, *op. cit.*, p. 26.

37. *Ibid.*, p. 127.

38. *Ibid.*, p. 128.

39. *Ibid.*, p. 38.

40. *Ibid.*, p. 42.

41. *Ibid.*, p. 41.

42. *Ibid.*, p. 89.

43. *Ibid.*, p. 157.

44. This is pointed out by Cassirer, *The Philosophy of the Enlightenment,* p. 232.

45. Clarke is the special object of Tindal's attack.

46. Tindal, *Christianity as Old as the Creation,* edition of 1798, p. 207.

47. *Ibid.*, p. 10.

48. The subtitle of the book is: *The Gospel, a Republication of the Religion of Nature.*

49. Tindal, *op. cit.*, p. 135.

50. *Ibid.*, p. 317.

51. The best example is Voltaire's *Philosophical Dictionary,* where not only the very plan of the work is modeled after Bayle, but many of the articles, such as "Tolerance," "Superstition," and "David" are nothing more than restatements and defenses of Bayle's position.

52. A brief, but excellent study of Bayle's attitude toward superstition in the form of an analysis of his general treatment of paganism, both ancient and modern, is to be found in Frank E. Manuel, *The Eighteenth Century Confronts the Gods* (Cambridge, Mass., 1959), pp. 24–40. Manuel emphasizes Bayle's rejection of the traditional allegorical interpretation of pagan myth and ritual and shows that for Bayle the pagans really believed in the divinities depicted in their myths. Manuel also shows that Bayle accounts for the prevalence of gross superstition by means of a psychological analysis of the pagan mentality, which is by implication relevant to superstition within Christianity.

53. Pierre Bayle, *Pensées diverses à un docteur de Sorbonne à l'occasion de la comète qui parut au mois de decembre 1680,* Section 60, critical edition by A. Prat (Paris, 1939), Vol. I, pp. 158–60.

54. *Ibid.*, Section 114, p. 303, where he states explicitly "that atheism is not as great an evil as idolatry."

55. *Ibid.*, Section 174, Vol. II, pp. 107–14.

56. *Ibid.*, Section 162, pp. 77–78.

57. *Ibid.*, Section 122, Vol. I, p. 320.

58. *Ibid.*, Sections 133, 134, Vol. II, pp. 5–11.

59. *Ibid.*, Section 138, p. 18.

60. *Ibid.*, Section 69: "That the pagans attribute their unhappiness to the negligence of some ceremony or other, and not to their vices," pp. 179–82.

61. Cassirer, *The Philosophy of the Enlightenment,* p. 161.

62. This treatment of Bayle's doctrine of toleration is largely based on Jean Devolve's analysis in his *Essai sur Pierre Bayle, religion critique et philosophie positive* (Paris, 1906), Section III, Chapter V, pp. 121–38. I differ from him, however, in viewing the notion of the reciprocity of compulsion and the right of the erring consciousness as two expressions of the same argument, rather than two distinct arguments based upon the sceptical principle.

63. This theme is developed at length in the *Critique générale de l'histoire du Calvinisme de M. Maimbourg* (1682) and its continuation, *Nouvelles lettres de l'auteur de la critique générale de l'histoire du Calvinisme de M. Maimbourg* (1685).

64. See especially Bayle, *Nouvelle lettres* in *Oeuvres diverses* (The Hague, 1737), Vol. II, p. 219b, where on the basis of the influence of environment in determining belief he attempts to prove that "the understanding is the concierge of the soul," and thereby justifies "the rights of the erring conscience."

65. Bayle, *Critique générale, Oeuvres diverses,* Vol. II, p. 87b.
66. For a discussion of Bayle's understanding and application of the principle see Devolve, *op. cit.,* Part II, Chapter III, pp. 97–111.
67. Bayle, *Commentaire philosophique, Oeuvres diverses,* Vol. II, p. 368a.
68. *Ibid.,* p. 368b.
69. *Ibid.,* p. 371b.
70. *Ibid.,* p. 372.
71. *Ibid.,* p. 374b.
72. Throughout the *Dictionary,* and especially in the famous article on "David," which he was forced to revise in the second edition, Bayle applied this principle to the rather scandalous actions of the Old Testament heroes in order to suggest that their deeds must be judged by the same standards as any one else's and that they cannot be recommended simply because of the stature of the individuals who performed them. In these articles Bayle laid the foundation for the deistic moral critique of the Bible which we have already encountered in Tindal and which was perfected by Voltaire.
73. Bayle, *Commentaire philosophique, Oeuvres diverses,* Vol. II, p. 384b.
74. *Supplement du commentaire philosophique, Oeuvres diverses,* Vol. II, p. 504a.
75. This point is discussed at length by Ludwig Feuerbach in his *Pierre Bayle, eine Beitrag zur Geschichte der Philosophie und Menschheit* (Leipzig, 1848), Vol. 6, *Sämmtliche Werke.* Feuerbach argues, esp. p. 159 ff., that although Bayle's fideism is a direct contradiction of the rationalistic standpoint suggested by the *Commentaire philosophique* and other early works, it is not the product of hypocrisy, but rather is sincerely meant, the result of an inner contradiction in Bayle himself. His sincerity is also defended by Emanuel Hirsch, *op. cit.,* Vol. I, p. 64, who bases his argument upon the personal sacrifices undergone by Bayle for his Protestant faith.
76. My discussion of this article is based heavily upon the essay by Richard H. Popkin, "Pierre Bayle's Place in 17th Century Scepticism" in *Pierre Bayle le philosophe de Rotterdam* (Paris, 1959), a series of studies edited by Paul Dibon, and Howard Robinson's *Bayle the Sceptic,* Chapter 10.
77. Pierre Bayle, *The Dictionary Historical and Critical of Mr. Peter Bayle* (London 1734–38), translated by Mr. Des Maizeaux, 5 volumes, Vol. 4, pp. 653b–54.
78. *Ibid.*
79. *Ibid.*
80. *Ibid.*
81. The analysis of the sceptical implications of modern philosophy is peripheral to Bayle's main argument, which is theological, but because of its great historical significance, it is worthy of mention. If, he argues,

secondary qualities—heat, color, smell—are to be regarded as nothing but modifications of the soul, despite our clear perception of them, why could not the same principle be applied to the alleged primary qualities? Although this position is not developed at any length, it is a clear anticipation of Berkeley, and Hume.

82. Bayle, *op. cit.*, p. 654b.

83. *Ibid.*; Popkin, *op. cit.*, pp. 5–6, shows that this claim went far beyond the scepticism of Sextus Empiricus, Montaigne, Huet, and Gassendi, who challenged the applicability of the principle of evidence, but not the principle itself.

84. *Ibid.*

85. *Ibid.*, p. 655a.

86. *Ibid.*

87. *Ibid.*, pp. 655b–56a.

88. Bayle, *Dictionary*, "Manichees," Vol. IV, pp. 91–94.

89. *Ibid.*, p. 94a–b.

90. *Ibid.*, p. 94b.

91. *Ibid.*

92. *Ibid.*, p. 95a.

93. *Ibid.*

94. *Ibid.*, pp. 95–96.

95. In this connection see Wilhelm Dilthey, who substituting Descartes for Bayle, writes: "As Descartes gave the direction to the French mind, and Locke determined the English, so was Leibniz the leader of our intellectual culture." *Leibniz und sein Zeitalter*, in *Studien zur Geschichte des deutschen Geistes, Gesammelte Schriften* (Stuttgart and Göttingen, 1959), Vol. III, p. 62.

96. This is not to deny that it exerted any influence outside Germany, but only to suggest that its foreign reception was on the whole unfavorable. W. H. Barber in his *Leibniz in France, from Arnauld to Voltaire* (Oxford, 1953) traces the French reaction in detail and shows that due largely to the antimetaphysical attitude of the Philosophes, the reception was, with some significant exceptions, hostile. In England the dominance of empiricism, in addition to the animosity caused by the dispute with Newton, accounts for the negative attitude.

97. The details of this correspondence and of Leibniz's other efforts in this direction are to be found in Jean Baruzi's *Leibniz et l'organisation religieuse de la terre* (Paris, 1907), and his *Leibniz, avec de nombreux textes inédits* (Paris, 1909). In his preface to the latter work Baruzi acknowledges that Leibniz was primarily concerned with the political and diplomatic aspects of unification, but nevertheless argues for the sincerity of his theological views.

98. Leibniz, Gerhardt, *Die philosophischen Schriften*, Vol. IV, p. 292.

99. See for instance: *A New System of the Nature and the Com-*

munication of Substances, Section 10, *The Second Letter to Clarke,* Section 9, *Discourse on Metaphysics,* Section 22.

100. George Friedmann, *Leibniz et Spinoza* (Paris, 1949), esp. p. 99.

101. This is formulated most explicitly in his letter to Christian Philip, January 1680, Gerhardt, Vol. IV, pp. 283–85.

102. Leibniz, Gerhardt, Vol. IV, p. 283.

103. *Ibid.,* p. 284.

104. Leibniz's criticism is here directed specifically to Descartes' statement in the Reply to the Sixth Set of Objections, Note 8, where he asserts: "To one who pays attention to God's immensity, it is clear that nothing at all can exist which does not depend on Him. This is true not only of everything that subsists, but of all order, of every law, and of every reason of truth and goodness; for otherwise God, as has been said just before, would not have been wholly indifferent to the creation of what he has created." *Philosophical Works of Descartes,* translated by E. S. Haldane and G. R. T. Ross (New York, 1955), Vol. II, p. 250.

105. Leibniz, Gerhardt, *op. cit.,* p. 285.

106. Leibniz, *The Principles of Nature and of Grace, Based on Reason,* Section 15, English translation by Leroy E. Loemker, in *Gottfried Wilhelm Leibniz, Philosophical Papers and Letters* (Chicago, 1956), Vol. II, p. 1041; Erdmann, p. 717b.

107. Fragment of a letter to Phillipe Naud, from J. Baruzi, *Leibniz avec de nombreux textes inédits,* p. 265.

108. Leibniz, Gerhardt, *op. cit.,* p. 300.

109. Leibniz, *Theodicy, Essays on the Goodness of God the Freedom of Man and the Origin of Evil,* English translation by E. M. Huggard (London, 1951), p. 51; Erdmann, p. 469b.

110. *Ibid.,* pp. 51–52; Erdmann, p. 469b.

111. Wilhelm Windelband, *A History of Philosophy,* English translation by James H. Tuft, Harper Torchbooks (New York, 1958), Vol. II, p. 506.

112. Leibniz, *op. cit.,* Part I, Section 6, p. 127; Erdmann, p. 505b.

113. *Ibid.,* Section 1, p. 123; Erdmann, p. 504a.

114. *Ibid.,* Section 8, p. 128; Erdmann, p. 506a.

115. *Ibid.,* Section 10, p. 129; Erdmann, p. 507a.

116. *Ibid.,* Section 20, p. 135; Erdmann, p. 510a.

117. *Ibid.*

118. Bayle, *Oeuvres diverses,* Vol. IV, pp. 796–98.

119. Leibniz, *op. cit.,* p. 197–98; Erdmann, p. 539b.

120. His relationship to Locke at this point can be seen from the relevant passage in the *New Essays,* Book IV, Chapters XVI–XIX. It is noteworthy that there is more of a basic agreement between these two men on this issue than on almost any other.

121. Leibniz, *Preliminary Dissertation*, Section 29, p. 91; Erdmann, p. 488a.

122. Werner Conze, *Leibniz als Historiker* (Berlin, 1951), esp. pp. 62–63.

123. See Leibniz's letter to Huet, Gerhardt, Vol. III, p. 12, where he argues that the primary purpose of studying history is to prove the truth of Christianity.

124. Leibniz, *op. cit.*, Sections 1–2, pp. 73–74; Erdmann, pp. 479–80.

125. *Ibid.*, Section 3, p. 75; Erdmann, p. 480a.

126. *Ibid.*; Erdmann, p. 480b.

127. *Ibid.*, Section 23, p. 88; Erdmann, p. 491a.

128. In this regard Leibniz's correspondence with Des Bosses, where he attempts to formulate a philosophic explanation of the possibility of the Catholic conception of the Eucharist is particularly noteworthy, since it led to a new attempt to delineate the nature of matter in terms of the principle of his philosophy. See especially letter of Feb. 5, 1712; Gerhardt, Vol. II, pp. 435–37.

129. Leibniz, *op. cit.*, Part I, Section 74, p. 162; Erdmann, p. 522b.

130. This judgment of the historical significance of Wolff's thought was made by Hermann Hettner, *Geschichte der deutschen Literatur im achtzehnten Jahrhundert* (Berlin, 1961), Vol. I, p. 163.

131. This point is particularly emphasized by Walther Arnsperger in his *Christian Wolffs Verhältnis zu Leibniz* (Weimar, 1887). Arnsperger starts from Wolff's express declaration in the foreword to his translation of the Leibniz–Clarke correspondence, that he had no special philosophic relation with Leibniz, had never conferred with him concerning philosophical affairs, and had no greater knowledge of his thought than was derivable from his few published works. Moreover, Leibniz himself said precisely the same thing in his letter to Remond, July 1714.

132. A clear statement of Wolff's mechanical world view can be found in his *Vernunfftige Gedanken von Gott, der Welt und der Seele des Menschen; auch allen Dingen überhaupt, der Liebhabern der Wahrheit mitgetheilet* (referred to as *V.G. v G.*), eighth edition (Halle, 1741), Section 557, pp. 336–37. Here Wolff defines the world as a machine, or composite thing, the changes of which are grounded in the mode of combination of its parts.

133. In *V.G. v G.*, anderer Theil, fourth edition (1740), Section 251, p. 416, Wolff presents a detailed account of his reasons for rejection of the Leibnizean concept of the monad. My account is here based largely on Paul August Heilemann, *Die Gotteslehre des Christian Wolff* (Leipzig, 1907), p. 47.

134. Wolff, *V.G. v G.*, Sections 928–38.

135. *Ibid.*, Section 975, pp. 601–2.

136. *Ibid.*, Section 988, p. 610.

137. I am here following Harry Levey's *Die Religionsphilosophie Christian Wolffs* (Regensburg, 1928), p. 80 ff., and similar views as expressed by B. Pünjer in his *History of the Philosophy of Religion* (Edinburg, 1887), translated by W. Harte, p. 523.

138. This is discussed in some detail by E. Hirsch in his *Geschichte der neuern evangelischen Theologie*, Vol. II, p. 76 ff.

139. Heinz Liebing, *Zwischen Orthodoxie und Aufklärung* (Tübingen, 1961), a study of the philosophy and theology of Georg Bernhard Bilfinger, a prominent member of this school, shows (pp. 108–9) how Bilfinger applied this principle in his scriptural justification of his concept of reason, which apparently was contradicted by Second Corinthians: 10.4. This was accomplished by a fairly subtle exegesis, which showed that Paul was here condemning the misuse of reason, but not reason itself. It is, however, not the details of the argument, but the fact that this school felt it necessary to find scriptural justification for their philosophic principles, which is of interest here.

140. Wolff, *V.G. v G.*, Section 993, p. 613.

141. Translated from the quotation in Hettner, *op. cit.*, pp. 196–97.

142. The relationship between Leibniz and Wolff on this point is expressed by Hettner, *op. cit.*, p. 170.

143. Wolff, *V.G. v G.*, Section 1018, p. 628.

144. *Ibid.*, p. 623.

145. My account is based upon *V.G. v G.*, Sections 1010–19, pp. 622–29. A substantially similar list is found in *Theologia Naturalis*, Vol. I, Section 451 ff. Levey, *op. cit.*, p. 86 ff., presents an analysis based upon both works.

146. Wolff, *V.G. v G.*, Section 1011, p. 624.

147. *Ibid.*, Section 1014, p. 625.

148. *Ibid.*, Section 1015, p. 627.

149. *Ibid.*, Section 1016, p. 627.

150. *Ibid.*, Section 1018, p. 628.

151. *Ibid.*, Section 1019, p. 629.

152. My discussion of neology is based primarily upon Karl Aner's comprehensive study of the entire movement in his *Die Theologie der Lessingzeit* (Halle, 1927), esp. Chapter III, "Der Übergang vom Wolffianismus zur Neologie."

153. Aner, *op. cit.*, pp. 146–48.

154. Thus argues Aner, *ibid.*, p. 155.

155. See E. Hirsch, *op. cit.*, Vol. IV, p. 25 ff. Hirsch points to the new use of the conception of fundamentals, especially in connection with Spalding, whose *Die Bestimmung des Menschen* (1748) was one of the most popular expressions of this humanistic tendency, and which laid the foundations for the "Humanitätsreligion" of Herder, Goethe, and Schiller. The extent of Spalding's influence is also suggested by Fichte's borrowing of his title for the popular expression of his own philosophy.

156. This discussion is based upon Aner, *op. cit.*, pp. 180–95, where Jerusalem's concept of revelation is treated as the prototype of the whole neological movement.

157. J. F. W. Jerusalem, *Nachgelassene Schriften* (Braunschwig, 1792), Erster Theil, p. 433.

158. Johann August Eberhard, *Neue Apologie des Sokrates oder Untersuchung der Lehre von der Seligkeit der Heiden* (Berlin, 1772), p. 62.

159. This emphasis is perhaps due to the fact that the book was occasioned and explicitly directed to the formal condemnation (1768) by the Sorbonne, and the orthodox Protestant attacks upon Marmontel's *Belisaire* (1767), wherein the hope was expressed that the noble heathen, especially Socrates, may find a place in the Christian heaven.

160. Eberhard, *op. cit.*, p. 211.

161. The general theme of the limitations and degree of truth in the heathen concepts of God is discussed at great length, pp. 196–244.

162. *Ibid.*, p. 250.

163. *Ibid.*, p. 252.

164. *Ibid.*, p. 299 ff.

165. *Ibid.*, p. 310. This follows, for Augustine, from the fact that the noble actions of the heathens do not flow from the true love of God.

166. *Ibid.*, pp. 364–65.

167. Eberhard, *op. cit.*, pp. 373–74.

168. *Ibid.*, pp. 395–96.

169. In this connection, Eberhard, *ibid.*, pp. 415–16, refers to Leibniz's letter to Bourguet of August 5, 1715 (Gerhardt, Vol. III, pp. 580–83), where the conception of the perfection of the world is shown to be understandable either as a static quality or as infinitely increasing. He claims that the latter is Leibniz's true opinion, and it is in relation to this that he justifies, against Leibniz, finite punishments in relation to the perfection of the world.

170. Eberhard, *op. cit.*, pp. 404–45.

171. For a discussion of the relation between Reimarus, Leibniz, and Wolff, see O. Pfleiderer, *The Philosophy of Religion on the Basis of Its History*, translated from the second German edition by Alexander Stewart and Allan Menzies (London, 1886), Vol. I, p. 102; and J. Engert, *Der Deismus in der Religions-und Offenbarungs Kritik des Hermann Samuel Reimarus* (Vienna, 1916).

172. D. F. Strauss, *Hermann Samuel Reimarus, und seine Schutzschrift für die vernunftigen Verehrer Gottes* (1862), *Werke* (1887), Vol. V, pp. 229–408. Strauss prefaced this study to his own edition of selections from the complete text, and it has served as the foundation for all subsequent studies of Reimarus' religious thought, including Engert's.

173. Strauss, *op. cit.*, p. 253.

174. *Ibid.*

175. *Ibid.,* p. 264. It is interesting that the opposition between the views of Reimarus and neology are readily apparent at this point. Both are offended by this conception, but whereas neology endeavors to show that it is unscriptural, and thus unChristian, Reimarus sees it as an integral part of Christian doctrine and consequently rejects this doctrine in its entirety.

176. *Ibid.,* p. 254. Reimarus is here following in the footsteps of Bayle and Tindal.

177. Gotthold Ephraim Lessing's *Gesammelte Werke,* edited by Paul Rilla (Berlin, 1956), Vol. VII, p. 674.

   178. Lessing, *op. cit.,* p. 684.
   179. *Ibid.,* pp. 687–88.
   180. *Ibid.,* p. 689.
   181. *Ibid.,* p. 691.
   182. *Ibid.,* pp. 692–93.
   183. *Ibid.,* pp. 693–98.
   184. *Ibid.,* pp. 698–702.
   185. *Ibid.,* pp. 702–8.
186. Reimarus is here largely reiterating the argument of Anthony Collins' *A Discourse of Freethinking, Occasion'd by the Rise and Growth of a Sect Call'd Freethinkers,* see esp. pp. 10–12 of the first edition.

   187. Lessing, *op. cit.,* p. 734.
188. A typical example is Reimarus' analysis of the Hebrew term "Ruach," p. 754, which he shows, directly following Spinoza, originally meant merely wind or breath, and not spirit. See *Theologico, Political Treatise,* Chapter I, "Of Prophecy," English translation by R. H. M. Elwes, from *The Chief Works* (New York, 1951), Vol. I, p. 19.

   189. Lessing, *op. cit.,* p. 795.
   190. *Ibid.,* Vol. VIII, p. 263.
   191. *Ibid.,* p. 305.
   192. *Ibid.,* p. 307.
   193. *Ibid.,* p. 309.

CHAPTER 2

1. Thus, commenting on the significance of Bayle's *Dictionary* for Lessing, T. W. Danzel, his first great biographer, wrote: "This book was one of the chief sources of Lessing's education, and perhaps no other person contributed as much to the particular form of his spiritual development as Bayle." *Gotthold Ephraim Lessing, sein Leben und sein Werke* (Leipzig, 1850), p. 220.

2. Lessing, Letter to Father, May 30, 1749, *Gotthold Ephraim Lessing's Gesammelte Werke,* edited by Paul Rilla (Berlin, 1956), Vol. IX, p. 22.

3. This fragment is generally dated somewhere between 1750 and

1755. It was first published by Lessing's brother Karl in his edition of Gotthold's *Theologischen Nachlass* (Berlin, 1784).

4. A typical attack was made by D. Carl Gottlob Hoffmann in his *Dritte und letzte gegründete Anzeige derer Herrenhutischen Grund- Irrtümer in der Lehre von der H. Schrift, Rechtfortigung, Sakramenten und letzten Dingen* (Wittenberg, 1751). This work was reviewed by Lessing in the thirty-fifth issue of the *Berlinische Privilegierte Zeitung*, March 23, 1751, where he condemns the work as a prime example of orthodox bigotry, which convicts people of a crime of the will, whose only fault is weakness of the understanding. This frank admission, however, of the intellectual weakness of the Moravians is significant and enables us to place his praise of this group in the fragment under discussion in its proper perspective. This review is published by Rilla, Vol. III, pp. 47-49.

5. Lessing, *op. cit.*, Vol. VII, p. 186.

6. *Ibid.*

7. *Ibid.*, p. 188.

8. *Ibid.*, pp. 188-89.

9. *Ibid.*, p. 189.

10. This judgment is expressed in regard to Lessing's total production at this time by Gottfried Fittbogen in his *Die Religion Lessings* (Leipzig, 1923), p. 69.

11. Lessing, *op. cit.*, p. 190.

12. *Ibid.*, p. 191.

13. *Ibid.*, pp. 192-93.

14. *Ibid.*, p. 197.

15. This was expressed in his review of Hoffmann's critique, see note 4.

16. This work was composed during Lessing's stay at Wittenberg (1752) and published, with several other "Vindications" of similar tenor, in the third part of his *Schriften* (1754).

17. Lessing admits as much when he asserts: "This can be regarded as a good addition to the article which Bayle devoted to this scholar in his Critical Dictionary." Lessing, *op. cit.*, p. 202.

18. *Ibid.*, pp. 201-2.

19. "Igtur his arbitrio victoriae relictis" is the particular passage in question. Lessing, *op. cit.*, p. 203.

20. *Ibid.*, pp. 203-5.

21. *Ibid.*, p. 207.

22. *Ibid.*, pp. 208-9.

23. *Ibid.*, pp. 209-11.

24. *Ibid.*, p. 211.

25. *Ibid.*, pp. 211-12.

26. *Ibid.*, p. 312.

27. *Ibid.*, p. 212.

28. *Ibid.*, p. 213.
29. *Ibid.*, p. 217.
30. *Ibid.*, pp. 219–20.
31. *Ibid.*, p. 220.
32. *Ibid.*

33. The fragment is generally dated either 1752 or 1753, in any event, before the advent of his friendship with Mendelssohn. It was first published by Karl Lessing in his edition of his brother's *Theologischen Nachlass* (1784).

34. For scholars such as Gideon Spicker, *Lessings Weltanschauung* (Leipzig, 1883), and Hans Leisegang, *Lessings Weltanschauung* (Leipzig, 1931), who endeavor to place Lessing's thought within a rigid philosophical framework, this fragment tends to assume great importance as the first systematic formulation of his metaphysics and as a key to the understanding of his later works. Thus, Spicker, for whom Lessing was "the greatest thinker between Leibniz and Kant" (p. 11), can say of this work: "Lessing's chief thoughts are in truth contained in these few paragraphs, and he never really progressed beyond the basic position outlined therein" (p. 7). Similarly, Leisegang views the work as "an entire Christian metaphysic in a nutshell" (p. 58). Others, however, such as Carl Hebler, *Lessing Studien* (Bern, 1862), who treat Lessing primarily as an "occasional thinker," dismiss the fragment as a youthful exercise of wit (p. 26). The debate concerning the sources centers largely around the question of the influence of Giordano Bruno's *Spaccio de la bestia trionfante*. This was affirmed by Otto Nieten, *Lessings religions- philosophische Ansichten bis zum Jahre 1770 in ihrem historischen Zusammenhang und in ihrem historischen Beziehungen* (Duisberg, 1896), pp. 31–36, and by Eric Schmidt, *Lessing, Geschichte seines Lebens und seines Schriften*, second edition (Berlin, 1899), Vol. II, p. 463, and pp. 511–12. This view, which was generally popular in the nineteenth century, was rather convincingly refuted by Eckhart Jacobi, *Lessings Weltanschauung* (Berlin, 1932), p. 30. Among twentieth-century scholars the Leibniz-Wolffian roots of the fragment are generally acknowledged, and there seems to be a universal agreement in the rejection of any Spinozistic influence at this date.

35. Aristotle *Metaphysics* XII, p. 1074b.
36. Spicker, *op. cit.*, pp. 13–14 to the contrary.
37. Lessing, *op. cit.*, Vol. VII, p. 197, English translation from *Lessing's Theological Writings*, translated by Henry Chadwick (Stanford, 1957), p. 99 (henceforth referred to as Chadwick).
38. In addition to the *Theodicy*, and the works of Wolff, which he studied at the University of Leipzig, Lessing was at this time probably also acquainted with *The Principles of Nature and of Grace* and with the *Monadology*, which was then known only in German and Latin translations.

39. Lessing, *op. cit.*, Vol. VII, p. 199; Chadwick, p. 100.

40. Cf. Leibniz, *Theodicy*, Section 218.

41. Such a reconciliation may be constructed on the basis of Pfleiderer's interpretation of Leibniz's concept of God in his *The Philosophy of Religion on the Basis of Its History*, Vol. I, pp. 77–78, where he argues that since the will is always determined by the understanding, in the case of a being with a perfect understanding which infallibly recognizes from eternity what is right, that it becomes meaningless to speak of choice, and hence of freedom. Thus, according to Pfleiderer, the essential aspect for Leibniz in his polemic with Descartes and Spinoza, is not really the freedom, for ultimately the Leibnizean system is completely deterministic, but rather the rationality of the creative act, and this rationality implies an objective standard, binding upon God and man alike, in terms of which the act may be judged. Moreover, this interpretation of the Leibnizean concept of God and doctrine of creation, which might possibly have been Lessing's, appears much more plausible in the light of Leibniz's more technical treatments of the subject, esp. *De rerum originatione radicali* (1697), wherein God is considered as the supreme mathematician, and creation as the solution of a maximum-minimum problem. Although Lessing was of course not familiar with this work, nor at that time, with any of Leibniz's more technical writings, I believe that he was already aware of the popular or exoteric character of the language of the *Theodicy* and consequently attempted to grasp its deeper meaning. This, however, can only be established by a complete analysis of Lessing's relationship to Leibniz, which I undertake in the course of this study.

42. Lessing, *op. cit.*, Vol. VII, p. 199, Chadwick, p. 100.

43. *Ibid.*, p. 200; Chadwick, p. 101.

44. Chr. Schrempf, *Lessing als Philosoph* (Stuttgart, 1906), pp. 34–35, suggests that the next topic with which Lessing intended to deal was the problem of evil, but that the work remained incomplete because the identity of will, thought, and creation in God renders the notion of alienation meaningless, and that since the most obscure consciousness of one's perfections still remains a consciousness thereof, which as such should lead to happiness, it is hard to find a place for suffering in this scheme.

45. The two men are generally reputed to have first become acquainted in either 1753 or 1754, through the efforts of a mutual friend, Issac Hess. The earlier date is suggested, but not insisted upon by Eric Schmidt, *op. cit.*, Vol. I, p. 256, and the later by H. Graetz in his *Popular History of the Jews*, English translation by Rabbi A. B. Rhine, fifth edition (New York, 1935), Vol. 5, p. 299. The determination of the precise date of their friendship is of some importance in connection with the question of possible mutual influence between Lessing's *The Christianity of Reason* and Mendelssohn's *Philosophical Conversations*.

46. Maupertuis, the head of the Academy, was a bitter antagonist of the Leibnizean philosophy. For a discussion of the history of this affair, see W. H. Barber, *Leibniz in France*, pp. 44–47.

47. The review was published in the *Berlinische privilegierte Zeitung*, March 1, 1755. It is contained in Rilla, Vol. III, pp. 142–44.

48. This is treated in the first "Conversation," *Moses Mendelssohn's gesammelte Schriften*, edited by G. B. Mendelssohn (Leipzig, 1843), Vol. I, pp. 191–202.

49. This is the subject of the second "Conversation," *Ibid.*, pp. 203–33.

50. Fritz Bamberger, in his Introduction to *Moses Mendelssohn's gesammelte Schriften* (Berlin, 1931), Vol. I, pp. xx–xxiii, traces the history of this argument and shows that it was first applied to Wolff by the Halle Pietists in order to suggest the dangerous, that is, Spinozistic implications of Wolff's philosophy.

51. It is very interesting that in his *Morgenstunden* (1785) Mendelssohn reiterates this conception of a "purified pantheism" which is reconcilable with morality and religion (Lecture XIV), and later (Lecture XV) interprets Lessing's thought in this light in order to defend his departed friend against Jacobi's charge that he had been a Spinozist. See *Moses Mendelssohn's gesammelte Schriften*, Vol. II, pp. 350–72. For Mendelssohn at least, Lessing's ultimate philosophical position entailed such a synthesis of Leibnizean and Spinozistic motifs.

52. See especially Lessing's letter to Mendelssohn of February 2, 1757, Lessing, *op. cit.*, Vol. IX, pp. 104–8, where Lessing specifically discusses the problem of feeling in relation to tragedy.

53. Lessing, *op. cit.*, Vol. IV, p. 105.

54. *Ibid.*, p. 243.

55. *Ibid.*, p. 244.

56. *Ibid.*, p. 247.

57. *Ibid.*, pp. 247–48.

58. *Ibid.*, p. 248.

59. *Ibid.*, pp. 248–49.

60. *Ibid.*, p. 250.

61. The question of Lessing's view of the relationship between morality and religion in his critique of Cramer is treated at length by Chr. Schrempf in his *Lessing als Philosoph* (Stuttgart, 1906), pp. 170–86, where he criticized E. Zeller and others who believed that Lessing identified them, and was thus a forerunner of Kant. Schrempf realizes that such an interpretation seems plausible in light of certain assertions of Lessing, especially in *Thoughts on the Moravians*, but argues instead that morality, for Lessing, is the foundation of all religion. It is the universally human realm, which unites all those who are divided by the speculative search after truth.

62. Lessing, *op. cit.*, Vol. VIII, p. 228.

63. Letter to Ramler, August 5, 1764; Lessing, *op. cit.*, Vol. IX, p. 235.

64. Quoted by Eric Schmidt, *op. cit.*, Vol. I, p. 455.

65. Letter to Michaelis, October 16, 1754; Lessing, *op. cit.*, Vol. IX, p. 49.

66. Lessing, *Pope ein Metaphysiker*; Lessing, *op. cit.*, Vol. VII, pp. 261–62.

67. Letter to Mendelssohn, April 17, 1763; Lessing, *op. cit.*, Vol. IX, p. 221.

68. Lessing, *op. cit.*, Vol. VII, pp. 307–8. This passage is especially significant as a barometer of Lessing's development, for in *The Christianity of Reason*, Section 9, he posited just such a harmony of the thing with itself as the speculative meaning of the Christian doctrine of the Holy Spirit.

69. It is interesting to note that although Lessing seems to have arrived at an essentially accurate understanding of Spinoza's position, he nevertheless still interpreted the Leibnizean doctrine of harmony in the narrow, Wolffian sense, wherein it is limited to the mind body relationship.

70. Lessing, *op. cit.*, Vol. VII, p. 308.

71. *Ibid.*, p. 309.

72. According to Gideon Spicker, *op. cit.*, p. 165 ff., this fragment was induced by Mendelssohn's Preisschrift, *Über die Evidenz in metaphysischen Wissenschaften* (1763), in which he argued that mathematics provides the knowledge of the possible, and metaphysics the knowledge of the real.

73. See A. Michaelis, *Der ontologische Sinn des Complementum Possibilitas bei Christian Wolff* (Berlin, 1937), p. 26.

74. Eric Schmidt, *op. cit.*, Vol. II, p. 511.

75. Lessing, *op. cit.*, Vol. VII, p. 305; Chadwick, p. 102.

76. *Ibid.*

77. This general line of criticism was formulated by Michaelis, *op. cit.*, p. 41 ff. who, however, makes no mention of Lessing in this context.

78. Christian Wolff, *op. cit.*, Section 14.

79. I. Kant, *Critique of Pure Reason*, B284, English translation by N. K. Smith, Macmillan & Co. (London, 1958), p. 250.

80. Lessing, *op. cit.*, p. 306; Chadwick, p. 103.

81. Spinoza, *Ethics*, Part I, Prop. XXV, Corrolary, Elwes, *op. cit.*, Vol. II, p. 66: "Individual things are nothing but modifications of the attributes of God, or modes by which the attributes of God are expressed in a fixed and definite manner."

82. See, for instance, the vigorous defense of its authenticity in Th. C. von Stockum, *Spinoza-Jacobi-Lessing, Beitrag zur Geschichte der deutschen Literatur und Philosophie des 18. Jahrhundert* (Groningen, 1916), p. 40.

83. Stockum, *op. cit.*, p. 31; see also F. H. Jacobi, *Werke* (Leipzig, 1819), Vol. IV, Part I, p. 55.

84. Jacobi, *op. cit.*, p. 70.

85. *Ibid.*, p. 59.

86. *Ibid.*, pp. 50–51.

87. *Ibid.*, p. 54.

88. *Ibid.*

89. *Ibid.*, p. 55.

90. *Ibid.*, p. 90.

91. *Ibid.*, p. 63. Although the same thesis has been seriously maintained, for example by Stein and Russell, Lessing's remark is here clearly meant in jest. This is evident from the fact that he supports it by reference to Leibniz's undated letter to Bourguet (Gerhardt, Vol. III, pp. 588–91), where Leibniz defends the possibility of conceiving of the world as perpetually retaining the same degree of perfection. Against Bourguet's objection that finite beings can only stand in a limited number of relationships at one time and, consequently, cannot receive all of their perfections simultaneously, Leibniz contends that there could never be any increase of perfection in one aspect of the universe, without a corresponding diminution in another aspect. On the basis of this passage, Lessing makes (p. 64) the utterly fantastic statement that Leibniz claimed that God is in a state of perpetual expansion and contraction and that this process results in the creation and conservation of the best of all possible worlds. However, Lessing soon withdrew this claim (pp. 64–65) in the face of Jacobi's objections. For Jacobi's subsequent reflections on this point, see *Beylagen zu den Briefen über die Lehre des Spinoza, Works*, Vol. IV, Part 2, pp. 42–44.

92. Jacobi, *op. cit.*, p. 65.

93. *Ibid.*, p. 68.

94. Such an assertion may be compared with Spinoza's letter to Oldenburg, Epistle LXXIII, English translation, Elwes, *op. cit.*, Vol. II, p. 298, where Spinoza asserts: ". . . my opinion concerning God differs widely from that which is ordinarily defended by modern Christians. For I hold that God is of all things the cause immanent, as the phrase is, not transcendent. I say that all things are in God and move in God, thus agreeing with Paul, and perhaps with all the ancient philosophers, though the phraseology may be different. . . ."

95. Jacobi, *op. cit.*, p. 61.

96. *Ibid.*, pp. 75–79.

97. Unless, of course, one interprets the notion of the world soul as an effect, in light of his conception of the Son of God as the identical image which results from the Divine creative self-contemplation. There is, however, no indication that this was Lessing's intent in this passage.

98. Highly significant in this regard is W. Dilthey's mention of the report of Klose to the effect that Lessing's interpretation of Spinoza was very much influenced by the work of J. K. Dippel, who in his *Fatum*

fatuum (1701) took issue precisely with this aspect of Spinoza's thought. See *Das Erlebnis und die Dichtung,* thirteenth edition (Stuttgart, 1957), p. 101.

99. Jacobi, *op. cit.,* p. 61.

100. *Ibid.,* p. 62. Both here and in the statement concerning the nature of God, Lessing is obviously referring to Spinoza's critique of final causes in the appendix to Part I of the *Ethics,* Elwes, *op. cit.,* Vol. I, p. 25, where he states: "All such opinions spring from the notion commonly entertained that all things in nature act as men themselves act, namely with an end in view. It is accepted as certain that God himself directs all things to a definite goal (for it is said that God made all things for man, and man that he might worship him)."

101. *Ibid.,* pp. 70–71.

102. We have already encountered such indications in *The Christianity of Reason,* but expressions of a deterministic view point are scattered throughout Lessing's early writings. Cf. the poem *Die Religion,* Lessing, *op. cit.,* Vol. I, p. 207.

103. Lessing's views in this regard are suggested by Jacobi's footnote (pp. 56–57), in which he states that Lessing following Leibniz (*Theodicy* Section 173) in finding the most obscure portion of Spinoza's thought to lie in his advocacy of a blind or geometrical necessity, and his treatment of the will and intellect of God. As we have already seen, the Leibnizean doctrine of providence is formulated explicitly in refutation of these views, and Lessing's agreement on this point is the one concrete indication in the conversation of his true view in this regard.

104. Lessing, *op. cit.,* Vol. VII, pp. 282–300. Generally dated either 1763 or 1764, it was first published by Karl Lessing in his brother's *Theologischen Nachlass* (1784).

105. Lessing's objective approach, which he shares with Spinoza, separates him from other similarly antisupernatural interpretations of the origin and development of the Christian religion, such as offered by Reimarus and the other deists, who with their unhistorical approach and vindictive attacks, are anything but objective. In distinction from these as well as from the orthodox, Lessing proposes to consider the problem purely in historical terms. Aside from Spinoza, Lessing's other great predecessor in this direction was Bayle.

106. Lessing, *op. cit.,* Vol. VII, p. 283. This passage implies the extension of Spinoza's principle of Biblical exegesis to the field of Church history. In this regard, see especially *Theologico-Political Treatise,* Chapter VII, English translation by Elwes, *op. cit.,* Vol. I, pp. 99–100, where Spinoza states: "I may sum up the matter by saying that the method of interpreting Scripture does not differ from the method of interpreting nature—in fact, it is almost the same. For as the interpretation of nature consists in the examination of the history of nature, and therefrom deducing definitions of natural phenomena on certain fixed axioms, so

Scriptural interpretation proceeds by the examination of Scripture, and inferring the intention of its authors as a legitimate conclusion from its fundamental principles. By working in this manner everyone will always advance without danger of error—that is, if they admit no principles for interpreting Scripture, and discussing its content save such as they find in Scripture itself—and will be able with equal security to discuss what surpasses our understanding, and what is known by the natural light of reason."

107. Lessing, *op. cit.*, Vol. VII, p. 282.

108. *Ibid.*, pp. 282–85.

109. *Ibid.*, pp. 285–87.

110. *Ibid.*, p. 287.

111. *Ibid.*, pp. 291–99.

112. *Ibid.*, p. 299.

113. *Ibid.*, pp. 280–81. This work was also published by Karl Lessing in his brother's *Theologischen Nachlass* (1784). Its date of composition is disputed, but it is generally placed somewhere between 1760–65, during the Breslau period.

114. Lessing, Chadwick, *op. cit.*, p. 104.

115. It should be kept in mind that at this time Lessing was not yet familiar with the work of Reimarus, which was, of course, unknown, except to his immediate family and close friends. Tindal, however, was a highly probable influence upon Lessing at this time.

116. Lessing, Chadwick, *op. cit.*, p. 104. Here Tindal's influence is quite apparent especially in regard to the parallelism between natural and positive religion and natural and positive law, for in a similar context Tindal asserts: "And in truth all laws, whether the law of nature, or those of particular countries, are only the laws of nature adjusted, and accommodated to circumstances." *Christianity as Old as the Creation,* p. 58.

117. Lessing, Chadwick, *op. cit.*, pp. 104–5.

118. *Ibid.*, p. 105.

119. See esp. Chapter XV, *op. cit.*, Vol. I, p. 190.

CHAPTER 3

1. Lessing, Letter to Moses Mendelssohn, Wolfenbüttel, January 9, 1777, Lessing, *op. cit.*, Vol. IX, p. 406.

2. A detailed discussion of the various interpretations of this passage is provided by Father Edward S. Flajole, S.J. in his monograph, *Lessing's Retrieval of Lost Truths*, "Publications of the Modern Language Association of America" (March 1959), Vol. XXIV, No. 1, p. 52 ff. Father Flajole here shows that the disagreement extends not only to the question of the nature of the truths which Lessing alleges to see "from afar" in Ferguson, but also to the purely factual question as to

which of Ferguson's works, *An Essay on the History of Civil Society* (1767) or *Institutes of Moral Philosophy* (1769), Lessing is here referring. In my opinion, however, the attempt which is made by Father Flajole, pp. 65–66, and several other scholars, esp. K. Aner, *op. cit.*, p. 351 ff., to show that Ferguson was a decisive influence upon Lessing's thought is completely futile. Both Father Flajole and Aner argue in this connection that the key to Lessing's positive appreciation of Christianity lies in his appropriation of Ferguson's concept of historical development. They believe that the latter's "perfectionism" furnished the means whereby Lessing was able to reconcile his monistic philosophy, which precluded the acceptance of the traditional concept of revelation, with a sincere adherence to some of the main principles of Christian thought. No one who has read *The Education of the Human Race* would deny that the notion of historical development plays a central role in Lessing's understanding of religion. However, his use of this notion is, as we shall see, grounded in his study of Leibniz. Thus, it seems manifestly absurd to trace the roots of Lessing's thought on this subject solely to his acquaintance with a relatively superficial thinker, whom he never again mentions. Moreover, it has also been suggested more than once that Ferguson's concept of historical development or perfectionism, is itself the product of Leibnizean influence. Windelband, *op. cit.*, Vol. II, p. 510; W. C. Lehman, *Adam Ferguson and the Beginnings of Modern Sociology* (New York, 1930), p. 194. Thus, rather than a decisive influence, we can see in Ferguson, at most, a thinker who called Lessing's attention to a train of thought to which he had not hitherto paid sufficient attention, the subsequent development of which takes place under the influence of Leibniz.

3. This is the view of Father Flajole, *op. cit.*, p. 53, and of the majority of scholars. Some, however, such as Leisegang, *op. cit.*, p. 114 ff., think that Lessing is referring primarily to metaphysical principles.

4. Father Flajole, *op. cit.*, p. 53 ff.

5. This whole treatment of Lessing's relation to neology is greatly indebted to Karl Aner's *Die Theologie der Lessingszeit* and to the monographs of Father Flajole, both the aforementioned one, and an earlier article, *Lessing's Attitude in the Lavater-Mendelssohn Controversy*, "Publications of the Modern Language Association of America," Vol. XXIII, No. 3, pp. 201–14.

6. Letter to Karl, February 2, 1774, Lessing, *op. cit.*, Vol. IX, pp. 596–97.

7. A large part of Ferguson's *Essay on the History of Civil Society* is devoted to an explicit refutation of Rousseau's primitivism, with its sharp distinction between natural and artificial. This critique of primitivism may well have helped Lessing transcend his own primitivistic position in *On the Origin of Revealed Religion*. Such an influence is suggested by the following passage from Ferguson: "If we are told,

that vice, at least, is contrary to nature; we may answer, It is worse; it is folly and wretchedness. But if nature is only opposed to art, in what situation of the human race are the footsteps of art unknown? In the condition of the savage, as well as that of the citizen are many proofs of human invention; and in either is not in any permanent station, but a mere stage through which the travelling being is destined to pass. If the palace be unnatural, the cottage is no less; and the highest refinements of political and moral apprehension, are not more artificial in their kind, then the first operations of sentiment and reason," fourth edition (London, 1773), p. 13.

8. Rilla, Vol. VII, p. 324.

9. Letter to Karl, March 20, 1777; Lessing, *op. cit.*, Vol. IX, p. 729.

10. Lessing, *op. cit.*, Vol. VII, p. 454.

11. *Ibid.*, pp. 459–60.

12. *Ibid.*, p. 466.

13. *Ibid.* Compare with Leibniz, *New Essays Concerning Human Understanding*, English translation by A. C. Langley, third edition (LaSalle, Ill., 1949), Book I, Chap. I, p. 70; Erdmann, p. 206b. "But at present I will put this investigation aside, and, accommodating myself to the received expressions, since in fact they are good and tenable, and one can say in a certain sense that the external senses are in part causes of our thoughts . . ." Leibniz is here talking about innate ideas rather than theological questions, but his language is so close to Lessing's as to suggest that this was the passage from which Lessing derived his general conception of the Leibnizean methodology. See also Leibniz, *op. cit.*, p. 272; Erdmann, p. 291, where, in a discussion of the use of language, Leibniz specifically refers to distinctions between the esoteric and exoteric methods of the ancient philosophers.

14. *Ibid.*, pp. 470–71.

15. Lessing made this assertion in ignorance of Leibniz's essay, *De rerum originatione radicali*, where he explicitly argues for such an infinite increase in perfection.

16. Lessing, *op. cit.*, pp. 471–76.

17. *Ibid.*, p. 476.

18. *Ibid.*, p. 478.

19. *Ibid.*

20. *Ibid.*, p. 479.

21. *Ibid.*, pp. 479–80.

22. *Ibid.*, p. 481.

23. *Ibid.*, pp. 482–83.

24. See especially G. Fittbogen, *op. cit.*, p. 83. Fittbogen sees Lessing's entire theological polemic as a disguised attack, under the cover of a "schien Theologie," and views the present work as a prime example of this method.

25. Letter to Karl, July 14, 1773; Lessing, *op. cit.*, Vol. IX, pp. 581–82.

26. Lessing, *op. cit.*, Vol. VII, pp. 491–96. Lessing severely criticized both here and elsewhere, the Chevalier de Jaucourt's life of Leibniz, appended to the 1734 and 1747 editions of the *Theodicy*, which was one of the standard sources of biographical information concerning Leibniz during the latter part of the eighteenth century. Here his most specific complaint is with Jaucourt's dating of the fragment in 1671, and he argues instead for early 1669 (pp. 491–92). This concern with the details of Leibniz's career, indicative of a profound interest in Leibniz, led to Lessing's own eventual attempt to write a biography of him, which, however, never got beyond the outline stage.

27. *Ibid.*, pp. 496–510. The text itself consists of seven syllogistic arguments by Wissowatius and replies by Leibniz. The arguments are rather banal and repetitive and need not be discussed in detail. In each case Leibniz rephrases Wissowatius' syllogism, and shows that when properly formulated it presupposes what it endeavored to prove. Thus, in his first argument, Wissowatius declares: "The one highest God is the Father, from whom all proceeds. / The Son of God, Jesus Christ is not the Father, from whom all proceeds. / Ergo, the Son of God, Jesus Christ, is not the one highest God." Against this Leibniz states the principle which he uses in response to all seven arguments: that the copula in the major premise is not properly conceived, and that all major premises which contain singular judgments must be reformulated as universal judgments. Thus, reformulated, the syllogism becomes: "Each, who is the one highest God, is the Father from whom all proceeds. / The Son of God is not the Father from whom all proceeds. / Ergo, the Son of God, Jesus Christ is not He who is the one highest God." Now, however, Leibniz argues, the word "all" may be understood to refer either to creatures, or also to the Son. If taken in the first sense, the major premise is acceptable, but the minor is not, for it is argued that creatures are created by the Son. If taken in the second sense, so that the "all" includes the Son, then the minor premise is acceptable, but the major premise must be rejected. Thus, Leibniz believes he has shown that taken in either sense, Wissowatius' syllogism is invalid, and since his purpose is not to prove, but merely to defend the doctrine of the Trinity against attack, this is deemed sufficient.

28. For an analysis of the similarities and differences between Socinianism and neology, and of how the relation between the two was understood in the eighteenth century, see K. Aner, *op. cit.*, pp. 45–59.

29. Thus, in a letter to Mendelssohn, May 1, 1774, Lessing, *op. cit.*, Vol. IX, p. 607, Lessing admits that Leibniz regarded the doctrine of the Trinity as "complete nonsense," but nevertheless asserts: "And still I am convinced that even here Leibniz thought and acted as Leibniz.

For it is undeniably better to defend an unphilosophical thing in a very philosophical manner, than unphilosophically want to reject or reform it."
30. Lessing, *op cit.*, Vol. VII, p. 527.
31. *Ibid.*, p. 528.
32. *Ibid.*, pp. 529–30.
33. *Ibid.*, p. 532.
34. *Ibid.*
35. *Ibid.*, p. 816.
36. *Ibid.*
37. *Ibid.*, p. 817.
38. Lessing, *op. cit.*, Vol. VII, p. 540, gave graphic expression to this feeling in a brief, unpublished satirical dialogue, *Herkules und Omphale*, which E. Schmidt, *op. cit.*, Vol. II, p. 213, dates at approximately the same time as a previously discussed letter to Karl—February 1774. The dialogue revolves around a discussion of a painting of the two legendary characters, where Hercules, in female garb, is seen performing womanly duties for Omphale. The theme of the dialogue is the analogy between this situation and the contemporary relationship between philosophy and theology. Thus, Hercules, or modern philosophy, is dressed in a simple frock, spinning sorites for the service of Omphale (theology), the intent being to suggest the perversion of roles on both sides, and the utter absurdity of the result.
39. Lessing, *op. cit.*, Vol. VII, pp. 819–20.
40. *Ibid.*, pp. 812–13.
41. *Ibid.*, p. 813.
42. *Ibid.*, pp. 821–22.
43. This is pointed out by G. Fittbogen, *op. cit.*, p. 95.
44. Lessing, *op. cit.*, p. 824.
45. *Ibid.*, p. 825.
46. *Ibid.*, pp. 826–27.
47. *Ibid.*, pp. 827–28.
48. *Ibid.*, pp. 831–33.
49. *Ibid.*, p. 833.
50. *Ibid.*, p. 834.
51. *Ibid.*, p. 850.
52. *Ibid.*, pp. 851–52.
53. Lessing, *op. cit.*, Vol. VIII, p. 11; Chadwick, p. 53.
54. *Ibid.*, p. 12; Chadwick, *Ibid.*
55. Although Lessing was somewhat influenced by Bonnet's biological speculations, he did not have much respect for him as a theologian. See letter to Mendelssohn, January 9, 1777; Rilla, Vol. IX, p. 408; and Father Flajole's article, *Lessing's Attitude in the Lavater-Mendelssohn Controversy.* The above passage seems very much like a direct attack on the conclusions of Bonnet's *Recherches philosophiques sur les preuves du Christianisme*, which was included in the second

volume of *La Palingénésie philosophique* (Geneva, 1769), where he asserts, pp. 398–400: "The whole argument leads me to the important conclusion that there is no ancient history so well attested, as that of the Messenger of the Gospel; that there are no historical facts supported by so great a number of proofs, or by such striking, solid and various proofs, as are those facts on which the religion of Jesus Christ is founded.

"Sound logic has taught me to make precise distinctions between the different kinds of certainty, and not to demand the rigor of demonstration in matters of fact, or in things which essentially depend upon testimony. I know that what I call 'moral certainty,' is not, and cannot be perfect or strict certainty; that this kind of 'certainty' is never anything more than a greater or less 'probability,' which is more or less successful in gaining the assent of the mind, as it approaches more or less to that indivisible point, in which complete certainty resides.

"I also know that if I adhere to nothing but evidence, in the strict sense, as to demonstration, and believe nothing but what my own senses attested to me, I must of necessity fall into the most absurd pyrrhonism; for what pyrrhonism can be more absurd, than that which seriously doubts all the facts of history, physics, and natural history, &c. and which completely rejects every kind of testimony? What life can be more miserable and limited than that of the man who trusts to nothing but the report of his own senses, and who refuses to accept any analogical conclusion?

"I shall not say that the truth of Christianity is demonstrated; this expression, admitted and repeated with too much complacency by the best apologists, would certainly be very improper. I shall say merely, that the facts upon which the credibility of the Christian religion is founded appear to me to be so probable, that, if I rejected them, I would be violating the surest rules of logic and renouncing the most common maxims of reason."

56. Lessing, *op. cit.*, Vol. VIII, p. 12; Chadwick, p. 53.

57. Fittbogen, *op. cit.*, p. 110.

58. Cf. Spinoza, *Theologico-Political Treatise*, p. 61: "The truth of a historical narrative, however assured, cannot give us the knowledge nor consequently the love of God, for love of God springs from knowledge of Him, and knowledge of Him should be derived from general ideas, in themselves certain and known, so that the truth of a historical narrative is very far from being a necessary requisite for our attaining our highest good."

59. Lessing, *op. cit.*, p. 14; Chadwick, p. 55.

60. *Ibid.*; Chadwick, p. 54.

61. This point is argued at some length by Chadwick, *op. cit.*, pp. 30–36, in an attempt to minimize Lessing's originality and historical significance. Chadwick, however, completely fails to come to

terms with the positive aspect of Lessing's thought, which is the true basis of both his originality and historical significance.

62. Lessing, *op. cit.*, p. 15; Chadwick, p. 55.

63. *Ibid.*, p. 16; Chadwick, pp. 55–56.

64. For a discussion of Ress, see E. Schmidt, *op. cit.*, Vol. II, pp. 241–42.

65. It was during this period that both his wife of a year and newborn child died. See E. Schmidt, *op. cit.*, Vol. II, p. 243.

66. Lessing, *op. cit.*, p. 25.

67. *Ibid.*, p. 29.

68. Cf. Spinoza's *Theologico-Political Treatise*, Preface, pp. 7–8, where Spinoza explicitly attacks the doctrines of infallibility, lamenting (p. 8) "that human commentaries are accepted as divine records," and as an alternative, he suggests his own method of Scriptural interpretation: "Making no assumptions concerning it, and attributing to it no doctrines, which I do not find clearly therein set down." Moreover, Spinoza's discontent with this doctrine, just as Lessing's, was based on the fact that it was the result of an arbitrary dogmatic, rather than demonstration or evidence.

69. Lessing, *op. cit.*, p. 31.

70. Such an objective consideration, which was only suggested in the present work, was actually undertaken in his *New Hypothesis Concerning the Evangelists Regarded as Merely Human Historians* (1777), which is one of the pioneer works in modern Biblical criticism. The decisive point is that it is only when everything is not seen to hinge upon the facticity of historical events, that an objective investigation of these events, and the books in which they are recorded, becomes possible. Thus, Lessing's attempt to separate the question of the truth of the Christian religion from the truth of its historical foundation may be said to have furnished the basic presupposition of "Higher Criticism."

71. Lessing, *op. cit.*, p. 36.

72. *Ibid.*, p. 37.

73. *Goeze's Streitschriften gegen Lessing*, edited by Eric Schmidt, in "Deutsche Literaturdenkmale des 18 und 19 Jahrhunderts," No. 43 (Stuttgart, 1893), p. 12.

74. *Ibid.*, p. 13.

75. *Ibid.*, p. 14.

76. *Ibid.*, pp. 14–15.

77. *Ibid.*, p. 15.

78. *Ibid.*, p. 16.

79. *Ibid.*, p. 17.

80. *Ibid.*, p. 20.

81. *Ibid.*, p. 21.

82. *Ibid.*

83. *Ibid.*, p. 122.

84. *Ibid.*, p. 45.

85. *Ibid.*

86. See E. Schmidt, *op. cit.*, Vol. II, p. 70.

87. This was recorded by Karl Lessing in his edition of G. E. Lessing's *Theologischen Nachlass*, p. 21. It is quoted by Rilla, Lessing, *op. cit.*, Vol. VIII, p. 154.

88. Lessing, *op. cit.*, Vol. VIII, p. 157.

89. *Ibid.* It should, however, be noted that Goeze was not far wrong in this regard, for it was Lessing's intent to show that although Reimarus' objections could be answered, this could only be accomplished at the cost of the doctrine of verbal inspiration.

90. *Ibid.*, pp. 156–57.

91. *Ibid.*, p. 160.

92. Henry Chadwick, editor of *Lessing's Theological Writings*, suggests in his introduction (p. 23) that: "With this claim Lessing imported into German Protestantism and many history books the legend that the fundamental principle of the Reformation was the right to exercise unrestricted private judgment."

93. Lessing, *op. cit.*, p. 161.

94. *Ibid.*, p. 163.

95. *Ibid.*, p. 176.

96. *Ibid.*, p. 167.

97. *Ibid.*

98. *Ibid.*

99. *Ibid.*, p. 169.

100. *Ibid.*

101. *Ibid.*, p. 171.

102. *Ibid.*, p. 173.

103. *Ibid.*, p. 179.

104. *Ibid.*

105. *Ibid.*

106. *Ibid.*, p. 180.

107. *Ibid.*

108. *Ibid.*, p. 181.

109. *Ibid.*, pp. 184–85.

110. *Ibid.*, p. 185.

111. Lessing admits as much in an oft-quoted letter to Karl, dated March 16, 1778, where in reference to the *Parable* and the *Axioms* he writes: "Because of your curiosity I am sending you a duplicate copy of my answer to Goeze. I will be pleased if this also gains your approval. And I think it will, to some extent, if you bear in mind that I must direct my weapons at my opponents, and that not everything which I write *gymnastikos* would I also write *dogmatikos*. Lessing, *op. cit.*, Vol. IX, p. 773.

112. Lessing, *op. cit.*, Vol. VIII, p. 188.
113. *Ibid.*
114. *Ibid.*, p. 189.
115. *Ibid.*
116. *Ibid.*, p. 190.
117. *Ibid.*, p. 193.
118. *Ibid.*, pp. 195–96.

CHAPTER 4

1. According to Karl Lessing, who first published it in his 1784 edition of his brother's *Theologischen Nachlass*, this fragment stems from the year 1780. It is interesting to note that this distinction between the religion of Christ, conceived of as a purely ethical faith, and the Christian religion with its positive doctrines is almost identical with Hegel's thesis in his early fragment, *The Positivity of the Christian Religion*, in *On Christianity: Early Theological Writings*, translated by T. M. Knox (New York, 1961), pp. 67–81, that Jesus' original intent was merely to stimulate the Jews to an ethical inwardness, but that because of the narrowness of the Jewish mentality, with its emphasis on an exact and mechanical fulfillment of an external law, this soon became perverted into a positive doctrine concerning the teacher.

2. Leibniz, *New Essays Concerning Human Understanding*, p. 43; Erdmann, p. 194a.

3. Here, as well as in many other instances, Lessing is a probable influence upon Kant, who in his *Religion Within the Limits of Reason Alone*, translated by T. M. Greene and H. H. Hudson (New York, 1960), writes, p. 143: "No inference regarding a religion's qualification or disqualification to be the universal religion of mankind can be drawn merely from its origin." And in his description of a religion which is "objectively natural," that is, intrinsically rational, but "subjectively revealed"—in fact communicated by revelation—he seems to be reiterating Lessing's argument against Goeze: ". . . the occurrence of such a supernatural revelation might subsequently be entirely forgotten without the slightest loss to that religion either of comprehensibility or of certainty, or of power over human hearts," p. 144. A highly similar view was also expressed by Hegel in *The Positivity of the Christian Religion*, p. 79, where he proclaims in reference to miracles: ". . . eternal truths are of such a nature that, if they are to be necessarily and universally valid, they can be based on the essence of reason alone and not on phenomena in the external world which for reason are mere accidents. . . ."

4. Leibniz, *op. cit.*, p. 73; Erdmann, p. 207b.

5. This was clearly recognized by Goeze and formed the basis of his charge that Lessing was a disguised naturalist who, like Tindal, only defended the Christian religion insofar as it was a reaffirmation of the religion of nature. See *Goeze's Streitschriften gegen Lessing*, p. 124.

6. The influence of Leibniz's psychology, and especially of the doctrine of "small perceptions" upon Lessing has been suggested before, for example by Otto Nieten, *op. cit.*, p. 79, where it is connected with religious feeling, but not formulated as an answer to the problem which I have delineated, and also by Gustav Kettner in his *Lessings Dramen im Lichte ihrer und unsere Zeit* (Berlin, 1904), pp. 220-25, where it is viewed as underlying the psychology of the characters in *Emilia Galotti*.

7. Leibniz, *op. cit.*, p. 46; Erdmann, p. 196a-b.

8. *Ibid.*, p. 88; Erdmann, p. 214b.

9. *Ibid.*, p. 50; Erdmann, p. 198a.

10. *Ibid.*, p. 180; Erdmann, p. 214b. Kurt Hildebrandt, in *Leibniz und das Reich der Gnade* (The Hague, 1953), emphasizes this aspect of Leibniz's thought and suggests, pp. 9-10, that Lessing was the first to grasp it and that the failure of others, that is, Kant, to do so, was one of the sources of the opposition between the advocates of pure reason and the champions of creative thought and intuition in German intellectual life of the eighteenth century. Hildebrandt, however, does not relate this discussion to the problem with which we are here concerned.

11. Once again we can discern an interesting parallel between Lessing and the young Hegel, who in a later draft of the *Positivity of the Christian Religion*, pp. 167-77, likewise rejects the extremely abstract conception of natural religion maintained by the Enlightenment, and suggests that a natural religion is not one which agrees with a mythical universal human nature, but rather one which is appropriate to human nature at a particular level of development. Moreover, in light of this he reaches a conclusion very similar to Lessing's: that the difference between a natural and a positive religion lies not so much in the content but in the form, that is, the manner in which it is apprehended.

12. However, these same scholars generally find the clue to lie in the distinction between the esoteric and exoteric methods, with the inevitable result that all of Lessing's positive assertions about the truth of the Christian religion are dismissed as merely an exoteric cloak for some hidden, esoteric truth, which generally turns out to be nothing more than natural religion. This general approach to Lessing's philosophy of religion was first formulated by Frederick Loofs in his *Lessings Stellung zum Christentum* (Halle, 1910). Against the tendency, prevalent in the nineteenth century to view Lessing as a sincere Christian (he specifically cites Ritter), Loofs argues (p. 20 ff.) on the basis of this passage that all of Lessing's positive assertions about Christianity are to be understood exoterically, and he sees much of their esoteric meaning in the concept of development, taken from Ferguson. However, he does acknowledge the difficulty of precisely determining the relationship between the esoteric truth and its exoteric formulation, and he

further admits that at some times the latter seems to assume a far more positive significance than at others. Following Loofs, this notion of the distinction between the esoteric and exoteric methods has become almost an axiom of Lessing scholarship. In addition to Fittbogen, *Die Religion Lessings*, who is its most subtle protagonist, this general view is maintained in a modified form by Benno von Wiese in *Lessing, Dichtung, Aesthetik, Philosophie* (Leipzig, 1931), and Arthur von Arx in *Lessing und sie geschichtliche Welt* (Leipzig, 1944). The most outspoken critic of this interpretation is Helmut Thielicke, who in his *Offenbarung Vernunft und Existenz, Studien zur Religionsphilosophie Lessings*, fourth edition (Gütersloh, 1957), argues (pp. 16–28) that rather than solving the problem, this distinction serves only to sharpen it, and that the real question concerns the meaning of Lessing's concept of revelation, that is, is it merely an exoteric cloak for a purely natural process, or does it indicate some sort of transcendent act of the Deity. Although Thielicke is, I believe, wrong in what he considers to be the real problem (my criticism of this point will be expressed in connection with the discussion of *The Education of the Human Race*), he is quite correct in pointing out that the emphasis on the distinction between esoteric and exoteric methods or standpoints serves rather to sharpen than to solve the problem of what Lessing meant by the truth of the Christian religion. There is no doubt that many of Lessing's defenses of orthodoxy against neology, and many of his remarks against Goeze and Reimarus are to be understood exoterically, or ironically. He had explicitly written to his brother Karl that the orthodox religious system is false, but he also, and here lies the heart of the problem, affirmed that it was not a patchwork of bunglers, that it contained significant insights, and that it was one of the supreme manifestations of the human spirit. Thus, the esoteric-exoteric distinction leaves us precisely where we started: namely with the question of the nature of that esoteric truth which Lessing claimed to have found in the Christian religion.

13. Jacobi, *op. cit.*, p. 63.

14. These are contained in the volume of "Collectanea" in *Gotthold Ephraim Lessings Sämtliche Schriften*, edited by Karl Lachmann and Franz Muncker (Leipzig, 1900), Vol. 15, pp. 512–22.

15. This is affirmed by the editors, *ibid.*, p. 512.

16. *Ibid.*, p. 512. This letter was first published in the Dutens edition (Geneva, 1768), Vol. V, p. 358, and is also to be found in Gerhardt, Vol. VII, p. 488.

17. *Sämtliche Schriften, op. cit.*, pp. 519–20, Leibniz, *New Essays*, p. 66; Erdmann, p. 205a.

18. *Ibid.*, pp. 517–18. The letter was published by Dutens, Vol. V, pp. 7–11, and is in Gerhardt, Vol. III, p. 605–7.

19. Leibniz, Gerhardt, Vol. III, p. 607.

20. Leibniz, *New Essays*, pp. 48–49; Erdmann, p. 197b.

21. Cf. Rudolf Zocher, *Leibniz's Erkenntnislehre* (Berlin, 1952), pp. 21–30.

22. Cf. Ernst Cassirer, *Das Erkenntnisproblem in der Philosophie und Wissenschaft der neuern Zeit* (Berlin, 1907), Vol. II, p. 182.

23. Leibniz, *New Essays*, p. 51; Erdmann, p. 198b.

24. In regard to Leibniz's conception of the levels of knowledge, and their relation to the ideal as realized in the divine mind, see Zocher, *op. cit.*, p. 30 ff.

25. Cf. *New Essays*, p. 95; Erdmann, p. 195b, *The Principles of Nature and of Grace, Based on Reason*, Section 5.

26. Cf. *New Essays*, p. 422; Erdmann, p. 344b.

27. Cf. *The Principles of Nature and of Grace, Based on Reason*, Section 16.

28. Leibniz, *Monadology*, Section 56; Loemker, *Leibniz's Philosophical Papers and Letters*, Vol. II, p. 1053; Erdmann, p. 709b.

29. *Ibid.*, Section 57.

30. Leibniz, *Discourse on Metaphysics*, Section 9.

31. Leibniz, Letter to Arnauld, October 9, 1687. *Discours de métaphysique et correspondence avec Arnauld*, edited by Georges Le Roy (Paris, 1957), p. 144. For similar, but more popular formulations, with which Lessing was no doubt familiar, see *Principles of Nature and of Grace, Based on Reason*, Section 14, and *The Monadology*, Section 83.

32. Zocher, *op. cit.*, pp. 26–27, comments on this precognitive grounding of the Leibnizean epistemology.

33. Lessing, *op. cit.*, Vol. VII, pp. 576–80. The fragment was first published by Karl Lessing in the second volume of his *G. E. Lessings Leben* (1795).

34. Heinrich Kofink, to whom this analysis of the fragment is greatly indebted, presents a good deal of evidence to date it late in 1776, or just before the beginning of the theological controversy. See his *Lessings Anshauungen über die Unsterblichkeit und Seelenwanderung* (Strassburg, 1912), p. 85.

35. Lessing's interest in Bonnet's biological speculations is documented by Jacobi in his account of his conversations with Lessing. Jacobi, *op. cit.*, pp. 80–81.

36. Lest such a synthesis appear incredible, it should be noted that Bonnet, *La Palingénésie philosophique*, Vol. I, pp. 263–307, himself acknowledges his indebtedness to Leibniz. Leibniz's influence on Bonnet is also discussed by Arthur Lovejoy, *The Great Chain of Being* (New York, 1960), Harper edition, pp. 283–87.

37. Cf. Leibniz's letter to Basnage (July, 1698), Erdmann, p. 153b.

38. Although this conception of additional senses probably comes from Bonnet, *op. cit.*, Vol. I, pp. 533–38, Vol. II, p. 384, it is not without intimations in Leibniz. Cf. *New Essays*, pp. 583–84; Erdmann,

p. 403b. "Suppose there were creatures in the planet Jupiter provided with six senses and that God in a supernatural way gave to a man among us the ideas of this sixth sense, he could not by means of words make them spring up in the minds of other men."

39. The necessary connection between a monad and a material body is a recurring theme with Leibniz, and provides the basis for his explanation of finitude or limitation. Cf. *New Essays*, p. 52; Erdmann, p. 199a. "I believe with the majority of the ancients that all genii, all souls, all simple created substances, are always joined to a body, and that there are never souls entirely separated."

40. Cf. Leibniz, *The Monadology*, Sections 66–70.

41. This idea is derived from Bonnet. See Kofink, *op. cit.*, pp. 93–94.

42. Lessing, *op. cit.*, p. 578.

43. *Ibid.* Lessing's adherence to this doctrine will be discussed in relation to *The Education of the Human Race.*

44. Leibniz, *A New System of the Nature and the Communication of Substances*, Section 14; Loemker, *op. cit.*, Vol. II, p. 747; Erdmann, p. 127b.

45. Lessing, *op. cit.*, Vol. VIII, p. 27. Cf. *New Essays*, p. 194; Erdmann, p. 259, where in reference to Locke's distinction between a feeling of uneasiness and pain, Leibniz writes: ". . . and very far from being obliged to regard this uneasiness as incompatible with happiness, I find that uneasiness is essential to the happiness of created beings which never consists in complete possession." For a similar statement see also *The Principles of Nature and of Grace, Based on Reason*, Section 11.

46. Lessing, *op. cit.*, Vol. VIII, p. 547.

47. For the history of this work, and a detailed discussion of Lessing's relationship to the masonic movement see Heinrich Schneider, *Lessing und die Freimäurer*, in his *Zwölf biographischen Studien*, (Munich, 1951), pp. 166–97.

48. Lessing, *op. cit.*, p. 548.

49. *Ibid.*, p. 549.

50. *Ibid.*, pp. 549–50.

51. *Ibid.*, p. 550.

52. *Ibid.*, p. 554.

53. *Ibid.*, p. 556.

54. *Ibid.*, p. 557.

55. *Ibid.*, pp. 558–59.

56. *Ibid.*, p. 559.

57. *Ibid.*, p. 561.

58. *Ibid.*

59. *Ibid.*

60. Cf. Leibniz, *Theodicy*, Part I, Section 20.

61. Lessing, *op. cit.*, p. 562.

62. *Ibid.*, pp. 17–23.

63. *Ibid.*, p. 562.

64. Lessing, *op. cit.*, pp. 562–63.

65. The original is found in the *Decameron* in the third tale of the first book.

66. A detailed analysis of the relationship and respective purposes of the two versions is given by G. Kettner, *op. cit.*, pp. 353–75.

67. This situation forms a close parallel to the Lavater-Mendelssohn controversy, in which Lessing was deeply interested. See letter to Mendelssohn, January 7, 1771, Lessing, *op. cit.*, Vol. IX, p. 408. The history of this controversy, and of Lessing's relationship to it is narrated by Father Edward S. Flajole in his monograph, *Lessing's Attitude in the Lavater-Mendelssohn Controversy.* Mendelssohn, like Nathan, was a Jew placed in the embarrassing position of having to defend his religious convictions without offending the powers that be. Thus, like Nathan, he was hesitant to give direct expression to his beliefs. However, due to the persistence of their adversaries, both were ultimately forced to do so. For the nature of Mendelssohn's response to Lavater's demands, see his *Schreiben an den Herrn Diaconus Lavater zu Zurich* (1769), and *Nacherinnerung* (1770).

68. Lessing, *op. cit.*, Vol. II, p. 401, English translation by William A. Steele, *Lessing, Laocoön, Nathan the Wise, Minna von Barnhelm* (London, 1930) (henceforth referred to as Steele), p. 164.

69. It is in this sense that one must understand Lessing's often misinterpreted remark: "Nathan's attitude toward all positive religions has long been mine." *Outline of a Preface,* Lessing, *op. cit.*, p. 332. What Lessing and Nathan are both rejecting is not the content of these religions, but their positive pretensions, that is, their claim to be the actual historical revelations of God, and thus the single true religion. This absolutistic connotation was intrinsically connected with the concept of "positive religion" as it was understood in the eighteenth century.

70. It is noteworthy that Hegel alluded to precisely this passage in connection with his rejection of the either/or approach to truth, so characteristic of the Enlightenment. See *The Phenomenology of Mind,* English translation by J. B. Baille (London, 1955), p. 98: "Against this view it must be pointed out, that truth is not like a stamped coin that is issued ready from the mint and so can be taken up and used."

71. Lessing, *op. cit.*, p. 402; Steele, p. 165.

72. This introduction of the magic power is Lessing's most significant modification of the original fable. See Kettner, *op. cit.*, p. 560.

73. Lessing, *op. cit.*, pp. 403–5; Steele, pp. 166–67.

74. *Ibid.*, p. 405; Steele, p. 167.

75. *Ibid.*

76. *Ibid.*, p. 406; Steele, p. 168.

77. *Ibid.*

78. *Ibid.,* p. 407; Steele, pp. 168–69.

79. Cf. Lessing's significant but generally neglected remark in the unpublished *Selbstbetrachtungen und Einfälle,* Lessing, *op. cit.,* Vol. VIII, pp. 408–9: "I have nothing against the Christian religion, rather I am its friend and will remain attached to it for life. It fulfills the purpose of a positive religion as well as any other. I believe it and hold it for true to the extent to which one can believe and hold for true something historical."

80. Lessing, *op. cit.,* Vol. II, p. 408; Steele, p. 169.

81. *Ibid.,* p. 378; Steele, p. 149.

82. *Ibid.,* p. 427; Steele, p. 183.

83. It is at this point that I differ from scholars such as G. Fittbogen, *op. cit.,* pp. 159–63, and G. Kettner, *op. cit.,* pp. 365–82, who contend that the parable implies the complete rejection of all revealed religion and the substitution of a "Vernunftreligion" or a "Humanität-religion." Such an interpretation, however, not only makes utter nonsense out of Lessing's whole polemic with orthodoxy, but it also involves the confusion of an ethical with a religious ideal. The notion of the universal brotherhood of man, which the play clearly advocates, is not a religion which is to supercede Christianity, but an ethical task confronting men who are admittedly and necessarily divergent in their beliefs. This is perfectly consistent with *The Testament of John* and *Ernst and Falk.*

84. Lessing, *op. cit.,* p. 433; Steele, p. 187.

85. Cf. *Hamburg Dramaturgy,* No. 79. Lessing, *op cit.,* Vol. VI, p. 402, speaking of the task of a dramatic poet, states: "The whole of this mortal creator should be a shadow of the whole of the eternal Creator. It should accustom us to the height that just as in Him all things are resolved for the best, so also will it be here."

86. Thus, in vindication of Lessing against Jacobi's allegations of Spinozism, Mendelssohn wrote in connection with *Nathan the Wise*: "Chiefly in regard to the doctrine of providence and divine governance, I know of no author who has presented these great truths with the same clarity, with the same power of conviction, and with the same degree of interest for the reader at heart, as he." *Moses Mendelssohn gesammelte Schriften* (Leipzig, 1843), Vol. II, p. 362.

87. Cf. G. Kettner, *op. cit.,* p. 398: "Lessing's drama has embodied the direction of providence in the strangely entangled destiny of a family. Over all the events and all the actions of the characters moves a higher power which purposefully guides everything to an unsuspected goal."

88. Implicit in this little episode (Act I, Scene 2) is an interesting bit of religious psychology. Lessing's description of Recha's behavior is obviously intended to suggest that the belief in miracles is not, as with Reimarus and the deists, the result of deliberate deception, but rather the natural product of an overexcited imagination, whereby an entirely

natural course of events is changed into a miraculous occurrence wrought by God precisely for the benefit of the recipient. This, in all essentials, was the view of Spinoza, for whom the belief in miracles is explained in terms of the imagination and confused ideas, rather than reason and adequate ideas, and is consequently dismissed as an expression of men's ignorant desire to believe themselves God's favorites. See esp. *Theologico-Political Treatise,* Chapter VI, p. 82, and *Ethics,* Part I, Appendix, p. 78.

89. Lessing, *op. cit.,* p. 333; Steele, pp. 118–19.

90. This is revealed in Nathan's poignant confrontation with the monk (Act IV, Scene 7), when he relates the wanton murder of his wife and children by bigoted Christians and tells how after days of bitterness he finally became consoled when he recognized that this was the will of God. Lessing, *op. cit.,* p. 447; Steele, p. 197. As Lessing endeavors to suggest, Nathan's subsequent wisdom was grounded in this resignation (*Ergebenheit*) to the will of God. The beneficent providence immediately rewarded him with a new child (Recha). Nathan humbly accepts the infant as a gift from providence and subsequently strives actively to fulfill his duty, and is now even ready, if providence so dictates, to surrender his beloved daughter to her blood relations. This scene, which as Fittbogen suggests, *op. cit.,* pp. 180–82, expresses Lessing's ideal of true piety, may be seen to bear a superficial resemblance to Part V of Spinoza's *Ethics,* but it is actually much closer to the Leibnizean concept of "Christian fatalism," which is a direct corollary to the doctrine of providence. See G. Kettner, *op. cit.,* p. 405.

91. The Leibnizean basis of Lessing's philosophy and especially of his concept of providence, that is, universal determinism, was argued at length by Robert Zimmermann in his *Leibniz und Lessing, eine Studie,* in *Sitzungsberichte Akadamie des Wissenschaften* (Vienna, 1855), Vol. XVI, esp. pp. 368–69, where he contends that Lessing advocated the "happy necessity" of Leibniz, rather than the geometrical necessity of Spinoza.

92. Lessing, *op. cit.,* Vol. VII, p. 567.

93. Cf. Charles Bigg, *The Christian Platonists of Alexandria* (Oxford, 1886), pp. 55–56, where he shows that in his controversy with the Gnostics over the divine authorship of the Old Testament, Clement treated the Old Testament, especially the Mosaic law, as a needed preparatory discipline in the divine education of the world and the individual. It is an interesting fact that both the Gnostic critique (from the standpoint of the anthropomorphisms and lack of a doctrine of immortality, etc.) and Clement's historically oriented defense seem to parallel closely the respective positions of Reimarus and Lessing. In addition, Adolph Harnack in his *History of Dogma,* English translation by Neil Buchanan, Dover edition (New York, 1961), Vol. II, p. 103, shows that Tertullian employed a conception of stages of revelation in his polemic

with the Montanists, and, pp. 305–7, that the same notion occurs in Iranaeus in regard to the question of the relation between the Old and New Testaments. It is highly probable that the main theme of the work was originally suggested to Lessing by his Patristic studies during his Breslau period.

94. This concept also has Patristic roots, and was especially treated by Origen. See Bigg, *op. cit.*, pp. 223–24.

95. Cf. Spinoza, *Theologico-Political Treatise*, Chapters I and XIII.

96. Cf. Leibniz's assertion in the Preface to the *Theodicy*, p. 49, Erdmann, p. 468a: "Ceremonies resemble virtuous actions, and formularies are like shadows of the truth and approach, more or less, the true light," and the conception of religious development implied in the phrase, p. 49, Erdmann, p. 469a: ". . . Jesus Christ completing what Moses had begun. . . ." Wilhelm Dilthey in his *Das Achtzehnte Jahrhundert und die Geschichtliche Welt, Gesammelte Schriften*, Vol. III, pp. 241–42, points to the analogy between these two passages and the main argument of *The Education of the Human Race*. However, in his major treatment of Lessing's thought in *Das Erlebnis und die Dichtung*, he unfortunately does not develop the implications of this analogy for an understanding of Lessing's total theological position. Furthermore, it should be noted that these relatively isolated passages stand in sharp contrast to the major arguments of the *Theodicy* and, indeed, to the essential outlines of Leibniz's official philosophy of religion. Rather than locating the decisive influence of Leibniz upon Lessing in these isolated passages, it is our contention that they are merely striking manifestations of the basic principles, that is, perspectivalism and development, which Lessing adopted on the basis of his total acquaintance with the Leibnizean philosophy, and whose full religious significance was perhaps not realized by Leibniz himself.

97. Herder's most systematic treatment of these themes and of the philosophy of history in general is, of course, to be found in his monumental *Ideen zur Philosophie der Geschichte der Menschheit*, (1784–91), but they are also to be found in his early sketch, *Auch eine Philosophie der Geschichte zur Bildung der Menschheit*, a document with which Lessing was in all probability familiar. In this work Herder attacks the unhistorical absolutism of the Enlightenment (his particular target was Isaac Iselin's *Philosophische Muthmassungen über die Geschichte der Menschheit* (1764), wherein all previous cultures, institutions, and beliefs are judged and found wanting in relation to the present stage of enlightenment. Although Herder views history in developmental terms (he posits three stages in the development of the human race in analogy with the three ages of man), he also believes that this development does destroy the relative significance of previous stages. With nations as with ages of life, he contends: "Each has within itself

the middlepoint of its happiness. The youth is not happier than the innocent, contented child; nor is the quiet old man more unhappy than the vigorously striving man. The pendulum always swings with the same force, when it goes furthest and all the more quickly strives, or when it wavers most slowly, and nears the state of rest. Meanwhile, it is still an eternal striving. Nobody lives in his age alone. He builds upon the past which is, and wants to be, nothing but the foundation of the future." J. G. Herder, *Sämmtliche Werke*, edited by Bernhard Suphan (Berlin, 1891), Vol. V, p. 512. Although Herder is here not specifically concerned with religion, the analogy between his general relativistic conception of history and Lessing's critique of Reimarus' attempt to judge the Old Testament in light of the hypostasized unhistorical natural religion of deism is readily apparent. What Lessing has done is to apply precisely the same arguments against Reimarus, which Herder uses against Iselin. The influence of Herder's essay on *The Education of the Human Race* is suggested by Robert T. Clark, Jr., in his *Herder, His Life and Thought* (Berkeley and Los Angeles, 1955), pp. 286–87. The Leibnizean basis of Herder's historical insights has often been noted. Cf. Rudolph Haym, *Herder* (reprint, Berlin, 1958), Vol. II, p. 296 ff., and esp. Cassirer, *The Philosophy of the Enlightenment*, pp. 230–31, where he asserts that Herder's metaphysics of history, with its recognition of the unique significance and necessity of every historical stage is based upon "Leibniz's central doctrine," and *Freiheit und Form, Studien zur deutschen Geistesgeschichte*, second edition (Berlin, 1918), p. 180 ff., where he explicitly links Herder's emphasis upon the uniqueness and intrinsic worth of each "Volk" with the Leibnizean monad.

98. Lessing, *op. cit.*, pp. 590–91; Chadwick, p. 82.

99. The latter view is held by the vast majority of scholars, including Loofs, but is opposed by Helmut Thielicke, who in his *Offenbarung, Vernunft und Existenz: Studien zur Religionsphilosophie Lessing*, takes issue with this view and contends that Lessing actually believed in a sort of transcendent revelation. However, in order to do this, he is forced to explain away all of the apparently pantheistic or monistic tendencies in Lessing's thought. Nevertheless, the book does have the virtue of posing this problem in all its sharpness, especially (p. 33 ff.) in connection with the question of the relationship between Sections 4 and 77 of *The Education of the Human Race*.

100. Cf. the famous last paragraph of Hegel's lectures: *The Philosophy of History*, English translation by J. Sibree, Dover edition (New York, 1956), p. 457: "That the History of the World, with all the changing scenes which its annals present, is the process of development and the realization of Spirit and this is the true *Theodicea*, the justification of God in History. Only *this* insight can reconcile Spirit with the History of the World—viz. that what has happened, and is happening every day, is not only not 'without God,' but is essentially

His work." Highly significant in this regard is the characterization of *The Education of the Human Race* as a "theodicy of history" by both Kuno Fischer, *Geschichte der neuern Philosophie* (Manheim, 1855), Vol. II, p. 575, and by Ernst Cassirer, *The Philosophy of the Enlightenment*, p. 192.

101. See esp. the famous slave boy scene in the *Meno* (St., pp. 81–87).

102. This is the true significance of Leibniz's remark in the *New Essays*, when comparing his views to Locke, he writes (p. 42; Erdmann, p. 194a): "His has more relation to Aristotle, mine to Plato."

103. Lessing, *op. cit.*, p. 600; Chadwick, p. 89.

104. *Ibid.*, pp. 601–2; Chadwick, pp. 89–90.

105. *Ibid.*, p. 594; Chadwick, pp. 84–85.

106. Lessing's argument is to be compared with that of William Warburton who, in his *Divine Legislation of Moses* (1737–41), not only contends against the deistic critics that the absence of the doctrine of immortality is no argument against the divine origin of the Old Testament, but further goes on to argue that it actually constitutes an additional proof of this origin. Warburton's argument contains three propositions: (1) that the doctrine of a future state of rewards and punishments is necessary for the well being of society, (2) that the utility of the doctrine has been admitted by all mankind, and (3) that this doctrine is not to be found in the Old Testament. From this Warburton concludes that since Moses omitted a sanction, which as an enlightened man he knew to be necessary for the well being of society, he must have been certain of miraculous interference. For a detailed account of Warburton see Leslie Stephen, *op. cit.*, Vol. I, pp. 344–77, and for the argument in question, pp. 356–57. In Section 24 Lessing gently chides this completely unhistorical argument.

107. Lessing, *op. cit.*, p. 596; Chadwick, p. 86. Cf. Spinoza's *Theologico-Political Treatise*, Chapter V, *Of the Ceremonial Law*, wherein the whole emphasis is on the fact that the Mosaic law was directed purely to the abject condition of the Hebrew society at the time.

108. Lessing suggests this (Section 22) by affirming that this doctrine "in a way is found, and in a way is not found" in the books of the Old Testament.

109. It was no doubt in virtue of this historically limited conception of Judaism that Hamann accused Lessing of being prejudiced against the Jews in *The Education of the Human Race*. See his letter to Herder and his wife, June 11, 1780, *Johann George Hamann Briefwechsel*, edited by Arthur Henkel, Vol. IV, p. 192.

110. Lessing, *op. cit.*, p. 605; Chadwick, p. 91.

111. As such it can be viewed in analogy with the acquisition of a new sense, which Lessing similarly suggests, reveals totally new

levels of insight. Moreover, it should be noted that this dual conception of development precisely parallels Bonnet, who postulated both the
increasing refinement of each sense and a qualitative advance through
the acquisition of new senses. This latter fact is pointed out by Kofink,
op. cit., pp. 89–90, who, however, does not discuss the parallel between
this and *The Education of the Human Race*.

112. Lessing, *op. cit.*, p. 605; Chadwick, p. 92.

113. Lessing's relationship to Locke on this point is very revealing.
Both conceive of the work of Christ as making practically effective
what had previously been only vaguely understood, and thus both point
to the pedagogical significance of the Christian revelation. However,
Locke's whole argument is directed toward establishing the historical
facticity of that revelation, while Lessing's main point is precisely the
irrelevance of this facticity.

114. Lessing, *op. cit.*, p. 606; Chadwick, p. 93.

115. *Ibid.*, p. 608; Chadwick, pp. 93–94.

116. *Ibid.;* Chadwick, p. 94.

117. This is in all probability an allusion to John Toland, who in
Christianity not Mysterious, p. 89, argued that the notion of mystery
as found in the New Testament and early Fathers referred to a previously
undisclosed matter of fact rather than to something inherently
incomprehensible.

118. Lessing, *op. cit.*, p. 610; Chadwick, p. 95.

119. *Ibid.*, pp. 610–611; Chadwick, p. 95.

120. Both aspects of this conception are clearly found in the
New Essays, Book I, Chapter II, wherein Leibniz presents his conception of innate practical principles. The implicitly rational content
of these "small perceptions" has already been discussed, but it is perhaps even more clearly expressed in the assertion, p. 88; Erdmann, p.
214b: "There are then in us truths of instinct, which are innate principles, which we feel and approve, although we have not the proof
of them which we obtain, however, when we give a reason for this
instinct." The second aspect, wherein these small perceptions function
as guides to the reason is likewise explicitly affirmed, p. 91; Erdmann,
p. 216a: ". . . at bottom these natural impressions, whatever they may
be, are only aids to the reason and indices of the plan of nature."

121. Cf. Thielicke, *op. cit.*, p. 33; and Chadwick, *op. cit.*, p. 39.

122. Lessing, *op. cit.*, p. 612; Chadwick, p. 96.

123. *Ibid.*, pp. 613–14; Chadwick, p. 97.

124. Cf. the remarks appended to the fragment, *That Man Could
Have More Than Five Senses*, Lessing, *op. cit.*, Vol. VII, p. 579: "This
my system is certainly the oldest of all philosophical systems. For it is
actually nothing but the system of the pre-existence of souls and metempsychosis, which was not only taught by Plato and Pythagoras, but even

before them by the Egyptians and Chaldeans and Persians, in short by all the wise men of the Orient.

"And already this must constitute a good prejudice in its favor. The first and oldest opinion is often in speculative things the most probable, because the sound human understanding soon begins to decay. This oldest, and as I believe, only probable system is only to be modified in two respects. First—." Kofink, *op. cit.*, p. 116, suggests, and I believe correctly, that two modifications or objections which Lessing intended to make to the ancient form of this doctrine concern (1) the regress of the human soul into animals and (2) the connection of this doctrine with a supernatural, transcendent realm, both of which contradict Lessing's conception of the steady, yet natural process of the human soul which underlies the formulation of this doctrine in *The Education of the Human Race*.

125. The question of Lessing's conception of his own religious-philosophical standpoint vis-à-vis the history of the race is treated by Thielicke, *op. cit.*, p. 44 ff., who argues quite cogently that Lessing took the limitations of his own historical perspective seriously, and that his philosophical and theological assertions must be understood accordingly. This, moreover, is a logical consequence of his perspectival conception of truth.

CONCLUSION

1. Aner, *op. cit.*, p. 358. By rationalism Aner means the theological position, typical of German idealism, which rejects the facticity of revelation, yet reaffirms the content of Christian doctrine.

2. I have modified Cassirer's assertion in *The Philosophy of the Enlightenment*, p. 194, that in *The Education of the Human Race* Lessing achieved a new synthesis of the rational and the historical, so that the historical is no longer opposed to the rational, but is rather viewed as the way to its realization, and the only place of its fulfillment. Although this insight is basically true, Cassirer formulates it in a highly misleading manner as a solution to the problem of the "ugly, broad ditch" between rational and historical truths which was delineated in *On the Proof of the Spirit and of Power*. In reality the radical gulf, which is ultimately identical with the opposition between necessary and contingent truths, is never overcome, but rather continues to underlie the argument of *The Education of the Human Race*. Thus, it would be better to say that in both works this "ugly, broad ditch" is not so much filled in as shown to be irrelevant.

3. Friedrich Hegel's *Lectures on the Philosophy of Religion*, English translation by E. B. Speirs and J. B. Sanderson (London, 1895), reprinted 1962, Vol. I, pp. 27–35.

4. Johann Gottlieb Fichte, *Die Anweisung zum seligen Leben,* edited by Fritz Medicus, *Der philosophischen Bibliothek* (Hamburg, 1954), Vol. 234, p. 97.

5. For a discussion of the relation between Lessing and Bultmann, see Thielicke, *op. cit.,* pp. 150–51.

Index

Natural religion, in deism, 4, 126
in English rational theology, 168-69
in Enlightenment theology, 10, 194
in neology, 38-39, 42, 85, 126
Leibniz on, 25, 27
Lessing on, 53, 57-58, 65, 77-78, 85, 99-100, 122, 124, 126, 134, 149, 163, 194, 202
Locke on, 8, 10
Reimarus on, 43, 45
Tindal on, 14, 15
Wolff on, 34
Naud, Phillippe, 173
Neology, 38-42, 175-76, 188
and Augustinianism, 40
and deism, 39, 85
and Leibniz, 33, 42
and natural religion, 126
and Reimarus, 177
and revelation, 80, 176
and Wolffianism, 38-39, 42
Lessing and, 65-66, 83-95, 96, 121, 124, 134, 156, 163, 165, 186, 189, 195; see also Eberhard, Jerusalem, Sack, Semler, Spalding
Newton, Isaac, 14, 52, 172
Nicolai, Christoph Friedrich, 84
Letters Concerning the Newest Literature (with Lessing and Mendelssohn), 63-66
Nieten, Otto, 179, 194
Nollet, Jean Antoine, 95

Oldenburg, Henry, 183
Origen, 201
Original sin, doctrine of, Lessing on, 156-57, 163
Locke on, 6-7
Neology on, 40

Pelagius, 2
Pfleiderer, Otto, 176, 180
Philip, Christian, 173
Pietists, German, 3, 52, 181
Plato, 52, 127, 152, 158, 203-4
Meno, 203
Plutarch, Essay on Superstition, 17

Pope, Alexander, Essay on Man, 62
Popkin, Richard H., 171-72
Protestantism; see Theology, orthodox Protestant
Pünjer, Bernhard, 175
Pythagoras, 204

Ramler, Karl Wilhelm, 67, 182
Raspe, Rudolf Erich, 124, 164
Reformation, 2-3, 53, 113, 192
Reformed Church; see Calvinism
Reimarus, Hermann Samuel, 42-49, 77-78, 80, 83, 103-4, 110, 121, 123-25, 148-50, 164, 176-77, 184-85, 192, 195, 199-200, 202
Apology for Rational Worshippers of God, 43-49
Impossibility of a Revelation Which All Men Can Believe on Rational Grounds, 45-47, 96-98
Lessing's critique of, 93-101
On the Decrying of Reason in the Pulpit, 44-45, 93-94
On the Purpose of Jesus and His Disciples, 48
On the Resurrection Narrative, 47-48, 100-101, 104-5
On the Toleration of Deists, 44
That the Books of the Old Testament Were Not Written to Reveal a Religion, 47, 98-100
The Passage of the Israelites Through the Red Sea, 47, 98
Treatises on the Foremost Truths of Natural Religion, 43
Remond, Nicolas, 128, 174
Ress, Johann Heinrich, 107, 122, 191
Defense of the History of the Resurrection of Jesus Christ, 104-5
Revelation, Bayle on, 19, 22
deistic critique of, 3, 11
Enlightenment conception of, 1-2, 10, 37-38, 80-81
in English rational theology, 4-6, 8-10, 168-69
in neology, 38-39, 42, 85, 90, 92-95